Divine Council, Ethics and Resistance in Psalm 82

Divine Council, Ethics and Resistance in Psalm 82

Erica Mongé-Greer

Foreword by
David G. Firth

James Clarke & Co.

James Clarke & Co.
P.O. Box 60
Cambridge
CB1 2NT
United Kingdom

www.jamesclarke.co
publishing@jamesclarke.co

Paperback ISBN: 978 0 227 18003 7
PDF ISBN: 978 0 227 18004 4

British Library Cataloguing in Publication Data
A record is available from the British Library

First published by Pickwick Publications, 2023

This edition published by James Clarke & Co., 2024,
by arrangement with Wipf and Stock Publishers

Copyright © Erica Mongé-Greer, 2023

All rights reserved. No part of this edition may be reproduced, stored electronically or in any retrieval system, or transmitted in any form or by any means, electronic, mechanical, photocopying, recording, or otherwise, without prior written permission from the Publisher (permissions@jamesclarke.co).

Written with compassion for the disenfranchised in every context.

"I want you to take care of everyone who's smaller than you."
—Peter Pan, *Hook* (1991)

Contents

Foreword by David G. Firth | ix
Preface | xi
Acknowledgments | xiii
Abbreviations | xiv

1. Current Approaches to Psalm 82 | 1
2. Psalm 82—A Textual Study | 42
3. Mythopoeia and Myth in Psalm 82 | 86
4. Poverty Centered Language in Psalm 82 | 115
5. Justice Centered Language in Psalm 82 | 139
6. Psalm 82 and Psalmic Hermeneutics | 161
7. Ambiguity as Means for Resistance | 175
8. Conclusions | 193

   Bibliography | 197

Foreword

PSALM 82 IS, BY any assessment, a strange text within the Old Testament. Readers familiar with the wider world of the Ancient Near East are perhaps less surprised by its reference to the gods and divine council, but the psalm remains something of an outlier. Despite its apparent oddity, it remains an important part of the Psalter. Its passion for justice as something which should be experienced remains an important contribution to the theology of the Book of Psalms. Yet although this concern has not been lost in studies of it, this has not been the dominant pattern of scholarship for the last century. Rather, the (not inconsiderable!) syntactical challenges of the opening verse and the references to the world of ANE mythology found there have come to dominate. As a result, the psalm's profound ethical challenge has been muted.

It is precisely because this book recovers the ethical concerns of the psalm, making them again central, that I believe it is an important contribution both to studies of this psalm and the Psalter more broadly. As an Old Testament scholar with a deep awareness of the wider world of the Ancient Near East, Erica Mongé-Greer is well placed to show how awareness of this wider world of which it is part is vital to its interpretation. Her work is not only an act of retrieval of the psalm's ethical thrust. It is also innovative in adapting an organon as a process by which the ethical significance of a text can be more fully understood. Her approach opens up the ethical significance of this particular psalm while also demonstrating a model that is potentially fruitful for understanding the ethical significance of other psalms. As such, this is not only a rich study of Psalm 82. It is also offering a theoretically informed model which is potentially significant for a wide range of texts. Having laid this foundation, I hope that Erica Mongé-Greer will continue to provide us with ethically informed readings of other Old Testament poems.

David G. Firth
Trinity College, Bristol

Preface

SHARING ABOUT MY WORK on the topic of justice advocacy for the poor, marginalized, and disenfranchised in the post-9/11 world of Trump and COVID has elicited many responses from people across all walks of life. On one very meaningful occasion, a woman whom I had never met before overheard me talking to an acquaintance in a Barnes and Nobles bookstore about my work on poverty language in the Psalter and correlations in ancient religious perspectives about the poor. She sought me out afterward and told me how important my work is and she 'just wanted to say thank you" for my effort. I realize there is irony in working on a topic that encourages ambiguity, acceptance, and ethical reflection in an academic context, where academia has earned a reputation of siloed, isolationist and elitist perspectives. I anticipate and work toward a collaborative and interdisciplinary future in academic research. This thesis incorporates biblical, theological, and literary theories from global perspectives about psalms, ethics, and resistance theory. It is only the beginning.

Psalm 82 is a Hebrew Bible text with a reputation for being particularly difficult to interpret. The most significant published scholarship on the Psalm was a study by Julian Morgenstern in 1939. Since that time scholars have been theorizing about the meaning of the Psalm and its origins. In that Psalm 82 is often analyzed for its meaning as a Hebrew Bible text, the central issue has been generally limited to the translation and interpretation of אֱלֹהִים in verse one and its subsequent use in the composition, which continues to be a source of much debate and speculation. Meanwhile, scholarship has largely avoided giving adequate attention to the profound ethical themes in the psalm. Central ethical themes revolving around righteousness, wickedness and a response to poverty in Psalm 82 have not been adequately recognized as an intentional contribution of the psalm.

This study develops a holistic approach to interpreting Psalm 82 by examining characteristics of the text that may uncover implicit ethics and social concerns about justice, and a concern for the poor and marginalized in the ancient Near Eastern world. Following Zimmermann's model for discovering implicit ethics in an ancient biblical text, this study explores multiple features of Psalm 82 that support an ethical reading. These features include its probable Northern Israelite compositional setting, intentional ambiguity, linguistic focus on the poor and marginalized in society, a mythological heritage, and its reception in the Second Temple Period as resistance literature.

Acknowledgments

I AM ETERNALLY GRATEFUL to have loved and known the love of a generous and supportive life partner. My research has been significantly impacted by my journey as a married woman, mother, daughter, and sister.

Abbreviations

AB	Anchor Bible
AIL	Ancient Israel and Its Literature
ApOTC	Apollos Old Testament Commentary
BASOR	*Bulletin of the American Schools of Oriental Research*
BBC	British Broadcasting Corporation
BBR	*Bulletin for Biblical Research*
BCOTWP	Baker Commentary on the Old Testament Wisdom and Psalms
BHS	Biblia Hebraica Stuttgartensa
BHQ	Biblia Hebraica Quinta
Bib	*Biblica*
BibInt	*Biblical Interpretation*
BWA(N)T	Beiträge zur Wissenschaft vom Alten (und Neuen) Testament
BZAW	Beihefte zur Zeitschrift für die alttestamentliche Wissenschaft
CBC	Cambridge Bible Commentary
CBSC	Cambridge Bible for Schools and Colleges
CBQ	*Catholic Biblical Quarterly*
DCH	*Dictionary of Classical Hebrew*
ExpTim	*Expository Times*
HAT	Handbuch zum Alten Testament
HBT	*Horizons in Biblical Theology*
HS	*Hebrew Studies*
HSCL	Harvard Studies in Comparative Literature

HTR	*Harvard Theological Review*
HTS	*Harvard Theological Studies*
HUCA	*Hebrew Union College Annual*
ICC	International Critical Commentary
IEJ	*Israel Exploration Journal*
Int	*Interpretation*
IRT	Issues in Religion and Theology
IVP	InterVarsity Press
JSCE	*Journal of the Society of Christian Ethics*
JBL	*Journal of Biblical Literature*
JBR	*Journal of Bible and Religion*
JNES	*Journal of Near Eastern Studies*
JRE	*Journal of Religious Ethics*
JSCE	*Journal of the Society of Christian Ethics*
JSOT	*Journal for the Study of the Old Testament*
JSOTSup	Journal for the Study of the Old Testament Supplement Series
JSS	*Journal of Semitic Studies*
KAI	*Kanaanäische und aramäische Inschriften*. Herbert Donner and Wolfgang Röllig. 2nd ed. Wiesbaden: Harrassowitz, 1966–1969
KTU	*Die keilalphabetischen Teste aus Ugarit*
LHBOTS	Library of Hebrew Bible/Old Testament Studies
NCBC	New Cambridge Bible Commentary
OBT	Overtures to Biblical Theology
OTE	*Old Testament Essays*
OTL	Old Testament Library
OtSt	*Oudtestamentische Studien*
PBM	Paternoster Biblical Monographs
R&T	*Religion & Theology*
RB	*Revue biblique*
RBS	Resources for Biblical Study
SBL	Society of Biblical Literature
SBLDS	Society of Biblical Literature Dissertation Series

SBLMS	Society of Biblical Literature Monograph Series
SBLSBS	Society of Biblical Literature Sources for Biblical Study
SBLStBibLit	Society of Biblical Literature Studies in Biblical Literature
SBS	Stuttgarter Bibelstudien
SCM	Syro-Mesopotamia Studies
SemeiaSt	Semeia Studies
SJOT	*Scandinavian Journal of the Old Testament*
SPCK	Society for Promoting Christian Knowledge
STI	Studies in Theological Interpretation
SubBi	Subsidia Biblica
SWBA	Social World of Biblical Antiquity
UCOP	University of Cambridge Oriental Publications
VT	*Vetus Testamentum*
VTSup	Supplements to Vetus Testamentum
WAW	Writings from the Ancient World
WTJ	*Westminster Theological Journal*
ZAW	*Zeitschrift für die alttestamentliche Wissenschaft*
ZKT	*Zeitschrift für katholische Theologie*

1

Current Approaches to Psalm 82

"As long as poverty, injustice and gross inequality exist in our world, none of us can truly rest." —Nelson Mandela, former president of South Africa

INTERPRETING PSALM 82 HAS been a complex discussion. Scholarship is filled with varied and broad interest in finding meaning in such a psalm, with unique features that do not fit easily in the religious context of the Hebrew Bible. Scholarship is still tackling questions about the text that were raised nearly one hundred years ago. The aim of this thesis is to identify meaning by considering new approaches to the reading and understanding the text in its ancient Near Eastern context.

Psalm 82:1 reads: אֱלֹהִים נִצָּב בַּעֲדַת־אֵל בְּקֶרֶב אֱלֹהִים יִשְׁפֹּט. The opening line of the psalm invites speculation about technical aspects—like syntax and grammar; as well as qualitative aspects—like cultural and religious relevance. The content elicits discussion about dating, provenance, and genre. And with all this, there is the underlying question of how and why the psalm was retained in its complex and unorthodox form by compilers of the Psalter.

There are aspects of Psalm 82 that have been overlooked for analysis. Past scholarship has been caught up in prioritizing a god-identity aspect of the psalm, i.e. identifying the אֱלֹהִים referenced in the opening lines through which the rest of the psalm finds its meaning. However, there are other features in the psalm that also demand attention. One aspect which has been explored to some extent is the psalm's literary heritage which draws on mythological elements. This deserves a more direct literary comparison by which the provenance of Psalm 82 can be situated culturally and literarily. Another aspect which demands further exploration is the psalm's resistance to easily conform to monotheistic expectations of the Hebrew Bible Psalter. The third aspect, which is perhaps the most neglected, is the concentrated linguistic focus on marginalized members of society—an ethical concern. This study seeks to bring to light a more meaningful reading of Psalm 82 by asking different questions and ultimately pursuing an ethical interpretation in light of ancient Near Eastern values concerning matters of justice for society's marginalized.

In the past, scholars have approached their interpretation of Psalm 82 by making the main issue one of securing the identity of the אֱלֹהִים and their (divine, or sometimes royal) agency throughout the psalm. This approach has led to a debate that largely begins with an underlying premise that the god of the Hebrew Bible is omniscient, omnipresent and omnipotent. It is this theological assumption that motivates attempts to disambiguate the identity of the divine in Psalm 82 and limits the imagination to exempt ambiguous readings which would allow for more polysemy in the text. This approach to interpretation is problematic for two reasons:

1. Psalm 82 does not seem concerned with making clear the identity of the אֱלֹהִים. Its use is obscured by awkward grammatical construction and multiple roots of meaning, suggesting intention on the part of the author. While identifying the אֱלֹהִים has presented a challenge for many scholars, it may be possible to consider an alternative to disambiguating its use in the psalm. This study will explore why the composer might be elusive in identifying the אֱלֹהִים and how the interpretation of Psalm 82 could be furthered through considering deliberate ambiguity as a means of drawing readers toward the central idea of justice for the poor.

2. Psalm 82 includes an intense concentration of language regarding marginalized persons that seems to suggest the psalm is largely concerned with addressing the problems in social order. While this issue is not completely ignored by past scholarship, its focus has generally centered on divine agency and clarifying a theology about who is in charge. Many approaches begin with a defense of God's innocence. Interpretations of Psalm 82 often rest on an eisegetical assumption that the psalm is somehow defending God and a limited group of chosen people, justifying theological focus from polytheistic views toward monotheistic practice. One of the problems with this is the arbitrary nature of such categories as polytheism and monotheism, a bilateral construct developed in modernity. This study will alternatively explore why and how Psalm 82 incorporates implicit ethical instruction in which the composer presents a social problem for ethical consideration among a broader community, regardless of theistic adherents.

Scholarship seems to have halted any further discussion of meaning for the psalm in its attempt to satisfy a need for disambiguating the interpretation of אֱלֹהִים in the psalm in such a way that continues to respond to the initial curiosities raised by Morgenstern in his 1939 thesis on Psalm 82.[1] This psalm represents a point of consternation in the Hebrew Bible: potentially ambiguous, potentially non-conformist, potentially resistant. This study explores these attributes as essential to interpreting Psalm 82 as an ethical text.

This study will demonstrate that the key to understanding Psalm 82 is recognizing its polysemy and contextual linguistic, literary, and social situation—it's ancient formation and origination (composition) as a text centered in a world where gods have opinions about justice for the poor, and its later canonical compilation in which it resists conformity with the dogma of religious Judaic monotheism in the Second Temple period. Not only does the psalm situate uncomfortably within the religious setting of Second Temple period Judah, but it is a text that resists the religious-political climate that Persian era Jews were seeking to secure.[2] Furthermore, though the language of Psalm 82 is often read in a Judeo-Christian liturgical context, the psalm does not promise a future theological dogma of Yahwhism. Neither does the text, which draws upon ancient language of אֱלֹהִים, and leans toward seeking righteousness as a distinct virtue, indicate that it belongs to future Judeo-Christian dogmatic categories of religion. The text is its own composition and must be read for what it is without limiting possibilities of interpretation based on religious priorities introduced many centuries since the composition first came to life.

This study will not attempt to defend the placement of Psalm 82 in the Psalter nor attempt to describe how it fits canonically as an Elohistic psalm or an Asaphite psalm. This study seeks to make sense of the ethical message contained in Psalm 82 by considering literary features of the psalm which acknowledge implicit ethics. For this approach, reasoning will follow Zimmermann's *Organon* model for identifying implicit ethics in ancient biblical texts.[3] This approach includes evaluating Psalm 82 in a way that tests for deliberate ambiguity as a means to guide the reader to the central message. Past scholarship has failed to fully explore the potential for implicit ethics and ambiguity in Psalm 82. Scholars have focused instead on a univocal reading of the psalm with attempts to reconcile difficulties by (sometimes)

---

1. Morgenstern, "Mythological Background."
2. Ezra–Nehemiah
3. Zimmermann, *Logic of Love*.

forcing a monologic reading. The following sections will summarize scholarship on Psalm 82 over the past century.

Several Decades of Interpretive Debate

When considering the ethical language in Psalm 82, it is surprising that in a century of scholarship the main focus of interpretation has not looked sufficiently at the matter of unmet justice. Instead, the focus has been on defining and confirming the identity of the so-called keepers of justice named in v. 1. Scholarship has tried to make sense of who is responsible for keeping justice, carefully preserving God's reputation. This effort detracts from what the text has to say about the implicit or explicit ethical imperative. The fact that there has been no clear consensus in the discussion may signal the need for an approach that allows for multiplicity in the psalm's framework. Past scholarship has been caught up in debate around the position and status of those in power, at the expense of a deeper consideration for the ethical value of the psalm and its obvious attention to weak members of society.

Psalm 82 is like a play, an unfolding drama that illustrates the importance of caring about those who are marginalized in society. While scholars are busy describing the set and costumes, they diminish the main concern of the text for the poor and the implications of injustice. The setting of Psalm 82 exists to enhance the message, and not the other way around. This study of Psalm 82 will acknowledge the research focused on the setting as peripheral to the main message and then focus more intently on the language of poverty to learn what this ancient composition has to say about ethics.

There are many variants of translation, and each depends heavily on guesswork about the origination or assumed context of the composition. For more than a century, scholars have focused on trying to define the setting of Psalm 82 in such a way that would defend and describe its inclusion in the Psalter. This has proven to be difficult, since scholars widely disagree about when, where, and why this psalm exists. The opening verse, Ps 82:1, does not fit comfortably within modern assumptions about the role of the divine, especially in a Judeo-Christian context, so translations/interpretations have varied widely during the past century. Scholars have argued for a variety of positions regarding this verse, based on their understanding:

- that the poetic phrase in v. 1 stands alone, as unique,[4]
- that v. 1 is connected to other Hebrew Bible texts,[5]
- that the psalm is connected to non-biblical Semitic texts,[6]
- that it is connected to Ugaritic literature and religion, via mythology,[7]
- that it affirms monotheistic perspectives in Israel,[8]
- that it denies monotheistic perspectives in Israel,[9]
- that its provenance is likely very early and Northern,[10] or
- that it was composed late, in Judah.[11]

These variations represent the ongoing conflict of meaning and interpretation. Obviously, many of these positions directly conflict with one another, nonetheless each is clearly argued, as will be presented in summary of scholarship in this chapter.

Though many aspects of Psalm 82 have been discussed in the existing scholarship, translating and interpreting the divine epithets is troublesome. Many scholars have set out to identify the אֱלֹהִים, its counterpart, אֵל, and the related בְּנֵי עֶלְיוֹן, epithets that are used in such an uncommon way in Psalm 82. While it is difficult to find obvious parallels in the Hebrew Bible, these epithets echo other ancient Near Eastern texts, particularly among those from Ugarit. Cognate linguistic comparisons have been useful to scholars attempting to make a clear statement about who the divine agents are and what they are doing in the psalm. This has resulted in various interpretations for the epithets in Psalm 82 that seem to fit with one justification or another, as outlined below.

Some scholars have focused their analysis of Psalm 82 on the translation of אֱלֹהִים. However, this is problematic because many other scholars

---

4. Nasuti, *Tradition History*.

5. Demonstrated connections to Dt 32:8, to Covenant Code in Exodus, plus multiple views on the Psalter, classification of Asaph Psalm (despite Nasuti's analysis), and canonical approaches.

6. Morgenstern, and others, on ANE readings of Ps 82, including apocrypha, Ugaritic and Assyrian cognates (Draffkorn).

7. Parker and Smith, *Ugaritic Narrative Poetry*; Smith, *Origins of Biblical Monotheism*; Trotter, "Death of the אלהים."

8. The Yahwhistic conclusions of the psalm are often emphasized.

9. Morgenstern and others look to polytheistic, mythological setting for explanations.

10. Rendsburg, *Linguistic Evidence*.

11. This is a minority view, relying on ideas that the psalm was redacted for a royal festival reading in Judah.

have made equally reasonable arguments to defend very disparate interpretations. Each of these interpretations depend on a variable translation of the epithet for אֱלֹהִים in v. 1. The problem with an interpretation of Psalm 82 that depends on a translation of אֱלֹהִים is that אֱלֹהִים can legitimately represent multiple concepts. There is a semantic range of meaning for אֱלֹהִים in the Hebrew Bible based on its use in various genres and within the Psalter. This will be described in more detail in Chapter Two.[12] The natural conclusion here is that the psalm allows for a range of interpreting the divine setting.

Frank-Lothar Hossfeld and Erich Zenger pointed out that the interpretations of Psalm 82 fit into three categories:[13]

1. Psalm 82 is about the death of gods of the nations,
2. Psalm 82 is about the condemnation of human judges,
3. Psalm 82 reveals the "antisocial behavior of Canaanite officialdom."

The categories Zenger identified as main avenues for interpretation among twentieth-century scholars center on the topic of how rule is conducted, rather than focusing on the ethical message of Psalm 82. His findings confirmed that the central issue at stake in Psalm 82 for scholarship over the past century has been focused on the identity of the אֱלֹהִים in v. 1. While there is mention of the language about the marginalized, it is clear the emphasis of the commentary is to determine that this is primarily sourced as evidence to support judgments about existing political systems, whether human or divine.[14] The aforementioned categories of interpretation center the discussion of meaning for the psalm on the rule of justice rather than the right of justice—a situation this study seeks to correct.

Pre-Twentieth-Century Scholarship

Scholarship on Psalm 82 can be dated by millenia. The Septuagint offers a reading variant in v. 1. Depending on one's view of sequence in Hebrew oral tradition, the accuracy of the Masoretic Text (MT) and the Septuagint (LXX) reflects either an emendation or correction.[15] The subtle difference

---

12. Textual study of Ps 82:1 analysis of אֱלֹהִים.
13. Hossfeld and Zenger, *Psalms 2*, 330–31.
14. Hossfeld and Zenger, *Psalms 2*, 334.

15. Although this reading does not appear in the BHS apparatus, it has been noted by scholars. Ackerman, "An Exegetical Study of Psalm 82." Salters, "Psalm 82:1," 225–39.

offers some clarity in affirming the divine council setting, but it does little to resolve the ambiguities in v. 1.[16]

Early translators Aquila, Origen, and Targum Jonathan follow the LXX in reading the second אֱלֹהִים as referent to the Hebrew God. Aquila omitted the construct form and translated "in the midst, (God) judges." This approach was also adopted by Symmachus and Jerome (*in medio Deus iudicat*). This view supports a scene in a divine council most likely based in Israel, with Israel's God at the head of a divine pantheon. Aquila reads "mighty ones" for אֱלֹהִים, whom he describes as ones who receive punishment for their wickedness, though this is not described clearly in the psalm. Syriac versions of the text similarly interpret the אֱלֹהִים as patron angels of nations outside of Israel receiving judgment from Israel's God. In the Peshitta, v. 1 indicates that God rules through these heavenly beings. Targum Jonathan also reframes v. 1 to read the אֱלֹהִים as "just judges" who thought too highly of themselves (v. 6) and therefore, they are condemned by an Israel-centered divine council. Ultimately, pre-twentieth-century LXX translators portray a divine council scene where multiple deities receive judgment[17] from God, whose judgment extends from within Israel.

Early translations and commentaries interpret Psalm 82 from a predetermined religious view that supports the just reign of one God who condemns non-Israelite nations. In traditional Jewish explanations, the אֱלֹהִים fit into two categories: 1) Israelite judges, or 2) the whole nation of Israel. These translations and commentaries are evidence of early attempts to conform the awkward grammar in the psalm to a monotheistic paradigm rather than allowing the ambiguity to stand. Ackerman proposed that the LXX represented an early tradition offensive to Jewish interpreters who wished to move the scene closer to Israel in a "deliberate attempt to tone down the polytheistic setting of this psalm."[18]

Early Christian commentators approached Psalm 82 with prejudice as well. Justin Martyr (c. 100 CE) focused on vv. 6–7 as a description of the fall and punishment of the first man and woman from the garden in Genesis. Jerome (fourth century) acknowledged a divine council and posited that the judgment either represents God condemning pagan gods to die, or the judgment addresses political leaders of Israel and/or Israelite judges, who are admonished for their wickedness. Augustine (fifth century) read

---

16. The LXX goes on to support the reading that the second אֱלֹהִים refers to God as the subject of the 3ms verb יִשְׁפֹּט and recommends a parallel reading of the אֱלֹהִים with those in vv. 6–7.

17. cf. Origin and Theodotion

18. See Ackerman for a full discussion of early translations and interpretive implications for the mythological setting in Psalm 82. Ackerman, "Exegetical Study," 3–5.

Psalm 82 as a rejection of the Jews. His interpretation dismissed ideas of divine beings and instead reads the psalm as God's judgment against the Jews. As early as the fifth century CE, there was no unified interpretation of Psalm 82.[19]

The sixteenth-century reformation shed new light on the Hebrew Bible as scripture, yet there was still no consensus in the translation and interpretation of Psalm 82. By this time, three categorizations had solidified for the condemned in the psalm: 1) rulers and judges in Israel,[20] 2) rulers and judges of the nations,[21] or 3) the members of God's divine council.[22] And so it was up until the twentieth century and, as it appears in the Hermeneia commentary, these are some of the categories still debated in scholarship today.[23]

---

19. Also see Ackerman for an extended discussion of the influences of early Christian church interpretations of Psalm 82. Ackerman, "Exegetical Study," 34–36.

20. Luther claimed the condemned אֱלֹהִים were judges of Israel, although, in his time, he applied this to German rulers. Pelikan, ed., *Luther's Works*, 38–72. Other scholars shared this view in various forms: Hengstenberg, *Commentary*, 29–38; Graetz, *Kritischer Commentar*, 479; Delitzsch, *Biblical Commentary*, 460–63; Kirkpatrick, *The Book of Psalms*, 494–97; Thalhofer, *Hauspräfaten und Dompropstes*, 530–31; Duhm, *Die Psalmen*, 211; Cheyne, *The Book of Psalms*; Kittel, *The Religion of the People*, 275–77; Berry, *The Book of Psalms*, 161–62; Perowne, *The Book of Psalms*, 101.

21. Calvin extended the אֱלֹהִים to include a larger group, beyond the Israelites. Calvin, *Commentary*, 327–34. Other scholars shared this view in various forms: Hitzig, *Urgeschichte und Mythologie*, 188–91; Baethgen, *Die Psalmen*, 257–59; Buttenwieser, *The Psalms*, 764–65; Ehrlich, *Randglossen zur Hebrèaischen Bibel*, 199–200; Caláes, *Le Livre des Psaumes*, 82–83.

22. Syriac commentaries suggest that the אֱלֹהִים are gods or angels. Ibn Ezra described the אֱלֹהִים as guardian angels set by God over the nations. Other scholars aligned themselves with this view. Gunkel was the first scholar to analyze and differentiate psalms according to literary types. He fostered comparisons with ancient Near Eastern sources. Gunkel made significant connections between ancient Near Eastern religious motifs and those in the Hebrew Bible. Gunkel described Psalm 82 as referring to angels in Post-Exilic Judah. He proposed that the psalms were developed first by early Israelite prophets, and then they were brought formally into the Jewish cult after the exile. Gunkel, *Introduction to Psalms*, 98–116, 330–57. Mowinckel disagreed with Gunkel on dating and application of Psalm 82, instead placing the psalm in pre-exilic Israel at a fall enthronement festival (*Thronbesteigungsfest*). Mowinckel, *Psalmenstudien*, 13–14, 213–14, 315–16. Variants on these theories followed: Weiser, *The Psalms*, 556–61. Kraus, *Theology of the Psalms*, 571. Wellhausen, *Die Kleinen Propheten*. Oesterley, *Ancient Hebrew Poems*, 373–74.

23. Hossfeld and Zenger, *Psalms 2*.

Twentieth-Century Scholarship

Two major works focused on Psalm 82 in the twentieth century: *The Mythological Background of Psalm 82* by Julian Morgenstern in 1939,[24] and *An Exegetical Study of Psalm 82* by James S. Ackerman in 1966.[25] Morgenstern raised the issues which had plagued interpretations since early Common Era in light of modern thoughts about mythology and the Hebrew Bible. This set into motion a complex conversation between scholars through articles and papers aimed at further clarifying how Psalm 82 fits into the Psalter and Hebrew Bible in light of its *newly* acknowledged mythical origins. As discoveries from Ugarit and Mesopotamia provided cognate linguistic and literary evidence to support translation work in Hebrew Bible studies throughout the twentieth century, scholars sought to recontextualize Psalm 82 for a new age of Semitic language scholarship. This section will explore the contributions of twentieth and twenty-first century scholarship regarding Psalm 82: first by reviewing the two largest contributions to scholarship, and then articles of contribution to the scholarship of Psalm 82.

In the late nineteenth century/early twentieth century, questions about Psalm 82 centered on the meaning of אֱלֹהִים. Some interpreted the term as royalty, for example Duhm, who envisioned the psalm as evidence of an Israelite psalmist crying out for justice and protection from foreign nations. Many scholars supported Duhm's interpretation,[26] and many opposed his view.[27] Some scholars defended a translation of אֱלֹהִים as foreign gods,[28] and many revised their statements over time, apparently affected by the conversation and the influence of archaeological data so as to alter their opinions.[29] Morgenstern summarized this debate as the center of the "deep-rooted, internal contradiction and resultant confusion," suggesting that there are only

---

24. Morgenstern, "Mythological Background."

25. Ackerman, "Exegetical Study."

26. Gesenius, *Gesenius' Hebrew Grammar*; Ewald, *Commentary on the Psalms*; De Wette, *Commentar uber die Psalmen*; Brown et al., *The New Brown-Driver-Briggs-Gesenius Hebrew and English Lexicon*; Olshausen, *Die Psalmen*.

27. Staerk, *Studien zur Religions*; Baudissin, *Kyrios als Gottesname*; Kittel, *The Religion of the People*.

28. Gunkel, *Introduction to Psalms*; Mowinckel, *Psalmenstudien*; Staerk, *Studien zur Religions*; Budde, "Ps 82:6f."

29. Notably, Duhm, who redirected his view from "Asmonean kings" to later join others in favor of "foreign kings." Kittel altered his view from "judges" to "gods" by 3rd and 4th editions of his commentary, and Staerk alternated between "kings" and "gods." Note Morgenstern's assessment of the difficulty in pinning down one definition for the אֱלֹהִים in early twentieth-century scholarship. Duhm, *Die Psalmen*. See further discussion in Morgenstern. Morgenstern, "Mythological Background," 30–31.

two basic interpretations of the אֱלֹהִים named in vv. 1b and 6, and only one could be right: 1) divine beings, or 2) human beings.³⁰

Julian Morgenstern approached Psalm 82 by noting that the difficulties of interpretation rely primarily on "the precise implication of the word אֱלֹהִים."³¹ He stated that most scholars in the time of his writing accept אֱלֹהִים as an emendation from the tetragrammaton. This is a view that developed as scholars abandoned ancient references to אֱלֹהִים meaning "judges"³² in favor of contemporary ideas about the significance of reception history. C. H. Gordon, Kittel, and Duhm, for example, revisited classical translations of אֱלֹהִים as judges, re-opening the door for more variety in interpretations.³³ While translations still relied on religious suppositions like the innocence of God, the conversation of meaning was once again a factor for evaluation. This line of discussion often challenged pre-modern interpretations. Morgenstern set the stage for future work on Psalm 82. Nearly every scholar since has picked up his premise that upon the translation of the word אֱלֹהִים hangs the balance of the interpretation of Psalm 82.³⁴

Morgenstern began parsing v. 1 with a discussion of divine and human realms. On the one hand, Morgenstern writes, Psalm 82 is *certainly* dealing with matters of judicial importance in the human realm, regarding human activity. He cited vv. 2–4 as dealing in a "perfectly literal manner with human beings and not with gods or angels."³⁵ On the other hand, with stated *equal certainty* he addressed the psalm as dealing only with divine beings, citing vv. 6–7 as evidence that "even if it were at all possible to interpret אֱלֹהִים in v. 6 as 'judges' or 'rulers,' certainly the specific term בְּנֵי עֶלְיוֹן, occurring nowhere else in the Hebrew Bible, can designate only divine beings and

---

30. Morgenstern, "Mythological Background," 30–31.

31. Morgenstern, "Mythological Background," 30.

32. Targum, Midr. Tehillim, and Rashi translate אֱלֹהִים as "judges." See previous discussion on pre-twentieth- century scholarship.

33. Gordon, "History of Religion"; Kittel, *The Religion*; Duhm, *Die Psalmen*.

34. Many articles open up with Morgenstern's premise that the difficulty in understanding the entire psalm lies in the correct interpretation of אֱלֹהִים in v. 1. Though most scholars note that interpretation is complex, and in some cases nearly impossible, they continue to hang an interpretation on their translation of אֱלֹהִים. Scholars have, however, continued to point out the difficulties. For example, Kraus, who noted "Psalm 82 is of such exceptional character in the Psalter at it could well be impossible to provide interpretations that are in every respect satisfactory." Kraus, *Psalms 1–59*, 155. Most notably, perhaps, Nasuti appeals to the possible ambiguous nature of Psalm 82, though he does not provide an analysis of the Psalm in light of this. Nasuti's perspective will be discussed in further detail in the manuscript. Nasuti, *Tradition History*.

35. Morgenstern, "Mythological Background," 32–33.

naught else."[36] His explanation for this is a text critical study of the psalm's mythological origin in which Morgenstern described Psalm 82 as a patchwork composition split into multiple excerpts from various source traditions which sometimes seem to stand in contradiction with one another. His thesis leaves no room for an ambiguous reading. Morgenstern seemed intent on justifying a singular interpretation in order to make theological sense of the psalm. This theological justification might have best addressed the major scholarly concerns of his time, but it does not address the complexities of the text in a holistic manner.

Morgenstern's approach to Psalm 82 lacks an appreciation for other important aspects in the psalm. The purpose of this study is to show that previous scholarship has not sufficiently demonstrated a clear path of interpreting Psalm 82; and that this path would be best served by considering a reading of Psalm 82 as shaped by intentional ambiguity. Morgenstern traced a discussion that attempted to clarify Psalm 82, justifying its placement in the Psalter. Morgenstern's scheme to work out a certain interpretation reached for conclusions he justified by working out a complicated rationale for dissecting Psalm 82 and evaluating each segment for its possible source in a text critical study. In all the textual juggling, however, the message of justice advocacy in Psalm 82 was lost.

Since Morgenstern, many scholars have contributed to the discussion, largely working within the paradigm established in his thesis. Scholars have taken up an opinion, siding with one or another of Morgenstern's proposed certainties, attributing these declarations firmly in defense, or in opposition, of each premise brought forth in Morgenstern's thesis. The scholarship on Psalm 82 has been primarily caught up in the back and forth of this discussion based on Morgenstern's framework.

Two decades after Morgenstern produced his thesis on Psalm 82, James Ackerman wrote *An Exegetical Study of Psalm 82*.[37] Whereas Morgenstern relied on the inner-biblical motif of fallen deities, Ackerman sought to consider Psalm 82 within a broader context of mythological influence, the evidence for which had since become more accessible. Ackerman read the psalm alongside contemporary attempts to relate YHWH worship to proto-Semitic worship of ʾEl. He also was influenced by the view that many psalms originated within "the pre-exilic Israelite cult, rather than later expressions of individual piety."[38]

---

36. Morgenstern, "Mythological Background," 32–33.
37. Ackerman, "Exegetical Study."
38. Ackerman, "Exegetical Study," vii.

Ackerman set Psalm 82 in its canonical context, as a part of Book 3, the Elohistic Psalter, and at home with the Asaph Psalms.[39] Taking a canonical approach, Ackerman explored the possibilities of Psalm 82's relevance within Israelite culture. The study was shaped by comparisons to ancient Near Eastern literature that provided evidence of deities judging and being judged for illicit behavior. He concluded with a description of God's responsibility to affect justice as the main idea of Psalm 82.

Ackerman explored the Hebrew lawsuit motif, drawing attention to the courtroom-like setting of the divine council. He noted trials of deities in comparative mythical context from ancient Near Eastern literature. From Mesopotamian literature, he included a case study of Enlil's trial in divine court from Sumerian myth as an example of primitive democracy. He also looked at the Enuma Elish wherein Marduk gathers a council of divine beings to judge the crimes of Tiamat, and he considered the Descent of Inanna who sat trial by divine council in the nether world. From Ugarit, he noted that Baʻal is brought to trial by Yam before the enthroned ʼEl, and from the Hebrew Bible, he noted that Isaiah 41–46 demonstrated evidence of a similar covenant lawsuit in prophetic literature.[40]

In addition to noting cases of divine beings on trial, he also noted trials in which divine council judge mortals. In cognate literature, Ackerman pointed to a trial in the Gilgamesh Epic, wherein legal proceedings are initiated against Gilgamesh and Enkidu by divine mandate for killing the Bull of Heaven.[41] He also considered the *Epic of Aqhat* from Ugarit, where the goddess Anat appeals to ʼEl for vindication against the mortal Aqhat. Although, in this case, Ackerman saw ʼEl as acting alone in judgment, rather than with a council.[42] In the Hebrew Bible, Ackerman presented his greatest cases: Dan 7:9–14; Isa 6:1–2; 1 Kgs 22:19–20; Job 1–2; Zech 3:1ff, and other prophetic passages.[43] Divine council in the Hebrew Bible often extended to mortal realms. Ancient Near Eastern divine council motifs extend judgment, deity to deity as well as to mortals.

After outlining the cognate literature to establish the presence of a theme of trial by divine council in the ancient Near East, Ackerman delved into the structure of judicial procedure. He found that the role of the divine assembly was established to witness events in the case. To a divine court,

---

39. Ackerman, "Exegetical Study," 175.

40. See Ackerman for a discussion of scholarship on covenant lawsuit in the Hebrew Bible. He engages scholars Frank Moore Cross, Herbert B. Huffmon, and Ludwig Koehler on the topic. Ackerman, "Exegetical Study," 169ff.

41. Ackerman, "Exegetical Study," 204–5.

42. Ackerman, "Exegetical Study," 206.

43. Ackerman, "Exegetical Study," 207–8.

one might present an accusation with recommendation of a sentence,⁴⁴ present an accusation through witnesses,⁴⁵ or present an accusation by complaint of damage done.⁴⁶ The divine council then carries out judgment with or without the involvement of witnesses.⁴⁷

Ackerman's catalogue of canonical evidence and cognate evidence of a divine lawsuit motif in the Hebrew Bible is impressive. Certainly, his contribution informs an aspect of the divine council and its correlates in mythological texts that had been overlooked in Hebrew Bible scholarship. However, after all of the setup about the importance of judgment by divine council in ancient Near Eastern trial texts, Ackerman found no parallel to Psalm 82 as an indictment against the gods in such a setting. The final chapter to Ackerman's work consists of a textual study of Psalm 82 where he evaluated the position of YHWH in v. 1, even though the tetragrammaton does not appear. In the end, Ackerman's conclusions hinged upon his translation of v. 1 in which he sided with certain traditions summarized in the previous section and defended his position that the Israelite God reigns over all other deities, who each represent nations surrounding Israel.⁴⁸ The remaining seven verses were interpreted following his assertion that YHWH is the leader of the divine council, in which God defends Israel against surrounding nations.

Ackerman made an interesting contribution to the understanding of judgment aspects of divine council in ancient Near Eastern literature. This might anticipate an ethical reading of the psalm. In the end, his exegesis of Psalm 82 defended a politically-oriented interpretation based on a Deuteronomic perspective of divine council. Rather than focusing on imagery of the poor and marginalized as victims, he took a metaphorical approach, defending the strength of the Hebrew God (and by proxy Israel) to rule over the patron deities of surrounding nations. Ackerman's contribution did little to advance the scholarship of Psalm 82 beyond the issue which Morgenstern had outlined a quarter century earlier.

While interest in the mythical provenance of Hebrew Bible texts grew in the twentieth century,⁴⁹ its application to Psalm 82 became obscure. Most scholars came to a position of agreement that Psalm 82 had something to do with the so-called myths of other ancient Near Eastern regional literatures,

---

44. For example, in Jer 26:11 and 2 Sam 19:21.
45. For example, in Deut 21:18–21 and 1 Kgs 21:13.
46. See 1 Kgs 3:17–21; Deut 22:13–21; and, with exception, Isa 3:13–15.
47. Ackerman, "Exegetical Study," 228.
48. This is a perspective drawn from Deut 32:8.
49. See discussion about myth and Psalm 82 in Chapter 3

but how and why the psalm engaged in such mythical language confounded scholars. Multiple explanations arose over the century following Morgenstern's analysis. The various translations and interpretations were no more settled than those which came before the twentieth century, for all its discoveries of ancient Near Eastern cognate linguistic influences and mythological awareness. Whereas Morgenstern thought to enlighten scholarship on the psalm by connecting it with its mythological provenance, the awareness brought another aspect about which to debate.

A number of scholars attempted to resolve the problems raised by Morgenstern regarding the difficulties in translating and interpreting Psalm 82. The psalm became famous for being difficult to translate. However, it is interesting to note Psalm 82 is not listed in a 1960 volume which claims to catalogue "problematic" MT Hebrew Bible texts which fall into one of three groups: a) practically untranslatable, b) adequate exegesis may be done with clues from other versions, and c) more than one translation is made possible by the MT.[50] This is evidence of assumptions that were made about the nature and translation of אֱלֹהִים in past centuries. As for the scholarship of the twentieth and twenty-first centuries, the interpretation of Psalm 82 continued to perplex scholars.

A series of articles over the next several decades followed in conversation about the significance of Psalm 82. Some of the scholarship focused on the reception of Psalm 82, discussing the difficulties in dating the psalm and identifying the location and reason of origin. Others focused on its canonical *raison d'être*, emphasizing a premise that because it is in the Hebrew Bible Psalter, it must contain a positive message about the Hebrew God. Nearly all scholarship prioritized commentary on identifying who are the אֱלֹהִים in v. 1. For all scholars, the identification of the אֱלֹהִים was in question, and the resolution of the matter would, it seemed, bring clarity.

In the mid-twentieth century, Hebrew Bible scholarship was flourishing in the western world. Biblical archaeology was well underway, the Nazis were defeated, and Israel was eager to establish its modern national heritage. Biblical scholars engaged more freely in comparative literature and literary theory as a method. This brought a renewed interest for some to revisit Morgenstern's proposal about the mythological provenance of Psalm 82.

Otto Eissfeldt introduced a perspective in the mid 1950s that helped make sense of the assumption that the Israelite God may have been a participant in the divine council of Psalm 82. This was difficult since the divine council motif was by this time identified as a remnant of Canaanite tradition, and therefore its inclusion in the Hebrew Bible did not sit well with

---

50. Hulst, *Old Testament Translation Problems*.

those who viewed the text as sacred scripture, unique and set apart from its environment. Eissfeldt made a startling proposal that the council described in Psalm 82 belonged to ʾEl, the Canaanite deity. Furthermore, the Israelite deity, YHWH, was seen as one of the unnamed אֱלֹהִים, merely a participating deity. Eissfeldt claimed that the psalm "clearly presents Yahweh in the congregation of El . . ."[51] Eissfeldt claimed that the setting itself, referent to divine council, provides sufficient implication for his view. He defended Psalm 82 as a polemic in which the psalmist calls upon YHWH as an attempt to invite reformation wherein YHWH should overtake El as supreme deity. Eissfeldt's reading introduced obscurity about who is the ruling deity when Psalm 82 is read in a mythological setting.

Eissfeldt's attempts to reconcile the Hebrew Bible psalm with its cognitive surrounding reflected literary theories about mythopoeia which were beginning to circulate at the time of this article. Eissfeldt viewed Psalm 82 as a religious expression of the world through an ancient lens. His view, which removed the Hebrew deity from center stage in a Hebrew text, invited further discussion about who the אֱלֹהִים *could* be in Psalm 82. Eissfeldt's proposal was revived by scholars in the early twenty-first century.[52]

In 1962, Mowinckel wrote about how the psalms were recognized in Israel's cultic setting. He noted that the primary purpose of Psalm 82 was to depict a contrast between YHWH and other regional deities. In his interpretation, YHWH is the speaker, passing judgment over all of the other deities. In his translation, "Yahweh stands out in the assembly of the gods,"[53] and the following verses describe a speech by YHWH in which all other deities are sentenced to death.[54] He placed Psalm 82 within a literary context that fits into the festival of New Year and Enthronement, alongside literature about how divine assembly gathers to determine the destiny of the year.[55] Furthermore, he asserted that the reference to gods and nations corresponds with Deut 32:8, in which the most high god portions out the nations amongst the sons of gods. He read Psalm 82 as a follow-up to the distribution of gods

---

51. Eissfeldt, "El and Yahweh," 25–37.

52. Trotter and Hossfeld discussed the evidence for deities uniting under the Canaanite god El in early Hebraic viewpoints. This will be presented later in this chapter. Trotter, "Death of the אלהים"; Hossfeld, "Ps 82."

53. In this translation, Mowinckel did not recognize ʾ *el* as a distinct, singular deity, rather he either followed the LXX tradition of ʾ *elim* or read it as a colloquial phrase meaning "divine council." Another interpretation that follows Mowinckel's reading may be found in the 1969 publication by Jüngling. Jüngling focused on imagining the divine environment of YHWH. His perspective also relied on reading YHWH as the speaker in Psalm 82. Jüngling, *Der Tod der Götter*.

54. Mowinckel, *The Psalms*, 64.

55. Mowinckel, *The Psalms*, 132.

among nations.⁵⁶ Again, this view supports a reading of Psalm 82 as justification for complaint against foreign powers assaulting Israel.⁵⁷

Mowinckel affirmed the setting of Psalm 82 in the geo-political realm. He developed this understanding by inserting the Hebrew deity into v. 1 which allows his reading to unfold upon that premise. Even given the understanding of אֱלֹהִים as YHWH, Mowinckel's description that the verses follow as a speech by YHWH is troublesome. For one thing, the speech patterns invoke human prophetic style and would be unusual to take as divine speech. For another, there is an appeal to the אֱלֹהִים to rise, which interferes with congruity of the speech, or it invokes a third person speaker. Mowinckel's reading of Psalm 82 as a nationalist composition dismisses its potential for application among a broader constituency.

Two years later, Cyril S. Rodd shed some light on Psalm 82 by looking at it from the first-century Gospel of John. He relied upon the use of Psalm 82 in John 10:3–6 for interpretation, which brings it into view alongside Isa 3:13–15. Rodd defended an interpretation of אֱלֹהִים as "lesser members of Yahweh's heavenly court."⁵⁸ Rodd followed Mowinckel in setting Psalm 82 as a ritual-psalm, spoken at the New Year festival in Jerusalem. He also viewed the psalm as depicting God denouncing other regional deities.

Rodd did point out that the central ethic of the Hebrew Bible as a whole is caring for the needy and defenseless. He made a case for Psalm 82 encouraging the king at the festival to follow this path of concern for the marginalized. To support this, he cited similar ethical passages in the Hebrew Bible.⁵⁹ Rodd's view brings to light the dual-focus of Psalm 82: the human side and the divine. This article re-raised the question that Morgenstern opened earlier that century—is Psalm 82 referring to the divine or to the human realm?

Later that decade, Tsevat produced an article that recommended compartmentalizing the psalm by reading the first seven verses as a narrative, aligned in form with other vision texts in the Hebrew Bible (cf. Isa 6:8; Ezek 9:8, 11:13; Amos 7:2; et al.). He substantiated his claim by asserting

---

56. He also cited the corroboration of this view in a Qumran fragment. Mowinckel, *The Psalms*, 150.

57. Mowinckel noted that Psalm 82 is a stylized form of national lament. Mowinckel, *The Psalms*, 220–1.

58. Rodd, *Psalms*. This view was also supported by Cook, who believed that arguments for interpreting אֱלֹהִים as human were weak and could not be supported. He read Psalm 58 as support for interpreting divine entities in Psalm 82:1. Cooke, "The Sons of (the) God(s)," 29–34.

59. Ps 72, Isa 11:3–5 and Jer 22:16; Isa 1:17, 23; 10:2; Jer 5:28; Amos 5, 7, 10,1 1; Zech 7:9–10; Ex 22:21–22; Lev 19:33–34; Dt 10:18–19; 24:17–22.

that v. 8 aligns with other Deuteronomistic writings. He concluded that v. 8 is a Deuteronomistic explanation for the proceeding verses.[60] Tsevat's comparison of Psalm 82 to features in Deuteronomy is not uncommon. As was brought up previously, Psalm 82 is often mentioned in connection with Deut 32:8. However, Tsevat's approach does not take into account the poetic or psalmic nature of the text.

Tsevat's appeal to restructure the Psalm opened the door to more questions about how and when this psalm was composed and received among early audiences. Tsevat appealed to the idea of a redactional force that would seek disambiguation through monotheistic propaganda. In his view, the psalm contains features from known *mythological* texts (referring here to genre or mode), and those references serve as a backdrop over which Deuteronomistic editors placed priority on a monotheistic view in which God assumes authority over any other deities. Tsevat's view is satisfying. It provides a way to disambiguate complex tensions in Psalm 82, but it does so at the expense of the apparent polysemy, narrowing the focus of the psalm to a deuteronomistic priority.

Tsevat's interpretation stemmed from his view that the Hebrew Bible is a pro-monotheistic source that recognizes a world wherein multiple deities are conceived by ancient Near Easterners, and therefore, they must be subjugated.[61] For him, this was the purpose of Ps 82:1. Tsevat's premise drives his interpretation. He conceded to one textual difficulty—that אֱלֹהִים must be an emendation from an earlier text that contained the tetragrammaton, (presuming that such a text existed). He based his reasoning on the grammatical awkwardness of the two-times appearance of אֱלֹהִים in one single verse. However, his focus quickly moved to align the source of justice with YHWH, theologically; and then he could read the tetragrammaton for the first occurrence of אֱלֹהִים in v. 1. Like others before him, Tsevat placed Psalm 82 in a political light, noting its expression of transition for the nation of Israel from a "primitive democracy," to an "absolute monarchy."[62] The emphasis on monarchy imagery is hotly debated in light of better readings of cognate ancient Near Eastern Literature.[63] The social political perspective is explored more in the late twentieth century and twenty-first century scholarship.

---

60. Tsevat, "God and the Gods in Assembly," 123–37.

61. Tsevat, "God and the Gods," 123–24.

62. Tsevat, "God and the Gods," 123–24.

63. Parker re-explored the logistics of the divine assembly motif in light of monarchical imagery in Psalm 82. A more thorough discussion on Parker's viewpoint is below. Parker, "The Beginning of the Reign of God," 532–59; Tate, *Psalms 51–100*, 335.

Tsevat's translation passed the test of his own interpretation, requiring that the reader assumes a pro-monotheistic position, which is not guaranteed in the composition of the psalm. The text alone does not necessitate this presumption, therefore, Tsevat's reading, while centered in a canonical interpretation, avoids the ambiguous nature of Psalm 82 and the natural tensions in the text by avoiding exegesis outside of Judeo-Christian priorities of monotheism.

In the late 1970s, Cyrus Gordon pressed into his study of Psalm 82 from a Semitic linguistic perspective, arguing that only those who seek interpretations that theologically "protect God" will translate אֱלֹהִים as human judges or rulers.[64] Gordon preferred to retain the divine aspect of אֱלֹהִים, which firmly protects the psalm in its Semitic linguistic heritage.

Again, the question that Morgenstern raised nearly half century previous was brought into view: does Psalm 82 speak to spheres of the divine or its human counterpart? Gordon's contribution was significant since his work established firmer connections between Ugaritic literature and Psalm 82. In this way, he furthered Morgenstern's work in connecting Psalm 82 linguistically with its mythological provenance.

By the late twentieth century, biblical studies as a field engaged more fully with cognate literature and accounted for sociological perspectives and cultural influences on the text of the Hebrew Bible. This brought a renewed attention to parts of the Hebrew Bible that seemed to be influenced by language and literature from surrounding cultures. Psalm 82 once again beckoned scholars to consider its origins and significance.

In 1980, Claus Westermann identified Psalm 82 as one of a handful of psalms that share motifs in common with psalms of lament and therefore connected to prophetic literature of lament.[65] As such, he proposed that Psalm 82 has commonalities with the theme and style of the community lament. Westermann identified the accusation of God as the "nerve center of all lamentation in the Psalms," in which the high god is lamented for having allowed suffering to come upon the people.[66] Though he did not cite Psalm 82 as a direct example, his description of the lament motif applies in that a deity, or deities, are accused. Psalm 82 contains two major features of the Westermann's lament motif: a request for divine attention of human suffering, and

---

64. Gordon, "History of Religion."

65. Westermann, *The Psalms*, 29. Westermann identified community psalms of lament as Pss 44; 60; 74; 79; 80; 83; and 89, as well as others that share common motifs or "reminiscences": Pss 82, 85, 68, 90, 106, and 115. He extended the genre into prophetic texts, including Jer 14; Isa 63:7–64:12; Hab 1; and also motifs in Isa 26; 33; 51; 59; Joel 1–2; Jer 3; and Isa 40:27.

66. Westermann, *The Psalms*, 32.

a request for divine intervention. The protest is marked by "how long . . . ?" and there is an inclusion of request for salvation and help.[67] However, Psalm 82 departs from the lament model in that its conclusion does not resolve with a vow of faithfulness. This is significant to reading Psalm 82 as a composition that wants a response beyond lament.

For Elmer Smick, who wrote in 1982, the central argument around Psalm 82 is monotheism. He argued that אֱלֹהִים could signify either divine beings or human authoritative beings. For Smick, the psalm moves "in both directions."

On one hand, Smick described a reading that views Psalm 82 as an Israelite complaint against ancient Near Eastern rulers.[68] Smick supported this reading by comparing the language of Psalm 82 to Isaiah 14 and Ezekiel 28 in which the rulers of Babylon and Tyre are described as heavenly rulers who eventually fall to Sheol. This canonically supports a reading of Ps 82:6–7 as a passage in which foreign deities come to death, after which, the final verse in the psalm asserts a monotheistic reign of God.

Smick referred to the deities in the Hebrew Bible literature as a "created reality," and Psalm 82 draws upon this mythical language, which he noted also appears in Job and Isaiah. Smick also draws upon later source material from the first-century-CE Gospel of John, Chapter 10, where Jesus of Nazareth references Psalm 82 as a matter of defense to Jews who question his given title as the *Son of God*. Smick concluded that the linguistic elements in Psalm 82 are reflective of a mythopoeic perspective that fits into the "god language from pagan sources."[69] In spite of this, for Smick, the position of God is not deflated in the mythological aspects of the psalm.

On the other hand, Smick emphasized the human world element of Psalm 82, "God's triumph is on earth not in heaven."[70] Therefore, the psalm is useful to the liturgy. Despite the claim of usefulness, Smick's interpretation did not focus much on the ethical insights offered in vv. 2–4 regarding concern for the poor and marginalized. His focus, instead, remained on how the psalm does justice to God. Although Smick accepted a plurality of possible meanings for the אֱלֹהִים in v. 1, he concluded that the purpose of Psalm 82 is meant to position YHWH as the highest in order of the gods, regardless of the fact that the name YHWH does not appear in the psalm. Smick advocated rightly for the truth or integrity of the text, presuming an early monotheistic value. He defended mythical god-language in the

---

67. Westermann, *The Psalms*, 31–34.
68.. Smick, "Mythopoetic Language," 88–99.
69. Smick, "Mythopoetic Language," 88–89.
70. Smick, "Mythopoetic Language," 88–89.

Hebrew Bible as a literary device which does not presuppose that the Hebrew religion followed other ancient Palestinian religions. For Smick, the complications in Psalm 82 could be ignored based on a presumption of monotheistic perspective.

In the late 1980s, Patrick Miller chimed in on the discussion about Psalm 82 calling it "one of the most overtly mythological texts in Scripture."[71] He identified the psalm as mythopoeic literature heralding two primary themes: "monotheism" and "justice in the human arena." His work follows Smick in that Miller also defended monotheism as the purpose of Psalm 82. Miller pointed to 1 Kgs 22:19–21 for an example of an image of YHWH seated in a council setting where others may come in to stand before or beside the ruling deity.[72] In his view, Ps 82:5 is a description of the consequence of injustice manifested in a kind of "cosmic disorder."[73]

Miller also compared the language in Ps 82:5 to language about idols in Isa 40–55, "the nothingness of the idols that have no capacity to see or know or discern anything,"[74] in order to propose that the subject of v. 5 are like Isaiah's divine idols. Miller then read that meaning back into v. 1, so that he described the אֱלֹהִים as idols as well. In this way, Miller justified his interpretation that Psalm 82 refers to multiple unnamed deities. For Miller, Psalm 82 describes an evolution of אֱלֹהִים as multiple deities who are then displaced by one God, who then subsumes the title of אֱלֹהִים.[75] It is for this reason that אֱלֹהִים may sometimes be used to represent a single deity, in particular the God of the Hebrew Bible.[76]

For Miller, the inclusion of a heavenly council scene in Psalm 82 is the mythopoeic expression of ancients who are describing an event in which multiple deities convene to gather under one deity, subjects to the rule of one.[77] This is an omnidirectional event; religious culture evolves toward monotheism, and not the other way around. Miller described Psalm 82 as an attempt by ancient Hebrews to situate monotheistic views in a polytheistic world. Furthermore, the event of a rise of monotheism in Psalm 82 is centered on portraying justice as "the cornerstone of the universe." Miller concluded that the psalm appeals to the order of justice in both human and cosmic realms.

71. Miller, "When the Gods Meet," 2–5.
72. Miller, "Cosmology and World Order," 56
73. Miller, "Cosmology and World Order," 69.
74. Miller, "When the Gods Meet," 2–5.
75. Miller, "When the Gods Meet," 2–5.
76. Miller, "When the Gods Meet," 2–5.
77. Miller, "When the Gods Meet," 2–5.

> The maintenance of justice and righteousness is the foundation of the universe, the responsibility of the divine council, and the issue upon which hang both the stability of the universe and the stability and effective reality of the divine world.[78]

He suggested that a good takeaway from the psalm for a modern reader is to "do justice," drawing on traditions of Hebrew prophets.[79] He also drew attention to the negative impact of human injustice on the physical earth.[80] Miller's work asserted that the divine council was reflective of social order because it was part of an ancient cosmology. Its appearance throughout the Hebrew Bible is reflective of ancient thought and it should not be dismissed without consideration for its role in declaring the rule and control of the cosmos in which there is a judge "who insures that the order of the world is truly a righteous order."[81] This conceptual description of divine interaction is the closest Miller gets to dealing with the social-ethical issues raised in Psalm 82 regarding care for the poor.

Niehr's paper followed, attempting to again address the confusion about whether אֱלֹהִים refers to the divine or to the human. His conclusions relied on a mythopoeic reading that takes into account that of an ancient pantheistic world in which the responsibilities of humankind and divine entities are inseparable. He wrote,

> Die vieldiskutierte Frage, ob in Ps 82 Götter oder Menschen angesprochen sind, ist dahingehend zu entscheiden, daß beide Gruppen gemeint sind. Dies beruht auf dem in Analogie zur Welt konzipierten Pantheon, so daß sich im menschlichen Handeln das Handeln der Götter zeigt.[82]

In this social context, human actions are reflective of the actions of the gods. This is an important acknowledgement of a composition's ability to reflect human social norms, attitudes, and values by describing them in a divine context.

Niehr concluded that the composition of Psalm 82 demonstrates an ambiguity which allows the text to conceptually play between heavenly and earthly realms. He described this by grouping verses within Psalm

---

78. Miller, "Cosmology and World Order," 68.
79. Miller, "When the Gods Meet," 2–5.
80. Miller, "When the Gods Meet," 2–5.
81. Miller, "Cosmology and World Order," 72.
82. "The much-debated question of whether gods or people are addressed in Ps 82 is interpreted to decide that both groups are meant. This is due to the designed-in analogy to the world Pantheon, so that in human action is the action of the gods." Niehr, "Gotter oder Menschen," 95–98.

82. In sum, vv. 1, 6, and 7 refer to events in the divine realm, while vv. 2–4 refer to events in the human realm.[83] His appeal was to the possibility of reading multiple subjects in the psalm which may have been reflective of expressed ambiguous tension. His reading promoted the idea that ambiguity is present when individual verses or groups of verses represent multiple points of view within a single psalm. Niehr appealed to an ambiguous reading of Psalm 82, but he did not fully explore the various ways that ambiguity could function within the composition.

Through Niehr's work, Psalm 82 represents a human realm which freely interacts with the divine. The ethical responsibilities of humankind and the deities are inseparable as human actions reflect the actions of the gods.[84] In this way, Niehr's work appeals to poetic ambiguity as a source for ethical interpretive means. In the following year, Hans-Joachim Kraus made a similar contribution. He wrote that the complexities inherent to Psalm 82 weigh on the translation. Kraus determined that any single interpretation may not be satisfactory due to the complex nature of the psalm.[85]

The contributions of scholarship at this point suggest that there is certainly more to explore in what it could mean for Psalm 82 to be read as an ambiguous composition, or what it means for the language to assert both divine and human attitudes at once. Niehr's contribution opened the door for further exploration of the usefulness of considering ambiguity as a means by which to read Psalm 82 ethically, which is exactly what this thesis explores.

In 1988, Harry P. Nasuti published his work on the tradition history of the Psalms of Asaph, including a discussion of Psalm 82. As an Asaph psalm, Psalm 82 potentially shares commonalities with this group of twelve psalms. In wider scholarship, two major commonalities among Asaph Psalms have been recognized: 1) Asaph psalms are seen as collective or communal lament (i.e. Ps 74, 79, 80, 83); and, 2) there is a connection to an Ephraimite tradition, by which Asaph psalms are seen to contain prophetic elements (i.e. Ps 50, 75, 81, 83).[86] Due to the prophetic nature of the Asaph psalms, as well as

---

83. This is several years after Morgenstern's proposal that the Psalm may be best understood by interpreting its elements based on probable origin of each composed section. Morgenstern also breaks up the psalm in a similar way, claiming that vv. 2–4 and vv. 6–7 come from different sources. Niehr, "Gotter oder Menschen."

84. Niehr, "Gotter oder Menschen." 95

85. Kraus, *Psalms 1–59*, 155.

86. Nasuti, *Tradition History*, 118.

Gunkel looked at speech patterns common to prophets in the Asaph Psalms as well as uses of imagery and eschatology in a similar manner, though his study is not quite as thorough as Nasuti's. Gunkel, *Introduction to Psalms*, 329ff.

a strong connection to Torah, Psalm 82 is largely considered to be prophetic and often compared to Deuteronomic texts. Though Psalm 82 is attributed to Asaph in the superscription, it stands apart in many ways.

Nasuti's study of the Asaph psalms is unparalleled. In his conclusion, he disclosed that he would not be comfortable placing Psalm 82 in any known Hebrew Bible tradition.[87]

> [I]t may be said that the theological and poetic distinctiveness of Psalm 82 is not matched by a similar linguistic distinctiveness which might lead to any decisive tradition-historical conclusions. In terms of the larger task of determining the tradition-history of the Asaphite psalms as a whole, Psalm 82 is, in effect, a neutral datum. With respect to the already observed Ephraimite tendencies of these psalms, Psalm 82 furnishes neither supportive nor contradictory evidence. Its theology may, of course, be seen to be similar to that expressed in certain Ephraimite sources, but it is part of the methodological caution of this study not to base its tradition-historical judgments on a criterion so open to diverse interpretation. Accordingly, in the present case, the tie to the Asaphite psalms (and possibly to the Ephraimite tradition stream of which some of these are a part) rests on the superscription alone.[88]

Nasuti's finding is significant because it contributes to a discussion about why Psalm 82 has been considered distinctive and complex by so many scholars in past centuries. Its uniqueness could also explain why there is difficulty in trying to justify a correct translation and interpretation of the psalm. Nasuti's observation about the nonconformity of the psalm informs this study, which seeks yet another way through the psalm.

Nasuti made note of several qualities in Psalm 82 that discounted its connection to the Hebrew Bible. In his exegesis of Ps 82:1, Nasuti acknowledged that the divine council scene may describe a heavenly realm, as others have noted, or it may refer to an assembly of humans.[89] This somewhat follows the sociological approach presented by Niehr.[90] Nasuti attempted to compare Psalm 82 with Psalm 58, but he was not able to justify a proper comparison between the two psalms due to the lack of a clear divine council

---

87. Nasuti, *Tradition History*.
88. Nasuti, *Tradition History*, 111.
89. He acknowledges the use of עֲדַת in Psalm 74:2 to reference an assembly of peoples. There is also suggestion of this elsewhere (cf. Psalm 7:8, 68:31; Jer. 6:18). Nasuti, *Tradition History*, 108.
90. Niehr, "Gotter oder Menschen."

scene in Psalm 58.[91] Nasuti noted that Psalm 82 is neither addressed to the people of Israel (as is the case in Psalm 81 and Psalm 50), nor to the wicked of the earth (as it is in Psalm 75). However, he made a case for connecting Ps 82:1 to another setting that corresponds to a legal/judicial matter in Isa 3:13, in which God judges those who despoil the poor. Nasuti classified the Isaiah passage as "the only example of such an overtly judicial setting."[92] While Isaiah 3 holds this in common with Psalm 82, Isaiah's passage is concerned with God's judgement of humans and does not include the judgment of other divine entities.[93] These unique characteristics make it difficult to situate Psalm 82 clearly within a biblical tradition.

Nasuti suggested that ambiguity contributes to the uncertainty of the tradition historical locus for Psalm 82. The first half of v. 2 refers to the עָוֶל, which may correspond to occurrences of the poor in other judicial settings, such as in Lev 19:15, 34, Deut 25:16 and related variations in Deut 32:4, Jer 2:5, 2 Chr 19:7, and Zeph 3:5. Psalm 82:2b may also have ambiguous connections to Ps 18:5[94] and Deut 10:17.[95] Nasuti's reticence to place the psalm in a shared category with these other judicial setting texts is evidence of the unique and ambiguous nature of Psalm 82. He concluded that Ps 82:3–4 shares traits more common to wisdom literature than liturgy regarding engagement with the topic of poverty. Furthermore, he noted the potential relationship between Psalm 82 and Proverbs or Job, but he also noted parallels between Psalm 82 and Amos, Isaiah, other Psalms, prophetic literature and legal texts.[96] Nasuti concluded that the obvious ambiguity prevents a clear association of Psalm 82 with any known Hebrew Bible tradition.

Nasuti's study also drew attention to terms in Psalm 82 that are often connected with "direct divine speech," such as the occurrence of יִמּוֹטוּ and מוֹסְדֵי in v. 5. Nasuti related these terms to other psalms, prophets and wisdom literature.[97] Again, Nasuti's study demonstrated that aspects of Psalm 82

91. Note that Parker will later compare the two psalms in conversation with one another. Parker, "The Beginning of the Reign of God."

92. Nasuti, *Tradition History*, 108.

93. The connection between Psalm 82 and Isaiah 3 may also be used to reverse interpret Psalm 82, which works as evidence for scholars who defend the judgment setting in Psalm 82 as human rather than divine.

94. Also note probable connection to 2 Sam 22:5.

95. Nasuti, *Tradition History*, 109.

96. Nasuti noted some of the following specific examples: prophetic tradition texts Isa 10:2; Amos 2:7; 4:1; 5:11; 8:6; Isa 11:4; 1 Sam 2:8 show concern for the poor, as do Ps 4:12; 72:13; and God is protector of the poor in Ps 113:7; Job 34:19; and Lev 19:15. Nasuti, *Tradition History*, 110.

97. Some parallels for use of מוֹט may be found in the psalms and prophets: Ps 46:3, 7; 61:4; Isa 24:19 and contrasting evidence in Ps 93:1; 96:10 (=1 Chr 16:30); 104:5.

might connect widely to ancient literature. These diverse connections support his conclusion that Psalm 82 is unique. Nasuti considered vv. 6–7 an expression of uniqueness that was even peculiar to the self-same psalm. The reference to בְּנֵי עֶלְיוֹן and the mortality of the gods is an obscure perspective for a Hebrew Bible text, even though these references may have more in common with other ancient Near Eastern texts outside the Hebrew corpus.

Finally, in v. 8, Nasuti made one clear parallel, aligning the appeal for proper rule over all nations with Deut 32:8, which describes a division of nations to "sons of God," (LXX, Deut 4:19). In this finding, he aligned with early interpretations, inclined to read Psalm 82 as a polemic against the nations.

> [I]n such a vein, this psalm may not be a purely theological polemic but may also be to some degree an oracle against the nations in which the fate of the nations' protective deities mirrors their own fate once God arises to 'judge the earth'.[98]

This description of Psalm 82 is in alignment with other prophetic texts, such as Amos' catalogue of offense of the nations. Nasuti engaged in this point with Tsevat's 1969 article, in which Tsevat attempted to place Psalm 82 in context with other Hebrew Bible texts that appeal to themes of justice.[99] Tsevat also concluded that while comparisons may be made, Psalm 82 must be interpreted independently, since it stands so uniquely among passages which share this theme. Even where connections seem apparent, Psalm 82 as a whole composition remains elusive, and invites new approaches to consider its meaning and significance.

One area Nasuti's study did not explore, is the unique use of the phrase בְּנֵי עֶלְיוֹן in Ps 82:6.[100] Morgenstern brought attention to this phrase in his study, asserting that the term appears nowhere else in the Hebrew Bible, emphasizing that this could "designate only divine beings and naught else,"[101] however, it has already been shown that there is much debate about the

---

Parallels for מוֹסָד which may indicate a practiced form may be found in Deut 32:22; 2 Sam 22:8, 16 (=Ps 18:8, 16); Isa 24:18; with usage of Prov 8:29 (Isa 40:12); Jer 31:37; Mic 6:2). Nasuti, *Tradition History*, 110.

98. Nasuti, *Tradition History*, 111.

99. Note also that Tsevat compared Psalm 82 with Psalm 58, as holding two themes together: a concern for justice and a conclusion of prayer. Nasuti also references a connection of Psalm 82 with Psalm 58 in v. 1, as a passage wherein the psalmist addresses divine beings. Tsevat, "God and the Gods."

100. It is fascinating that Nasuti does not deal with this. He claims that vv. 6–7 use "common language" but "thoughts expressed are almost unique to this psalm." Nasuti, *Tradition History*, 111.

101. Morgenstern, "Mythological Background," 33.

divine or human nature of language as represented in Psalm 82. The inclusion of unusual phrases invites a discussion that fosters curiosity and creative scholarly exploration.

As a unique text with distinctive features, Psalm 82 raises many questions that may best be resolved in light of an expression of intentional ambiguity. The distinctiveness of Psalm 82 invites the reader to consider its meaning more carefully, relying on ambiguous tension in the text for interpretation. The Asaph Psalms have been widely considered to be connected to prophetic texts, and while there are good reasons to hold Psalm 82 as separate in this regard, the implications of a broader orientation cannot be ignored by virtue of its connection and placement in the psalter among other Asaphite Psalms.

Nasuti's study gives a clear and detailed analysis of the Asaph Psalms and contextualizes their placement in the Ephraimite tradition, that is in reference to its influence by Northern religious practices. Psalm 82, however, eludes clarity. The psalm seems neither clearly linked to the Ephraimite tradition, nor does it contain "linguistic evidence which would decisively link it to a *traditio* outside the Asaphite Psalms or to a tradition stream other than that of the Ephraimite."[102] Nasuti's only recommendation relies on an appeal to ambiguity. This present study picks up on Nasuti's recommendation, which aligns also with other late twentieth century scholarship by Niehr and Kraus, to explore ambiguous tension in Psalm 82 in order to examine implicit ethics in the psalm.

Though some interest in the polysemy of Psalm 82 was introduced in the late 1980s, the nineties brought a resurgence of scholarship which continued an ongoing debate about the nature of the אֱלֹהִים in Psalm 82—divine or human. This decade marked a significant increase in the use of cognate literature from Ugarit for interpretation.

Marvin Tate published a commentary in which he categorized Psalm 82 as an Elohistic Psalm, which served as a foundation for his determination that the אֱלֹהִים in v. 1 represents the tetragrammaton.[103] His conclusions built on the work of Smick.[104] Tate's interpretation reflected this assertion. He wrote, "there is no good reason to doubt that God is the speaker in vv. 2–4 and v.7." However, he admitted to some uncertainty in vv. 5–6. Tate left no room in his commentary for ambiguity. His interpretation flowed alongside his translation of the אֱלֹהִים as YHWH.

---

102. Nasuti, *Tradition History*, 116.

103. This has been argued by virtue of the *Elohistic Psalter* as evidence of connections (Psalm 14–53). Tate, *Psalms*, 334.

104. Smick, "Mythopoetic Language."

A theological position fueled Tate's interpretation of Psalm 82. "(God) is clearly in charge, presiding over the meeting... he is surely Yahweh, the Great God..."[105] Tate's conclusions about YHWH depend on a theological reading. Because he did not engage with other possibilities for interpretation, nor did he explore a reading which relies on the acceptance of ambiguous tensions pointed out by earlier scholarship, Tate's reading offered a partial solution to interpreting Psalm 82.

Also in the early nineties, R. B. Salters considered a translation of Psalm 82 that leaned on the Septuagint. Based on a reading of the LXX, Salters proposed emending עֲדַת־אֵל to בַּעֲדַת־אֵלִים, claiming that it is more likely that an ancient editor dropped the plural form rather than add it.[106] Salters made a strong case for the reading of two possible early texts, one plural and one singular. His argument for preferring the plural reading is informed by the Targum and Peshitta, which both suggest a reliance on a pluralized version.[107] Salter observed the lack of textual notes on Ps 82:1 in the MT critical apparatus in light of the fact that the LXX includes confirmed readings that diverge. This oversight might be taken as a sign of implicit complexities in the text that justify further exploration. This is also evidence that a translation of deity-language in Psalm 82 should not be so simply cast in one direction without considering the polysemous nature of a text that has been categorized so many times as mythological poetry. Though Salters adamantly argued in favor of one reading, his presentation demonstrates a need for considering the obscure in Psalm 82.

By the mid-90s, there was a renewed interest in the identity of the אֱלֹהִים of Psalm 82. Responding to the decades-long discussion, W. S. Prinsloo wrote an article titled "Psalm 82: Once Again, Gods or Men?" He claimed that the crux of the issue for translating Psalm 82 lies in the interpretation of אֱלֹהִים in vv. 1b and 6a.[108] He took a stand against the use of a Near Eastern *religionsgeschichtliche* background as a concrete connecting point to other ancient Near Easter myths. His work emphasized a priority for the final form of the text over a potential reconstruction. Prinsloo's interpretation of Psalm 82 relies on a chiastic structure of poetic elements between vv. 1b and 8,[109] which draws attention to a reading that focuses on the contrast between the אֱלֹהִים in v. 1, and the אֱלֹהִים in v. 8.

---

105. Tate, *Psalms*, 334.
106. Salters, "Psalm 82:1," 225–26.
107. Salters, "Psalm 82:1," 225–26.
108. Prinsloo, "Psalm 82."
109. Prinsloo, "Psalm 82." See also Tate, *Psalms*.

> By using all sorts of rhetorical aids and applying metaphorical and mythological language, the writer wishes to convince his readers of the greatness of Yahweh. In contrast to this the gods are shown up as nonentities and impotent beings.[110]

Through the chiastic structure, Prinsloo recognized an inclusion between the first and last verses of the psalm in v. 6, whereby God is the first-person speaker. For Prinsloo, the psalm is about the greatness of God. Prinsloo's translation efforts reasserted a theological position that relied on monotheistic claims, supposing that mythological elements in the poem mostly function as polemic.[111] Prinsloo's interpretation ends with a declaration that v. 8 is the climax of ultimate support, a comforting reminder that God will rise up and take control, making everything good again. Although Prinsloo's work attempted to disambiguate the psalm, the challenges of conformity suggest that there is more flexibility in the psalm than Prinsloo allowed in his final interpretation.

Biblical scholarship in the nineties also focused more on connections between Mesopotamian literature and the Hebrew Bible. It is through this lens that Simon Parker confronted the question posed by Morgenstern about divinity of the beings in Psalm 82.[112] Parker contextualized the psalm linguistically within Ugaritic influence. The use of the terms אֱלֹהִים (vv. 1,7), עֲדַת־אֵל (v. 1), and בְּנֵי עֶלְיוֹן (v. 6) demonstrate his point.[113] Parker's main contention is with scholarship that assumes that YHWH presides over the divine council. Instead, he proposed that the Psalter consists of a particular group of literature in the Hebrew Bible that may be considered independent literary units.[114] Parker's reading resisted a canonical approach, claiming that Psalm 82 should be read for its unique contribution among the psalms. He acknowledged that the compilers of the Elohistic Psalter and the Psalms of Asaph held an understanding, in their own time, that the Israelite God presided over other deities, but that it was not the case for the composer of Psalm 82.

> As long as we read the psalms as a book, such contextual interpretation is appropriate. But the Book of Psalms, more than any other biblical book, and more obviously than any other biblical book, consists in large part of quite independent literary units,

---

110. Prinsloo, "Psalm 82."

111. See also Schlisske's discussion of demythologizing texts. Schlisske, *Gottessöhne und Gottessohn*, 44.

112. Parker, "The Beginning of the Reign of God," 533.

113. Parker, "The Beginning of the Reign of God," 533.

114. Parker, "The Beginning of the Reign of God," 533–34.

almost every one of which was originally designed for use on its own. (The present liturgical use of the psalms continues to fulfill that design.) While principles of organization are discernible for some groups of these units, the present literary context of each psalm is, for the most part, no more relevant to its individual interpretation than is the literary context of a hymn in a modern hymn book or a poem in an anthology. The first principle of interpretation of virtually any psalm requires that it be understood and explained as an independent literary unit. Accordingly, Psalm 82 in its pristine integrity is the object of the following study.[115]

Parker shifted the attention of scholarship on Psalm 82 from its received form in the biblical canon to its presumed composition in an early Northern ancient Near Eastern setting. In this context, YHWH, though not named in the psalm, was likely present among other the other deities.

Parker focused on linguistic and literary features of Psalm 82. He looked closely at the root meanings of verbs modifying the אֱלֹהִים in v. 1 to conclude that the אֱלֹהִים are members of a divine court, attending to a higher deity.[116] He asserted that the God of Israel was one of these members in v. 1.[117] Furthermore, Parker looked at the structure of the psalm and identified two sections: vv. 1–5, which introduces the protagonist, sets the location, and describes the initial action, as well as introducing the first speech and its addressees, and vv. 6–8, wherein the protagonist recognizes that because of the injustice, the deities are not divine at all—they are more like mortals. Parker compares this outlook with the divine speech made to the King of Tyre in Ezek 28:2: "You said: 'I am God . . .' But you are a mortal, and not God . . . you will die the death of a battle casualty." The near repetition in Psalm 82 confirmed for Parker that vv. 6–7 may be read as a speech. Parker proposed that YHWH is the one making this speech. Then, he described v. 8 as a proclamation of God as the "true inheritor of the world" in response.[118]

Parker's argument centered on how Psalm 82 established the God of Israel as a powerful deity in an ancient Near Eastern context. He appealed to a consideration of divine order and re-order in the psalm—"Psalm 82 presents us with the critical moment of the cult: the setting to rights of the world."[119] Furthermore, the right order of things involves a ruling deity that

115. Parker, "The Beginning of the Reign of God," 534.
116. Parker, "The Beginning of the Reign of God."
117. Parker's translation work follows also with Gordon, who considers alternative meanings for נִצָּב. Gordon, "History of Religion," 131.
118. Parker, "The Beginning of the Reign of God."
119. Parker, "The Beginning of the Reign of God," 559.

takes a stand against injustice. Parker's analysis suggests there is some ethical value in the composition of Psalm 82.

Parker did more to develop an approach to Psalm 82 that incorporates mythological features than any other scholar since Morgenstern. Writing more than a half-century later, Parker had access to more resources. He noted how remarkable it is that Psalm 82 is not cited in many studies of myth in the Bible in his time, drawing attention to the works of Rogerson,[120] Petersen,[121] and Otzen,[122] asserting that Psalm 82:1–7 is "a genuine and thoroughly Israelite myth."[123] The connections he made drew attention to the mythical provenance of Psalm 82, encouraging a reading of the psalm which is not bound by canonical interpretations.

Twentieth century interpretations of Psalm 82 tended toward prioritizing the disambiguation of deities within the psalm. Scholars seemed especially drawn to the mythological provenance of Psalm 82 as a way to understand how and why the psalm included unique language, uncommon in the Psalter. While a few scholars pointed toward the polysemy of the language and grammar, most scholars presumed a monotheistic category for the psalm and built their work around that presumption. There was very little discussion of the ethical language in Psalm 82, as most scholars took it for granted that if God was the ruling deity, then there was an automatic priority for justice. Yet, for all the scholarship which was generated, questions about Psalm 82 continued to circulate, and twenty-first century scholars continued to revisit the same questions raised by Morgenstern 80 years hence.

Twenty-First-Century Scholarship

The twenty-first century saw a resurgence of interest in mythological connection between texts in the Hebrew Bible and other ancient Near Eastern literature. Psalm 82 was examined as inclusive of the divine council motif. Its role in the Psalter was viewed in light of prophetic discourse and its relationship to other divine council narratives, such as Job 1–2.

Michael Wilcock wrote in 2001 that Psalm 82 portrays God as a judge in a prophetic vision granted to the psalmist.[124] Wilcock considered four potential interpretations for the identity of the אֱלֹהִים in v. 1: "gods

120. Rogerson, *Myth in Old Testament*.
121. Petersen, *Mythos im Alten Testament*.
122. Otzen et al., *Myths in the Old Testament*.
123. Parker, "The Beginning of the Reign of God," 543.
124. Wilcock, *The Message of Psalms*.

of heathendom," "principalities and powers," "human beings, rulers or judges or priests of Israel," and "the people of Israel themselves."[125] Each of these proposed categories falls into one of the two categories that Morgenstern presented— divine or human. Wilcock drew upon the reference to Psalm 82 in John 10 to conclude that the people of Israel are esteemed as אֱלֹהִים in Ps 82:1.

Wilcock's study drew attention to the concern for the weak and the rights of the poor in Psalm 82. He described this as a value close to the heart of God. His interpretation presented the psalm as an allegory for Israel as "the assembly," which is complete in the coming of Christ. Although Wilcock sufficiently assessed the importance of the psalm for its appeal to care for the poor, his work relied on presumptions from a future Judeo-Christian perspective which cannot be guaranteed by the Psalter.

In 2004, Chalmers made a point to connect Psalm 82 with Ps 89:6–8,[126] which described the placement of YHWH among other deities. Through an exploration of polemic language, Chalmers concluded that YHWH takes on the traditional role of the Canaanite deity El for divine assembly motifs that appear in the Hebrew Bible. Chalmers cited attributes of El which are reflected in the Hebrew Bible as parallel with descriptions of God. Notable among these attributes are kingly qualities (Exod 15:18, Deut 33:15, and Num 24:21), wisdom, age and compassion, as described in Jon 4:2 and Hos 11:8, and creator/father imagery, in Gen 49:25 and Deut 32:6.[127] Chalmers described these characteristics of El as a match for the character of YHWH in the Hebrew Bible. He affirmed a sameness between the ancient Near Eastern deity El and the Israelite God, YHWH, yet it remains unclear whether the El referenced in Ps 82:1 necessitates a Yahwistic interpretation.

In the same year, Brueggemann looked at a typology of function within the Psalter, describing Ricoeur's influence in determining how psalms interpret order-disorder-reorder,[128] however he did not apply this process to Psalm 82 until a later work.[129] Later scholars will consider the social implications of ordering justice in Psalm 82 following Brueggemann's work, but there is still room for this to be explored more fully.

The following year, scholars demonstrated renewed efforts for interpreting the divine council in Psalm 82. Reviving Eissfeldt's proposal that God is one of several deities represented in the divine council, Frank-Lothar

---

125. Wilcock, *The Message of Psalms*, 40.
126. Chalmers, "Who is the Real El?," 611–30.
127. Chalmers, "Who is the Real El?," 613.
128. Brueggemann, *The Psalms*, 1–26.
129. Brueggemann and Bellinger, *Psalms*.

Hossfeld and Erich Zenger (2005)[130] provided an even more compelling reason to situate the divine council in an Ugaritic context. Zenger stated that the setting of Psalm 82 "evokes the traditional Canaanite ideology of a hierarchical assembly of the gods in which El sits on his throne surrounded by gods as his heavenly council."[131] The commentary proposed the mythological reading as a way of reaffirming a setting in antiquity, interpreting Psalm 82 as a text that demonstrates the political rise of the Israelite deity, YHWH, into power over the deities of nations that historically held more sway in the ancient Near East.

Eissfeldt's argument was dismissed by Trotter, whose work is explored in more detail below, as insufficiently supported and came to agree with Zenger's more nuanced discussion, concluding that a divine council motif in ancient Israel would indeed recognize El as the ruling deity.[132] Considering that forty years had passed since James S. Ackerman refused to accept a paradigm in which YHWH may be considered subordinate to El,[133] Trotter's reassurance did little to resolve the question about who the אֱלֹהִים represented. It did, however, open doors for further and more detailed work in cognate literature.

In 2007, Dirk Human edited a volume on *Psalms and Mythology*, demonstrating an increasing interest in mythological language in the Psalter. Work on Psalm 82 was conspicuously absent. The following year, however, Dirk Human published an article on the psalm, "Psalm 82: God Presides in a Deflated Pantheon to Remain the Sole Just Ruler," the title of which explains his position. He argued that v. 8 acts as a response in which the Hebrew God takes on the role of a sole ruling deity, charged with care over all the nations. In this view, Human returned the conversation to one centered on the matter of monotheism and the nature of divine council.[134]

Human's view was supported also in *God in Translation: Deities in Cross-Cultural Discourse in the Biblical World*, a volume in which Mark S. Smith looked at the translatability of language about gods in the Hebrew Bible. He presented Psalm 82 alongside a letter (ARM 26 196) that was sent to King Zimri-lim by his servant, Shamash-Nasir. Smith defended that "both represent divine conflict in the context of multiple divinities."[135] Smith saw

130. Hossfeld and Zenger, *Psalms 2*.
131. Hossfeld and Zenger, *Psalms 2*, 332.
132. Trotter, "Death of the אלהים."
133. Ackerman, "Exegetical Study," 306–36.
134. See also Gordon who wrote about the Divine Council as seminal to understanding the portrayal of God in the Pentateuch, Former and Latter Prophets, Psalms, Job and Daniel. Gordon, "Standing in the Council," 190–204, 190.
135. Smith, *God in Translation*, 131–139.

Psalm 82 as a corrective in this ancient Near Eastern context, an example of a prophetic call for the god of Israel to assume control overall the nations, and thereby end what he referred to as translatability.[136]

Also in 2007, Min Suc Kee furthered work on the exploration of divine council motifs in the Hebrew Bible. This will be explained more in the following chapters. Kee aligned Psalm 82 with other major type-scenes of divine council in the Hebrew Bible. He followed Tate's Elohistic reading of Psalm 82, affirming that a common feature of divine assembly texts in ancient Near Eastern literature pictures members of heavenly council as seated at the beginning of a meeting. His research implies that a standing deity indicates active participation. Kee's assertion was that when based on evidence from cognate literature, the opening verse in Psalm 82 describes a deity who is expressing honor or protection.[137] While Kee's particular focus on divine council motifs added to Tate's proposal that the Hebrew God is running the show in Psalm 82, it also begins with a presumption of YHWH as Most High, a supposition that is not necessarily evident in Psalm 82. There is room for further consideration about how the divine council is functioning within the psalm.

Kee also noted the aspects of judgment present in Psalm 82. He suggested that further studies should demonstrate how the divine council reflects human gatherings of justice, such as the *Tent of Meeting*, as an "earthly counterpart of the heavenly council since its functions and, above all, some of its visual descriptions (see Exod 33:7–11), outstandingly correspond to those of the heavenly council."[138] His recommendation encourages a reading of Psalm 82 that explores ethical values for the human realm. Themes of justice and righteousness are not limited to divine realms.

In 2012, James M. Trotter wrote a lengthy article that traced an outline of interpretation for אֱלֹהִים in Psalm 82 from Morgenstern to his present in 2012.[139] He began by acknowledging the difficulties inherent to the psalm, citing Morgenstern's thesis from 1939 as a focal point. Trotter agreed with others that the central defining matter for interpretation in Psalm 82 is the identity of אֱלֹהִים in v. 1.[140] His stated thesis is that the אֱלֹהִים are clearly divine-human kings who rule over nations in the ancient Near East. His study clarified that these divine monarchs are not human judges, tyrannical foreign

---

136. Smith, *God in Translation*, 138–139.
137. Kee, "The Heavenly Council," 259–73.
138. Kee, "The Heavenly Council."
139. Trotter, "Death of the אלהים."
140. Trotter begins with the same premise as Morgenstern. Morgenstern, "Mythological Background," 30.

rulers, nor deities of the pantheon.[141] Trotter defended his view as a new reading of Psalm 82, however, it is a nuanced version of previous interpretations. Morgenstern already pointed to the works of Duhm,[142] Staerk,[143] and others who vacillated between kings and gods.[144] Trotter's main contribution was to affirm that Psalm 82 is difficult to translate and that main approaches consider the identity of אֱלֹהִים to be the central issue of interpretation. Trotter considered three aspects of Psalm 82 essential to interpreting the composition: 1) the identity of the אֱלֹהִים in vv. 1–6. 2) the setting of event(s) in the psalm, and 3) the role of YHWH. It is by these three aspects that Trotter evaluated previous scholarship and defended his interpretation.

According to Trotter's article, the setting of Psalm 82 within an ancient Near Eastern context based on divine council motifs is central to its meaning. He particularly addressed parallels in Ugaritic, Mesopotamian, and Hebrew literature.[145] He dated Psalm 82 as an early Israelite composition, connecting the psalm with old Northwest Semitic and mythological texts, leaning on literary and linguistic cognates such as the divine council scene established in v. 1.[146] Trotter's work leaves no room for ambiguity in reading v. 1, as he systematically dismissed various previous arguments as unnecessary, or uninsightful. Although Trotter succeeded in summarizing so many variants on the interpretation of Psalm 82, his proposal lacks a sufficient discussion of why the scholarship is so diverse. His extensive summary of previous approaches begs the question, "Why do so many accomplished scholars offer such diverse theories on Psalm 82?" Trotter's article did not address this.

After dismissing the views of Kraus, Mullen, and Tsevat, who supported the idea of a theoretic original text which included the tetragrammaton, and also the contribution Marvin Tate,[147] Trotter proposed his interpretation of אֱלֹהִים as divine kings. This proposal supports an uncompromising monotheistic interpretation. Trotter was not the first to approach an interpretation of Psalm 82 from a defense of monotheism, but by the twenty-first century, defending monotheism in the Hebrew Bible was increasingly less

---

141. Trotter, "Death of the אלהים." 221
142. Duhm, *Die Psalmen.*
143. Staerk, *Studien zur Religions.*
144. Morgenstern, "Mythological Background."
145. Trotter, "Death of the אלהים" 223–24.
146. Trotter followed work by Cross to note other Hebrew Bible instances of divine council, particularly I Kgs 2, Job 1–2, Zech 3–6. Cross, *Canaanite Myth and Hebrew Epic.*
147. Trotter, "Death of the אלהים."

popular.¹⁴⁸ For Trotter, his translation of the אֱלֹהִים as divine kings made a clear path of interpreting the rest of the psalm in support of God's role as supreme ruler in the ancient Near East.

Trotter's summary of scholarship is extensive, and more than any other, it recognizes the multiplicity within which Psalm 82 has been received. Trotter attempted to disambiguate an interpretation of אֱלֹהִים in order to make sense of the entire psalm. His approach succeeded in confirming the continued difficulties and polysemic tendencies of Psalm 82. His interpretation failed to focus on the ethical purpose of the psalm, in favor of exploring the more captivating mythological overtones of divine council.

Trotter's thesis and conclusion appealed to a similar finding presented in Morgenstern, that the אֱלֹהִים should be interpreted as human kings operating in a human realm, albeit by divine right. The same questions are advanced from Morgenstern's thesis and resolved in a similar way. Avoiding the ambiguous nature of Psalm 82, Trotter attempted to clarify the divine references by justifying its application in the human realm in his appeal to the ancient concept of kings as divine. In this way, he married seemingly divergent realities in order to make sense of the psalm's contradictory features. Trotter's theory fits into the broad category which Morgenstern discussed in his introduction, that two possible interpretations for אֱלֹהִים remain: divine beings and human beings. Even more specifically, Morgenstern already considered variants within the category, including human judges and ancient Near Eastern kings, e.g. foreign kings by Duhm and kings in general, as sometimes favored by Staerk.¹⁴⁹ While Trotter's conclusion may have shed variant light on how Psalm 82 may be understood given its application in comparison to Ugaritic mythological texts that were not previously available, it failed to recognize the text of Psalm 82 apart from the framework so firmly established by Morgenstern nearly a century previous.

Susan Gillingham wrote on the interpretation of Psalm 82 in a *Festschrift* for John Barton that was published in 2013. Gillingham approached the psalm from an Elohistic view. She stated that Psalm 82:8 "reaffirms the absolute authority of ' *Elohim* who alone is judge of the nations."¹⁵⁰ She asserted that since the psalm does not explicitly include a reference to the tetragrammaton, the אֱלֹהִים must be considered a reference to God. Her

---

148. Tilde Binger included a lengthy discussion about the proclivity of biblical scholarship to rely on a presumption of monotheism and the inherent pitfalls it brings for interpretation. Binger, *Asherah*.

149. Duhm ultimately supported other scholars in favor of "foreign kings," especially those which have oppressed Israel, and Staerk alternated between "kings" and "gods." Morgenstern, "Mythological Background," 30–31.

150. Gillingham, "Praying to the Gods," 63-73.

contribution affirmed the views of previous readings, such as Tate and others, that because of the inclusion of Psalm 82 in the Psalter, an interpretation must include an identity for the Israelite deity. While there is a precedent for this reading, it excludes potential ways of understanding Psalm 82 that might better serve the reader in addressing central themes of justice and righteousness in the composition.

In 2015, Brueggemann and Bellinger approached Psalm 82 as a courtroom scenario, in which the presiding judge is the "high creator God who is the God of Israel."[151] This commentary picked up on Brueggemann's earlier work on patterns of disorder and order in the psalms. Here, the authors interpreted Psalm 82 as a mythopoeic expression by Israel that operates with "assumptions common in Israel's world of polytheism."[152] Again, in this translation, the issue of monotheism is at stake. In a juris perspective, Psalm 82:1–2 are read as a courtroom scenario, vv. 3–4 is the case on trial, v. 5 is the verdict, and v. 6 is the sentence, the consequence of which is death. God presides over all other deities.[153] In this model, vv. 7–8 adjourn the court and establish a new paradigm voiced by an Israelite human, which establishes God's concern for justice in all the world.[154]

This reading of Psalm 82 is firm and simplistic. It ignores certain complexities in order to bring a decisive theophoric message. The translation is appropriate to the text, but it cannot be the only way to read and interpret Psalm 82, as it does not address in full the complexities referenced in the beginning of the commentary. The translation relies on a modern understanding of ancient mythopoeic assumptions in Israel's world. The authors framed this understanding by considering monotheistic presumptions in the composition. These ideas have been brought to surface in scholarship across the past several decades, yet the psalm continues to invite variant

---

151. Brueggemann and Bellinger, *Psalms*.

152. Brueggemann and Bellinger, *Psalms*, 345.

153. Another twenty-first-century reading that presents YHWH as the speaker in Psalm 82 comes from McClellan who attempted to resolve the difficulties of understanding Psalm 82 by reading the psalm as a "gods-complaint" which he described as a complaint set into the mouth of YHWH, directed at the gods of the nations. McClellan admitted to the difficulties previously addressed regarding reading Psalm 82 as a lament due to the reference to divine council. However, his article sought to fit an interpretation neatly through a comparison with Psalm 74, through which he concluded that if the divine council framework had not been present in the psalm, then Psalm 82 would be read as a complaint against YHWH. His argument for a modified complaint model, which he called a "gods-complaint" relies on the premise that YHWH is the only righteous deity, therefore, it is YHWH who must make complaint against other deities. McClellan's reading follows presumptions already discussed in this thesis. McClellan, "The Gods-Complaint," 835, 851.

154. Brueggemann and Bellinger, *Psalms*, 355.

readings. This present thesis seeks to address the nature of the complexities in Psalm 82 so that multiple readings, such as the one proposed in this 2015 volume may be simultaneously considered as valid interpretations.

In a review of the study of Psalm 82 from Julian Morgenstern to the present, scholars have not progressed much further in understanding the psalm than to continue the debate which hinges upon identifying the subject(s) described in v. 1 and how each identified subject may then be perceived to act upon, or within, the following verses.[155] This same debate extends before Morgenstern's significant contribution in 1939, in which he catalogues various interpretations of אֱלֹהִים up to his own contribution.[156] The fact that the interpretation of אֱלֹהִים is not clearly defined up to this point suggests a certain amount of ambiguity is at play in the psalm. The fact that nearly a century later scholars remain divided on the matter confirms that Psalm 82 is not only a difficult passage in the Hebrew Bible, but a passage that embraces the semantic range of אֱלֹהִים, a topic pursued more substantively in the next chapter.

The following study explores an alternative approach to interpreting Psalm 82 by looking at features of the text that have not been adequately explored in past scholarship. Specific focus will be given to Psalm 82 as ethical, mythological, and ambiguous. Furthermore, this study will attempt to determine how such a composition may be received as an ethical text by various communities. The psalm may have been composed in an early Northern setting and later received for compilation by a Southern Judaic religious community. In a modern setting even, the liturgical practice of reciting the psalm presents its ethical influence.

An Ethical Approach

As an ancient Northern Semitic text, Psalm 82 should not be necessarily bound to a strictly monotheistic or even an exclusive Israelite reading. Its presence in the Hebrew Psalter demonstrates that the psalm may apply to an Israelite context, either by the psalmic composer or compiler, but it may just as easily speak to broader issues of justice in the ancient world view. That this question remains part of the ongoing discussion indicates the need for a different approach to interpretation. Psalm 82 contains polysemous features that should be reflected in an interpretation of the

---

155. Recent scholarship yet to be considered seems to follow in the same manner: The inclusion of El in Psalm 82:1 clearly places the psalm in the realm of ancient Near Eastern mythology. Norton, *Psalms*. Gillingham. *Psalms 73–150*.

156. Morgenstern, "Mythological Background," 30–31.

psalm. This study will go on to show that tensions in the psalm may be resolved by an awareness of ambiguity. Considering the content of Psalm 82 as potentially shaped by intentional ambiguity may offer the reader an opportunity to hold various competing interpretations in balance in such a way that allows them to focus on the central message of the psalm. It allows for more direct access to understanding the ethical implications of Psalm 82. In order to identify implicit ethics in an ancient composition, Zimmermann's model will be introduced here.

Reading Psalm 82 as ethical relays moral significance by implicit means. Implicit ethics in an ancient text reveals moral virtue reflective of the society from which it stems. Zimmermann examined methods of uncovering moral-ethical components in an ancient biblical text in his book *The Logic of Love*.[157] He drew from the *Organon* applied to Aristotle's work to consider eight approaches that serve a singular purpose to analyze and draw attention to implicit ethics in an ancient text.[158] The main idea behind the *Organon* is to conceive a structure by which various aspects of a text contribute toward support of an ideal, like spokes in a wheel. Each aspect is distinct, but they all contribute to support the whole. For this study, it applies to identifying ethical significance in the composition of Psalm 82. This thesis presents a thorough study on various aspects of the psalm to determine how each offers support for an ethical understanding of the psalm. Applying the *Organon* method to Psalm 82 should result in a revelation of underlying components that point to a "theory of conduct" which identifies social concerns for an ancient community.[159]

The model of *Organon* considers different approaches which each inform by their own logical means the uncovering of implicit ethics in the text to reveal moral significance as an intended message for the audience. The value of this model is in its ability to examine various means that may or may not be interconnected by nature. The means are comparable by recognition of a common outcome—uncovering implicit ethics in the text. Each identified feature of the text reveals moral significance that encourages an ethical reading of the text. Zimmermann examined eight potential approaches that may apply to an ancient textual paradigm.

The first approach has to do with the textuality of language.[160] One example of textuality through linguistic form is the use of imperatives. In Ps 82:3–4, four imperatives are expressed to communicate what behaviors

---

157. Zimmermann, *The Logic of Love*.
158. Zimmermann, *The Logic of Love*, 31.
159. Zimmermann, *The Logic of Love*, 29.
160. Zimmermann, *The Logic of Love*, 33.

ought to be practiced regarding the poor. Zimmermann demonstrated that imperatives are used to directly express ethics in ancient texts.[161] Another linguistic affect is ambiguity. Ambiguous constructions in the text prompt the reader to consider alternative approaches and insight. Ps 82:1 and verses following contain ambiguous features that encourage reader participation in making judgment of, and on behalf of, the subjects in the psalm.

The second approach has to do with ethical norms or values expressed in conduct of the individual or group.[162] An example of expressed ethical norms includes grammatical forms like rhetorical questions. Rhetorical questions may demand either negative or affirmative responses.[163] A rhetorical question appears in Ps 82:2 in a manner common to prophetic texts in the Hebrew Bible and in ancient Near Eastern literature. The question acts as an accusation against those who are doing wrong.

The third approach has to do with ethical genres. The genre of an ancient text may serve in a particular manner to invite reader response or participation that assumes a common understanding of societal concerns. Psalm 82 is a poetic and mythological composition. Genres associated with each of these two qualities serve to motivate readers to reflect and draw conclusions about (moral) significance.

The fourth and fifth approaches draw from significant cultural norms, or ethical points of contact.[164] For Psalm 82, this includes ancient Near Eastern values regarding concern for the poor as seen through legal texts, cognate linguistic analysis, and through other mythological and poetic literature. Through understanding the significance of moral values in society, it is possible to evaluate the moral significance communicated in the psalm. Comparing the text to others within the self-same culture encourages a process of reflection which allows the moral significance to come to light.

The sixth approach has to do with the freedom of a moral agent to act.[165] This asks questions about who is addressed. In Psalm 82, the subjects explicitly addressed are identified as powerful beings with defined social responsibilities to enact justice. However, an implicit subject is the audience or reader of the text, who has the opportunity to respond and become shaped by the message of moral significance communicated in the psalm.

---

161. Zimmermann, *The Logic of Love*, 111.
162. Zimmermann, *The Logic of Love*, 43.
163. Zimmermann, *The Logic of Love*, 116.
164. Zimmermann, *The Logic of Love*, 43ff.
165. Zimmermann, *The Logic of Love*, 73–74.

The seventh approach examines the history of how the text has been received across time.[166] Psalm 82 has its probable origin in an early northern Levantine setting, among mythopoetic communication, but it is also received in a later context as practiced liturgy among the Jewish religious community. The moral significance revealed by implicit ethics in the psalm carries a diachronic force that extends across culture as well.

The eighth approach examines the realm of validity of the text.[167] An ethical reading of Psalm 82 brings the psalm from its time and place of origin, through its acceptance in different historical settings, and into the present world. An ethical message revealing moral significance extends hermeneutically beyond the original audience. It is by this means that Psalm 82 may be considered in a present-day discussion about how and why it may be important for a community's leadership to oblige the poor.

This study will examine four aspects of Psalm 82 as support for an ethical reading: textual characteristics of the composition in Chapter 2, the mythological heritage of Psalm 82 in Chapter 3, the linguistic and cultural significance of poverty in the Psalter in Chapters 4 and 5, and the reception of the psalm as resistance literature in the Second Temple Period in Chapter 7. This thesis will also take a brief look at how the socio-linguistic and literary heritage of Psalm 82 fits into a broader hermeneutic of formational liturgy in Chapter 6.

Conclusion

In conclusion, Psalm 82 has long been considered one of the most difficult passages in the Hebrew Bible to clearly contextualize. Its features have attracted scholars for several years to contemplate various interpretations. Scholarly arguments have competed to defend different traditions and describe how the psalm fits into the Hebrew Bible.

The questions that Morgenstern raised about Psalm 82 remain the same questions at the center of contemporary scholarship. There has been little to no consensus on the meaning of mythology, even though most scholars claim that Psalm 82 is a mythological text. The unique language in Psalm 82 has not been adequately resolved: how it fits or does not fit within the Psalter. Furthermore, there is a degree of ambiguity on the textual level.

In an attempt to avoid dissecting the psalm for the purpose of disambiguation, a more comprehensive approach will be considered in this study. Reading the psalm as shaped by ambiguity resolves this by encouraging a

---

166. Zimmermann, *The Logic of Love*, 82–83.
167. Zimmermann, *The Logic of Love*, 91.

regard for the text as a whole, difficulties and all. Furthermore, by accepting ambiguity as a means of understanding implicit ethics, the inherent conflictive certainties force the reader to involve themselves on a literary level. This not for the purpose of weighing two views to affirm one in favor of another, but for the purpose of exploring an interpretation that lies in the space between the words, a consideration for a holistic approach.

Scholarship has failed to develop a full appreciation for the inherent ambiguity in the psalm, relying instead on an appeal to disambiguate to make sense of interpreting who is acting and why. After a century of discussion over Psalm 82, a review of the scholarship demonstrates the need for a different approach. Rather than continuing to rely on a framework that served its purpose to point out complexities in Psalm 82 in the early twentieth century, it is now time to revisit the text of Psalm 82 itself. It is time to seek clarity by considering the shape of ambiguity in Psalm 82 for the purpose of better understanding a central concern for justice and social ethics.

2

Psalm 82—A Textual Study

"The world is a dangerous place, not because of those who do evil, but because of those who look on and do nothing." —Albert Einstein, theoretical physicist

THIS DISSERTATION SEEKS TO show how Psalm 82 is shaped by ambiguity for the purpose of specific ethical instruction regarding care for the societally marginalized. This chapter will describe the text of Psalm 82, taking into consideration the meaning of words and the structure of phrases and word groupings that support an ethical reading. Discovering the textual facets of the psalm is one aspect of Zimmermann's *Organon* model for reading an ancient text ethically. This chapter will consider the texture of language and its contribution to such a reading.

I will begin by presenting a translation of the psalm, followed by a description of structure and an outline that demonstrates the relationship between phrases within the poem. Then, I will describe the possibilities of meaning for each line of poetry, including a discussion of interpretation for difficult words and concepts. The intent is to establish a framework for understanding how Psalm 82 may be read, while exploring possibilities of interpretation with a focus on an ethical reading.

Psalm 82 in Translation

Due to the difficulties in translating Psalm 82, this work will consider various means by which Psalm 82 might be read. My interpretation here will focus on the structure of the poem as a means by which to determine how ambiguity functions in Psalm 82. Furthermore, the textual character and shape of the psalm supports an ethical reading.

PSALM 82—A TEXTUAL STUDY

מִזְמוֹר לְאָסָף	A psalm for Asaph
אֱלֹהִים נִצָּב בַּעֲדַת־אֵל	' elohim[1] stand[2] in the council of El,[3]
בְּקֶרֶב אֱלֹהִים יִשְׁפֹּט:	in the midst of ' elohim, there is judgment.[4]
עַד־מָתַי תִּשְׁפְּטוּ־עָוֶל	How long will judgment be unjust,
וּפְנֵי רְשָׁעִים תִּשְׂאוּ־סֶלָה:	favor granted to the wicked?[5]
שִׁפְטוּ־דַל וְיָתוֹם	Provide justice for the poor and the orphan,
עָנִי וָרָשׁ הַצְדִּיקוּ:	the afflicted and needy; maintain their right!

1. Due to a great amount of discussion about how the word אֱלֹהִים functions in v. 1, I have chosen to leave it untranslated, so as to consider the semantic range of meaning it could have conveyed in the ancient world and thereby bring the modern reader a bit closer to the context of this verse. The case for range of meaning will be discussed in this chapter.

2. The Nifal ms participle נִצָּב is attributively modifying אֱלֹהִים. This use is ambiguous in two ways: temporally and in number. Regarding temporal ambiguity: Joüon-Muraoka's Hebrew Grammar describes an attributive participle as *atemporal*, for which the translation must rely on context. Joüon-Muraoka noted that when the participle is modifying past events, it typically includes an idiomatic definite article. In this case, the Hebrew participle occurs without a definite article, leaving it open to interpretation. Joüon and Muraoka, *A Grammar*, 383–84. Furthermore, Burnett demonstrated that the collective singular sense of verbs modifying plural divine beings is a somewhat normal grammatical feature of ancient Near Eastern literature, particularly with the use of אֱלֹהִים and variants. Burnett, *A Reassessment*. This discussion is taken up in more detail in this chapter.

3. While the role of the council of El is not fully grasped in relation to the Hebrew Bible, its significance drives us to consider ancient Near Eastern mythology. Norton confirms this in the BHQ apparatus. Norton, *Psalms*.

4. Though the verb here is parsed as a simple imperfect form, its use with a divine entity is suggestive of an anticipatory request and the translation should reflect the purpose of the council, as shown. Also note that the following verse seems to address the subjects of v. 1 as plural. It may be that ambiguity allows the reader to hold onto the concept of judgment for a yet to be determined subject, and that is where the poem leads toward implicit ethics. Right judgment is under trial, and it is those who are responsible for judgment whose character is under scrutiny. This is explained and discussed in the commentary below. Furthermore, the verb may be taken as jussive by context. A petition-type formula in v. 8, supports a petition in v. 1.

5. Literally, "lifting the faces," a phrase often used to express favorable or partial treatment.

פַּלְּטוּ־דַל וְאֶבְיוֹן	Deliver the poor and afflicted
מִיַּד רְשָׁעִים הַצִּילוּ:	from the hand of the wicked; save them!
לֹא יָדְעוּ וְלֹא יָבִינוּ	They do not know; they do not understand.
בַּחֲשֵׁכָה יִתְהַלָּכוּ	They walk around in darkness.
יִמּוֹטוּ כָּל־מוֹסְדֵי אָרֶץ:	All the foundations of the earth are shaken.
אֲנִי־אָמַרְתִּי אֱלֹהִים אַתֶּם	I had said you are all gods;
וּבְנֵי עֶלְיוֹן כֻּלְּכֶם:	all of you, sons of *Elyon*.
אָכֵן כְּאָדָם תְּמוּתוּן	Nevertheless, each one shall die as a mortal,[6]
וּכְאַחַד הַשָּׂרִים תִּפֹּלוּ:	shall fall as one of the princes.[7]
קוּמָה אֱלֹהִים שָׁפְטָה הָאָרֶץ	' *elohîm*, rise up[8] and judge[9] the earth!
כִּי־אַתָּה תִנְחַל בְּכָל־הַגּוֹיִם:	For it is you who are in possession of all the nations.

Psalm 82 is a brief composition, packed with language about justice that seeks to make things right for the poor and marginalized in society by admonishing the powerful. The poetic texture is reminiscent of other ancient Near Eastern cognate literature, poetic mythological texts that tell stories about the gods and their interactions. The text offers a glimpse into a society that is trying to sort out the identity of its inhabitants. Psalm 82 offers

6. A collective singular is used here to represent the group.

7. There is a possible reference to the Ugaritic "gracious gods" myth in which the Princes are the "divine pair Dawn (Shahru, sh-h-r) and Sunset (shalmu). Note that *Bt-Shlm* (daughter of Sunset) is a Phoenician personal name, and also *Ykn-Shlm* (Sunset exists). Both contain cognate roots to the Hebrew. There is a linguistic connection also with the name of Israel's capital city—Jerusalem (*Yr-Shlm*).

8. The imperative verb here includes a paragogic *he*. The precise function of this is unknown, although it is considered to add emphasis to the imperative form. Joüon-Muraoka summarized a few other theoretical possibilities based on its appearance in Hebrew Bible texts (i.e. as an honorific or a politeness or nicety, especially toward one of lower status, an emphatic gesture, or a poetic form). Joüon-Muraoka concluded that there is no way to determine its effect on meaning except to consider it emphatic without particular bearing on its interpretation. Joüon-Muraoka, *A Grammar*.

9. Here is another case where the singular verb may be indicating that the אֱלֹהִים refers to a singular deity or a plural collective, representing the אֱלֹהִים as 2mp addressees, consistent with the previous six verses.

a perspective that pertains to those who have power and authority as well as the very least of society's members, the destitute and the have-nots.

The central text of the psalm draws a picture of expectation for right judgment, while inner layers of the poem deal with the perversion of injustice and its consequences. The shape of the poem invites the reader as a participant in the poetic narrative.

Rife with allusion and intrigue, Psalm 82 describes a hyperbolic scenario that yields a lesson of ethical morality—when right judgment fails, everything suffers. The psalm implicates the highest class of beings imaginable with a charge of neglecting their primary duty to justice, the consequence of which is the mistreatment of the most vulnerable in society, the shared earth, and the status of those high beings. Psalm 82 challenges the right of the powerful to ignore justice.

Psalm 82 is also ripe with ambiguity. The composition relies on ambiguous language and style to invite a diverse audience into the scenario as participants. The poet begs for a consideration about who is at fault and how they failed society.

Finally, the composer brings the reader to an appeal for change. The final verse alludes to the first verse, returning the reader to conclude whether or not the so-called gods actually understand their duty and what is at stake. In this chapter, I will argue that nothing has been clearly resolved in the psalm's conclusion. It is left to the reader to determine what should, or could, be done. The cycle of injustice—poverty, desperation, and death is familiar to the reader. A shrouded conclusion begs the reader's input. The reader is tasked to become the judge of virtue.

I. Prologue [82:1a^1]

II. Status quo of societal justice [82:1a^2–1b]

   A. אֱלֹהִים exist(s) in divine council [82:1a^2]

   B. Right justice should take place [82:1b]

III. Perversion of the norm: the lowly are at risk due to lack of justice [82:2–4]

   A. Right judgment is not taking place [82:2]

      1. Challenge of justice [82:2a]

      2. Accusation of partiality [82:2b]

   B. Justice for marginalized groups [82:3–4]

      1. Appeal to offer right judgment [82:3a]

      2. Appeal to make right the marginalized [82:3b]

    3. Save those in need [82:4a]

    4. Bring them to safety from the wicked [82:4b]

IV. Everything is wrong: obscurity, darkness, instability [82:5]

    A. Lack of knowledge/understanding [82:5a¹]

    B. Walking in darkness [82:5a²]

    C. The land is shaken [82:5b]

V. Perversion of the norm: gods are in danger due to lack of justice [82:6–7]

    A. Challenge to the authority of אֱלֹהִים from the council [82:6]

        1. Divine status challenged [82:6a]

        2. Birthright challenged [82:6b]

    B. Death/demotion

        1. Status from divine to mortal [82:7a]

        2. Loss of elite status [82:7b]

VI. Appeal for correction of societal justice [82:8]

    A. אֱלֹהִים should be doing right justice [82:8a]

        1. Rise to action [82:8a¹]

        2. Judge properly [82:8a²]

    B. All nations depend on אֱלֹהִים for justice [82:8b]

The above outline of Psalm 82 reflects the style of an ancient Near Eastern poetic narrative text.[10] This structure fits with the approach here. Psalm 82 includes poetic features that support an ethical reading. There is a kind of inclusion formed between v. 1 and v. 8, which both describe a scene in a heavenly realm. However, in this study, I will argue for a progressive reading, whereby the reader might feel very distant from the realm of the אֱלֹהִים in v. 1, but in v. 8, the reader has become part of the process of justice-making. At the center of the narrative is a climax which lays out the stakes of injustice, the most central of which is that the stability of the earth is at risk in v. 5. The instability of the earth itself is a symptom of other things that are going wrong (described in the verses before and after v. 5): the poor are suffering at the hand of the wicked (vv. 3–4), and the אֱלֹהִים are falling (vv. 6–7). By the conclusion of the poem, the reader has seen enough and should be able to draw an ethical conclusion.

10. This is more fully considered in Chapter 3.

Psalm 82:1: Assembly of the Gods

Psalm 82:1 includes two clear components: the first is the introduction, contextualizing the psalm among the Asaphite Psalms and the second is the opening scene for the verses that follow. This section will provide a brief overview of what it means for a psalm to be Asaphite, then a longer sub-section will attempt to explain who is/are the subject(s) of v. 1 and what they are doing.

מִזְמוֹר לְאָסָף Psalm 82:1a, An Introduction

Psalm 82 is identified as an Asaphite psalm (v. 1a). There are twelve psalms in the Hebrew Bible attributed to Asaph.[11] These psalms include three features which distinguish them from the larger corpus of the Psalter. Though Psalm 82 offers several unique features,[12] as discussed in the previous chapter, it also contains features broadly common to other Asaphite psalms, including the following:

1. Asaph psalms are largely prophetic in voice, aligning much of the text with prophetic writings elsewhere in the Hebrew Bible.[13]

2. Asaph psalms are heavily connected to books of Torah, including specific references to creation, the lineage of Jacob and Joseph (Genesis) as well as phrases and references to the song of the sea, deliverance from Egypt, and Mosaic teachings (Exodus).[14]

Asaph psalms contain about one-third of all occurrences of עֶלְיוֹן in the Psalter, and about 15% of all occurrences in the Hebrew Bible.[15]

Psalm 82 has been classified as having prophetic voice and style, it demonstrates a connection to Torah, with specific parallels in Exodus 22, 23 and Deuteronomy 32, and it includes one occurrence of עֶלְיוֹן.[16] However, the way in which the composition of Psalm 82 engages these themes

---

11. Psalms 50; 73–83
12. Nasuti, *Tradition History*.
13. Johnson, *The Cultic Prophet*.
14. Goulder, *The Psalms of Asaph*.
15. The word עֶלְיוֹן occurs 8x in Asaph Psalms, 22x in Psalter, and 52x in the rest of the Hebrew Bible.
16. These various features are broadly engaged by scholars whose contributions are summarized in Chapter One.

is quite different from other compositions, even from those among other Asaphite psalms.[17]

Psalm 82:1b אֱלֹהִים נִצָּב בַּעֲדַת־אֵל בְּקֶרֶב אֱלֹהִים יִשְׁפֹּט׃

Psalm 82 opens with a divine council type scene that is common to ancient Near Eastern texts. The most common Hebrew Bible comparison is the scene set in the introduction of Job, in which YHWH is seated in a divine council, and activity regarding judgment is carried out within that cosmos realm. The event of divine council is considered an exceptional gathering, in which deities must travel some distance from their earthly realm counterpart in order to hold such a meeting.

> The gods are not envisioned in Ugaritic mythology as living together in 'heaven,' but rather at different locales around the earth, primarily on the mountains. The gods must make substantial journeys to get from one divine abode to another. Regular communication between them is portrayed as relatively rare and primarily through messengers.[18]

References in the Hebrew Bible to such an event should be considered in the same manner. The divine council type scene in the Hebrew Bible implies communication between deities in a style common to cognate literature.

Divine council scenes exist in the Hebrew Bible as direct references and allusions. Min Suc Kee created an extensive list in his article, "The Heavenly Council and Its Type-scene."[19] Kee concluded that the common elements of a divine council "type-scene" prepares the reader to hear a particular kind of text. It is a tradition that provokes a judgmental scene for the hearer or reader of the text. Kee identified major type-scenes of heavenly council in the Hebrew Bible: 1 Kgs 22:19–23; Isa 6; Job 1–2; Psalm 82; Zech 3; and Dan 7:9–14. He also pointed to a number of passages that relay short events or references to the council type scene: Jer 23:18, 22a; Job 15:8; Ps 25:14; Ps 49:20; 73:15; Amos 8:14; Isa 14:13. Some address multitudes of divine beings: Exod 15:11; Dt 32:8; Ps 86:4–5; 97:7,9; Dt 4:19; 17:3; Judg 5:20; Ps 148:2–3; Isa 14:13; Job 38:7; Neh 9:6; Jer 8:2; Deut 33:2–3; Zech 14:5. Others imply an event: Gen 1:26; 3:22; 11:7; Ps 29:1–2; 58:1–2;

---

17. This was largely covered in Nasuti's Text Critical work on the Asaph Psalms. Refer to the more detailed explanation in Chapter One. Nasuti, *Tradition History*.

18. Smith, *The Ugaritic Baal Cycle*, 43.

19. Kee, "The Heavenly Council."

89:6–9; Isa 24:33. Psalm 82 includes a direct reference to the divine council scene and takes on the characteristics described by Kee. The type scene prepares the audience to receive a particular kind of text, one that provokes sensibilities of justice, involving both divine and human realms.

Working out who are the אֱלֹהִים is one of the primary questions at the center of an ongoing discussion about how to interpret Ps 82:1. Translations have made sense of v. 1 in many different ways. They fall largely into two categories: אֱלֹהִים are mortal/human and אֱלֹהִים are divine entities (God/god/gods). Morgenstern described this dichotomy as the primary framework for possible interpretations in his thesis,[20] and it has been the central point of discussion for scholars ever since. Furthermore, the BHS apparatus for the MT does not mention any potential anomalies in the verse. Evidence has been cast for both definitions, and there has been no resolution on the matter in nearly a century.

This study considers intentional ambiguity as a means of reading the psalm in a broad context. Given the semantic range of use for אֱלֹהִים in the Hebrew Bible, Psalm 82 can easily bear leaving the word אֱלֹהִים undesignated, in which case the reader is left to decide the significance of its use which may be determined by cultural or theological influences. This process encourages a weighted focus on the message of justice in the psalm rather than a didactic context of judgment prescribed by a particular translation of אֱלֹהִים. An ambiguous reading empowers the reader to engage as a participant in the ethical case of justice central to Psalm 82.

The texture of language and imagery in Psalm 82 provides support for an ethical reading. One of the "spokes" of the *Organon* "wheel" involves assessing textual characteristics of the text. The possibilities for inclusion extended by a semantic range of meaning for אֱלֹהִים makes way for a diverse readership to consider ethical implications of the text.

The Semantic Range of אֱלֹהִים

The perceived issues in Ps 82:1 have been resolved in many different ways. As demonstrated in the previous chapter, some scholars have attempted to translate אֱלֹהִים strictly following verbal forms, while others attempt to justify the verbal forms based on grammatical technicalities. One complication arises because the words modifying אֱלֹהִים potentially imply both singular and plural subjects. For example, נִצָּב (which modifies the first use of אֱלֹהִים) and יִשְׁפֹּט (which appears at the end of v. 1) are verbal singular forms; however, the prepositional phrase בְּקֶרֶב, which modifies the second use of אֱלֹהִים

---

20. Morgenstern, "Mythological Background."

in v. 1, indicates plurality. To further complicate matters, in the Hebrew Bible אֱלֹהִים is commonly translated in the singular form with specific reference to God, and sometimes accepts the plural. The composition of Psalm 82 offers a range of options for translation. As was examined in Chapter One, scholars from the twentieth and twenty-first century have offered a variety of approaches in translating אֱלֹהִים. These range from reading the first occurrence as singular, and the second as plural, to conjecture about replacing אֱלֹהִים with the tetragrammaton. With an understanding of the grammatical possibilities for reading the Hebrew text of Ps 82:1, there are a number of technically acceptable ways to translate אֱלֹהִים.

The potential for polysemy in Ps 82:1 relies on the apparent flexibility of Hebrew grammar for a singular verb to modify a plural subject. This is sometimes referred to as a collective singular. In Ps 82:1, the subject אֱלֹהִים is technically plural, but since אֱלֹהִים is sometimes used as an epithet for God, it can be read singular in the context of the Hebrew Bible. In Ps 82:1a, the *nifal* ms participle נִצָּב modifies the first of two occurrences of אֱלֹהִים, indicating a singular verbal form. At first, this signals the reader to identify a singular subject. However, upon further consideration of the grammar, it is evident that נִצָּב may be modifying a plural אֱלֹהִים.

There are two ways to test the validity of subject-verb agreement in translating Hebrew. The first is by context, and the second is by considering grammatical possibilities by looking elsewhere in the language and possible translations. The mythological and poetic nature of Psalm 82 allows for a possible contextual reading that includes multiple deities. Several interpretations mentioned in Chapter One consider this a possibility. The limits of connections between Psalm 82 and Near Eastern mythological texts will be explored in Chapter Three.

The grammar test is a little more complicated. After consulting several resources, it seems that a case can be made for either reading, meaning אֱלֹהִים could refer to God, or a group of deities. When two possibilities exist for translation, a text may be considered ambiguous.[21] This section will attempt to identify the most syntactically straightforward translation.

Three grammar studies support a potentially plural reading of אֱלֹהִים in Ps 82:1. While a straightforward approach considers a singular verbal form to modify a singular subject, Joüon-Muraoka's *Grammar of Biblical Hebrew* noted two exceptions in the Hebrew Bible: 1) a *nifal* ms participle modifies a collective singular noun in 1 Sam 13:16 (וְהָעָם הַנִּמְצָא), and 2) a *qal* ms participle modifies a collective singular noun in Josh 5:4 (כָּל־הָעָם הַיֹּצֵא). In both

---

21. This is one of the recommendations of Empson's *Types of Ambiguity* which is explored in more detail in Chapter 7.

cases, the plural collective noun is הָעָם. The fact that a singular noun is used to represent a group of living beings and is, in this instance modified by a singular verb, provides evidence for potential ambiguity in reading אֱלֹהִים as a plural, singular collective. The grammar also notes that there is a tendency for adjectives, or attributive participles which essentially act as adjectives,[22] to occur in the singular when they modify a plural noun of "excellence or majesty," for which Joüon-Muraoka's grammar referenced אֱלֹהִים, קְדֹשִׁים, as well as cognate examples.[23] This also supports a potential plural reading of "gods" for אֱלֹהִים. Furthermore, Waltke-O'Connor's *An Introduction to Biblical Hebrew Syntax* addressed the adjectival nature of a passive participle such as נִצָּב in v. 1, and affirmed its translation in the gerund or other adjectival forms.[24] Waltke-O'Connor did not deal very clearly with collective singular translations, but did mention plurals of majesty, in which plurality acts to intensify the quality or character of a subject.[25] This aspect is also affirmed by Joel Burnett in his study, *A Reassessment of Elohim*. Burnett provided examples of how אֱלֹהִים is modified by singular verbs in ancient Near Eastern cognate languages, even when the subject is clearly plural.[26] Burnett's study explored the context and grammar possibilities of occurrences of אֱלֹהִים in Hebrew Bible passages that relate to ancient Near Eastern texts. However, he did not attend to the particularities of Psalm 82.

In Psalm 82:1b, another occurrence of אֱלֹהִים is possibly modified by a singular verb form; this time it is the *qal* ms imperfect verb יִשְׁפֹּט. As explored in Chapter One, many scholars take this second occurrence of אֱלֹהִים to be plural. The obscurity lies in identifying the actual subject of the singular verb. A straightforward reading would indicate that the verb is modified by the nearest noun. However, this presents the same issue surrounding אֱלֹהִים as exists in Psalm 82:1a—a plural noun modified by a singular verb.

Some translation acrobatics must be attempted to fit everything into a strong monotheistic paradigm. Many take the second occurrence of אֱלֹהִים as plural in order to make sense of the verse, and that requires some creative syntactical work. The final verb יִשְׁפֹּט is sometimes translated to modify the אֱלֹהִים in v. 1a, and other times the בַּעֲדַת־אֵל in v. 1a, and still yet, the אֱלֹהִים in v. 1b. Waltke-O'Connor translated Psalm 82:1 "God presides in the great

---

22. Waltke-O'Connor suggests that a passive participle which follows a noun (such as נִצָּב in v. 1) acts adjectivally. Waltke and O'Connor, *Hebrew Syntax*.

23. Joüon-Muraoka noted that this phenomenon occurs in both Hebrew and related examples in Aramaic (i.e. עֶלְיוֹנִין). Joüon-Muraoka, *A Grammar*, 469–70, 514.

24. Waltke and O'Connor, *Hebrew Syntax*, 619.

25. Waltke and O'Connor, *Hebrew Syntax*, 120–22.

26. Burnett, *A Reassessment*.

assembly; he gives judgment among the divine beings."²⁷ Waltke-O'Connor did not explain the syntax here, but it demonstrates how Ps 82:1 can be translated in such a way to conform to a monotheistic reading, even though it is difficult to identify a clear subject for the יִשְׁפֹּט verb.

An alternative approach allows for a poetic nuance, reading the verb as a standalone concept. Joüon-Muraoka gave a possible explanation for how an imperfect verb may indicate an aspect of repeated action or durative action, noting cases where the imperfect form of a verb parallels a participle. Joüon-Muraoka specifically cited Psalm 82:1 as an example of this grammatical feature. The authors interpreted the יִשְׁפֹּט verb participially: "Judgement is happening."²⁸ This use seems to best reflect thematic tendencies in divine council scenes to indicate an arena of judgment, as mentioned in the previous section. It also provides a more syntactically straightforward translation. There is no need to search back in the verse to identify a preferred subject.

Following the grammatical possibilities, it appears that there is more than one way to appropriately translate Psalm 82:1. Since אֱלֹהִים may represent either a single deity or a group of deities, and both translations fit the context and the grammar, a case could be made for intentional ambiguity in the composition. The reason for this could indicate a blended audience wherein some hear "God" and others hear "gods" for אֱלֹהִים in v. 1. The next section will explore the semantic range of אֱלֹהִים in the Hebrew Bible and ancient Near Eastern cognates. Considering Psalm 82 as a composition meant for a diverse audience could explain how it can be read so many different ways. However, the ethical themes of concern for the poor are a timeless message that extends to all of humanity, regardless of their view of the divine.

The proto-Semitic origins of אֱלֹהִים indicate a multivalent linguistic history that extends into the Hebrew Bible. This section will trace origins of the word and focus on its use in the Hebrew Bible, particularly in the Psalter, in order to more fully consider the cultural and literary background of אֱלֹהִים and its semantic range. Hebrew Bible references correlate with occurrences of אֵל and אֱלֹהִים in old Northwest Semitic texts, Hebrew inscriptions, and Bronze Age Ugaritic texts. Furthermore, conclusions will inform an attempt to understand how an ancient audience might have responded to the term אֱלֹהִים in Psalm 82.

The various ways that אֱלֹהִים is translated in the Hebrew Bible is representative of a developing Israelite religious culture as they discovered and

---

27. Waltke and O'Connor, *Hebrew Syntax*, 505.

28 Joüon-Muraoka, *A Grammar*, 338. Joüon-Muraoka also noted Ps 145:20, 33:16.

formed their identity in the ancient Near East. In the Levant, proto-Semitic cultural influences drew upon ancient ideas about God and worship that evolved from Phoenician, Hittite, Assyrian and Egyptian practices before formation within the confines of an explicit Israelite cultural group. The word אֱלֹהִים is borrowed from proto-Semitic deific language before its adoption into Israelite religion.

In *A Reassessment of Biblical Elohim*, Joel S. Burnett explored the possible origins of אֱלֹהִים in the Late Bronze Age, noting its earliest parallels in cuneiform documents from Amarna, Qatna, Taanach, and Ugarit, and he identified its closest Semitic roots in coastal Phoenician.[29] Without context, אֱלֹהִים is plural, and its form is connected with the name of the proto-Semitic most high deity, El, אֵל,[30] a term also referenced in Ps 82:1. While scholars have proposed that the plural form was derived from the singular proper name, Burnett provided evidence for early parallels in the plural form and demonstrated that though they are connected, it is difficult to show the exact morphology, allowing room for negotiation in forming a translation.[31]

The word אֱלֹהִים appears approximately 2600 times[32] in the Hebrew Bible. Usually, the context of the composition or narrative provides clues to how אֱלֹהִים is functioning as either an epithet for God, or as a reference to a group of deities,[33] who are often enemies of God. Peter Machinist saw this as a matter of thematic duality, arguing that אֱלֹהִים is the "key term in Psalm 82, whose recurrent double usage, referring to the God of Israel/*Elohim* and to the other gods/*elohim* in the divine council, and the play on this duality tie the text together."[34] The idea that אֱלֹהִים can represent multiple meanings is accepted, yet it remains difficult to interpret Psalm 82 without resolving the tension. Psalm 82 provides exceptional insight into ancient Near Eastern constructs of divine council and the roles and responsibilities of the אֱלֹהִים. This will become further evident after looking at the broader context for the use of אֱלֹהִים in the Hebrew Bible and in the ancient Near East.

By the Late Bronze Age, Phoenician writings demonstrated a prolific use of אֱלֹהִים as a "noun of abstraction (i.e. 'divinity') and to designate a

---

29. Burnett, *A Reassessment*, 7–8.

30. Another proto-Semitic term connected with אֱלֹהִים is אלוה.

31. Burnett, *A Reassessment*, 5.

32. Approx. 800 times in Torah, approx. 500 times in the Writings, approx. 50 times in Wisdom Literature, approx. 350 times in the Psalter, and approx. 900 times in the Prophets for a total of 2600 occurrences in the Hebrew Bible.

33. A notable exception exists in 1 Sam 28:13–14 where the identification of the אֱלֹהִים is applied to the human prophet's ghost.

34. Machinist, "How Gods Die," 194.

particular god as 'deity.'"³⁵ These texts have linguistic and literary links with the Hebrew Bible. For example, the Deir 'Alla inscription contains a narrative closely related to Numbers 22. The narrative gives an account of the prophet בִּלְעָם, who is notable in both texts as a foreigner who engages with אֱלֹהִים. The ink-on-plaster inscription is thought to have been on display in an international market, and it has been suggested that the אֱלֹהִים referred to are divine entities in a nonspecific way, "a designation which, by virtue of both its plurality and its non-specificity (and its placement), would have lent itself to the accommodation of a diversity of deities and worshippers."³⁶ This possibility provides evidence for the practice of ambiguity surrounding the use of אֱלֹהִים as a way of engaging multiple audiences toward a condensed message. The broad use of אֱלֹהִים and its cognates in the Levant from as early as fifteenth century BCE³⁷ suggests that אֱלֹהִים was widely adopted for generic application to imply divinity or refer to a deity that aligns with any particular hearer's beliefs.

On a related note, evidence was presented in 2017 by K. Lawson Younger that the concept of using one deific name to represent more than one potential deity was practiced in Aram, with regard to a local deity—the Moon God. A unique dedicatory inscription was found on the Bull Stela at et-Tell on the northern shore of Galilee which reads lšm, "belonging to the name ..." followed by a symbol that is meant to represent a Moon God. Younger proposed in 2017 that the symbol may provide a "fill in the blank formula" so that a person could adapt as needed. His theories are based on the evidence that there were different proper names attributed to moon gods throughout the region.³⁸ While this is suppositional, it demonstrates the uncertainty in relating cultural cognition of a deity to textual language about a deity. Determining the application and use of אֱלֹהִים is no exception.

In the Hebrew Bible, Gen 1:1³⁹ provides the first appearance of אֱלֹהִים, noted as *Creator of heavens and earth*, and then, thirty-four verses later, in Gen 2:4b,⁴⁰ a parallel construction reads יְהוָה אֱלֹהִים, which includes the Tetragrammaton, and indicates the deity as Maker of earth and heavens. The dual inclusion of these forms indicates evidence of competing traditions, both of which were too important to let go of by the compilers and/or redactors of the Hebrew Bible. Perhaps this was no concerning matter for

---

35. Burnett, *A Reassessment*, 29.
36. Burnett, *A Reassessment*, 39.
37. Burnett, *A Reassessment*, 8.
38. Younger, "'The Gods of Aram.'"
39. Gen 1:1: בְּרֵאשִׁית בָּרָא אֱלֹהִים אֵת הַשָּׁמַיִם וְאֵת הָאָרֶץ
40. Gen 2:4b: בְּיוֹם עֲשׂוֹת יְהוָה אֱלֹהִים אֶרֶץ וְשָׁמָיִם

the ancients, but it complicates matters for modern westerners who typically like to have theologies neatly packaged for delivery and consumption. The references to multiple nuances for the name of God in the Hebrew Bible suggests efforts of intentional inclusion in antiquity.

As the Hebrew Bible narrative continues from Genesis, the Israelites did not formally learn God's name per se until Exodus 3, after following the stories and lives of a multitude of generations, wherein Exod 3:15 reveals the name of God as

What does seem to be true is that the Hebrew Bible itself demonstrates some ambiguity about the nature and character of the Hebrew God as אֵל and as אֱלֹהִים; and also as distinct from אֵל and distinct from אֱלֹהִים. These variant occurrences of אֱלֹהִים demonstrate complexity of language as well as ideologies about what to call God.[41] A first look at common translations of Psalm 82:1 demonstrates the controversy—

- where אֱלֹהִים represents God proper as well as a generic plural sharing one space: "God has taken his place in the divine council; in the midst of the gods he holds judgment" (NRSV); "God presides in the great assembly; he renders judgment among the 'gods'" (NIV); "God takes his stand in his own congregation; he judges in the midst of the rulers" (NASB); "God is standing in the divine assembly; among the gods he exercises authority" (TFT);[42] "God is standing in the divine assembly, in the midst of the gods he pronounces judgment" (Tate);[43] "God takes His stand in the divine assembly, in the midst of the gods He renders judgment" (Alter);[44] "Elohim steht in der Versammlung der El, inmitten der Elohim richtet er *(jišpōṭ)*" (Rokay);[45] "God stands up, in the assembly of El, in the midst of the gods he judges" (Handy);[46] "God presides over the pantheon; in the midst of the gods

---

41. The larger discussion here involves naming the deity. In many cases, the Hebrew Bible refers to God through descriptions, adjectival phrases that define God's character. Often it is shown through a narrative or interaction. God is named by virtue of how the godself appears to a human in relationship. For example, in the story of Hagar from Genesis 20, when Hagar cried out to *El Roi, The God who sees,* or *the God who sees me,* was she crying out to God whose name she already knew, or had already heard about, and thought to implore in that moment of personal crisis? Or was she describing a God whose presence was making itself known, or seen, to her in that moment?

42. Goldingay, *The First Testament.*

43. Tate, *Psalms.*

44. Alter, *The Book of Psalms.*

45. Rokay, "Vom Stadttor zu den Vorhöfen."

46. Handy, "Sounds, Words and Meanings."

He rules" (Gordon);⁴⁷ "God takes his stand in the court of heaven, to deliver judgement among the gods themselves" (CBC);⁴⁸ "'Yhwh' stands in the divine assembly, He gives judgment in the midst of the gods" (Tsevat);⁴⁹ "God presides in the divine council, in the midst of the gods adjudicates" (ABC);⁵⁰

- where אֱלֹהִים represents God proper who is proclaiming judgment against other אֱלֹהִים: "God stands in the congregation of the mighty; he judges among the gods" (NKJV); "The True God stands to preside over the heavenly council. He pronounces judgment on the so-called gods" (VOICE); "When all of the other gods have come together, the Lord God judges them" (CEV); "There's God standing in the Houses of Parliament, surrounded by people who think they are God, and telling them that they're not" (Sissons);⁵¹ "God calls the judges into his courtroom, he puts all the judges in the dock" (Message);⁵² "The mighty God doth stand within th'assemblie of the throng: and he it is that righteously doth judge the gods among" (BPB).⁵³

- Additionally, two translations attempt to preserve the Hebrew and embrace the potential ambiguity in translation: "Elohim standeth in the Adat El; He judgeth among the elohim" (OJB); "Elohim [God] stands in the divine assembly; there with the elohim [judges], he judges" (CJB).⁵⁴

Psalm 82 reflects an ongoing issue for translation continuity in the instance of אֱלֹהִים in the Hebrew Bible, but it is not the only psalm to suggest that אֱלֹהִים has a semantic range of meaning.

Psalm 45, included among the *Elohistic Psalms*, along with Psalm 82, is one that obscures the normal modern understanding of אֱלֹהִים as a name

---

47. Gordon defended God as presiding over the pantheon, making the law. He suggested that El, the Ugaritic God, is the high god, but once all are eliminated, El becomes the only god. Gordon, "History of Religion," 130–31.

48. Rogerson and McKay, *Psalms*, 163–65.

49. Tsevat made an explicit note that there is "no textual or linguistic difficulties." He stated that YHWH is the clear agent. He also stated that it is possible to read the psalmist as the speaker in v. 5. Tsevat, "God and the Gods."

50. Dahood, *Psalms II*, 268–71.

51. Sissons, "Psalm 82 Re-written."

52. Peterson, *The Message*.

53. *The Bay Psalm Book*.

54. These translations are published versions of the Bible. A broader variety of translations have been suggested by scholars and in commentaries, which are discussed in chapter one.

for God. In this psalm, אֱלֹהִים represents a human king throughout the poetic narrative, but also may stand in for the Tetragrammaton in at least one instance. Psalm 45 is a song of love for a human king, called אֱלֹהִים, who has been blessed by אֱלֹהִים (God). Psalm 45:2 describes a clear context for reading the psalm as a missive of admiration for the king, who is called a son of humankind, בְּנֵי אָדָם, in v. 1, who is blessed by אֱלֹהִים.[55] Further along in the psalm, the king is addressed again as אֱלֹהִים, apparently an acceptable title for a monarch: an epithet for this enthroned king, as he is described, and subject of this love song. Again in v. 8, a blessing of anointing is recognized for the king from אֱלֹהִים אֱלֹהֶיךָ, and in this case, there is a note that some manuscripts present the Tetragrammaton to clarify how אֱלֹהִים is being used in this one instance.[56] At the very least, this shows some acceptance of semantic flexibility for the use of אֱלֹהִים, even within one single written psalm. More likely, it confirms that אֱלֹהִים had a wide semantic range of use in an ancient Near Eastern literary context.[57]

Psalm 138 provides another example of a variant use of אֱלֹהִים. The psalmist addresses God, as is made clear in several verses wherein the second person directive is accompanied by the Tetragrammaton. For example, in v. 4, which reads יוֹדוּךָ יְהוָה, "(they) shall all praise you, *yhwh*." The Tetragrammaton appears a total of six times in this verse, making the subject of address clear. The emphatic use of the Tetragrammaton in Psalm 138 to represent God then draws attention to the appearance of אֱלֹהִים in v. 1. In this context, the אֱלֹהִים exist alongside the Hebrew God. The psalmist praises YHWH, נֶגֶד אֱלֹהִים, "before (the) gods." There is no grammatical issue, nor is there any instruction to read this phrase differently. It must be understood that this is a normal use of the word אֱלֹהִים, in which it is distinct from the personal name of God.

In other Hebrew Bible texts, the term אֱלֹהִים appears in varied use as well.[58] In Exodus 3, the Hebrew God reveals the godself to Moses, which

---

55. BHS note on Ps 45:3 that this instance of אֱלֹהִים may be read as the Tetragrammaton.

56. BHS note on Ps 45:8 that this phrase is sometimes written יְהוָה אֱלֹהֶיךָ

57. See critical commentary about the *Elohistic Psalter* in Chapter 6.

58. Though several cases may be made for the flexibility of use that אֱלֹהִים represents in the Hebrew Bible, the examples offered here have to do with the identity of the אֱלֹהִים and the role of אֱלֹהִים in justice. For a discussion of some other difficult appearances of אֱלֹהִים, see Slivniak's study of Ruth 1:15–16; Gen 32:25–33; and Exod 32. Slivniak drew conclusions about the polysemous nature of אֱלֹהִים in the Hebrew Bible text, although he does not offer a solution to help ground understanding. Instead of considering ambiguity, he reached for a postmodern reading in order to engage the idea that ancient Israelites were pluralists as evidenced by their linguistic diversity. Slivniak, "Our God(s) is One," 3–23.

marks a significant shift in the intention of the Israelites to worship YHWH as the high god, if not the only god. In chapters 3 and 6, there is an appeal to distinguish אֱלֹהִים from the Tetragrammaton, which comes to stand for the name of God. In Exod 3:15, God is revealed to Moses as אֶהְיֶה אֲשֶׁר אֶהְיֶה, sometimes translated "I am who I am," the one previously known as אֱלֹהֵי אֲבֹתֵיכֶם, the אֱלֹהִים of your ancestors. Several verses later, in Exod 6:2, further clarification is given as אֱלֹהִים (speaking) shares with Moses a proper name, the Tetragrammaton, אֲנִי יְהוָה. Furthermore, there is an explicit explanation that the name of God as יהוה was not previously revealed to the patriarchs, which acts as an apologetic for their worship of the same God by another title.[59] The biblical authors in this pivotal point in Israel's history demonstrate a desire to distinguish the god they worship, and the god of their ancestors, as a distinct אֱלֹהִים. Even though there is some clarity in this particular narrative, the names and titles of the Hebrew God continue to maintain a semantic range throughout the biblical text.

In the Covenant Code, Exod 21:6 and 22:7–8, אֱלֹהִים is often interpreted as "judges." The אֱלֹהִים are presented in such a way that fits with the function of household deities in the broader cultural context of the ancient Near East as mediators of justice for personal disputes. Anne Kilmer made a convincing case for the relationship of אֱלֹהִים with such deities, providing specific textual comparisons to support her findings that the use of אֱלֹהִים in Exodus shares strong parallels with the Akkadian Nuzi texts, in which אֱלֹהִים relates to the word *ilāni*.[60] In her argument, Kilmer defended a translation of "household gods" for אֱלֹהִים, rather than the traditional rendering of "judges." In Akkadian Nuzi texts, the *ilāni* are called upon for judgment when a legal decision cannot be reached between two human parties. The *ilāni* become "the source of legal decisions obtained by supernatural means."[61] They are divine keepers of justice.

Kilmer's conclusions are supported by Burnett's research. In his exploration of the meaning of אֱלֹהִים in the Hebrew Bible, Burnett found similar evidence to show that אֱלֹהִים in Exodus 21 and 22 is being used as a title, representing "unspecified domestic or communal deities whose authority in legal matters is recognized."[62] The function of the *ilāni* and the אֱלֹהִים in these texts warrant consideration for their symmetry. This

---

59. It appears that El is confirmed as YHWH in Exodus 6. Hood read Exod 6:3 as evidence that God avoided appearing as YHWH until this moment. Ibn Ezra affirmed a perspective of Israelite reform toward a named deity which is why YHWH is considered to be revealed in the Mosaic texts. Hood, "I Appeared as El Shaddai," 167–88.

60. Kilmer, "Ilāni/Elohim," 216–25.

61. Kilmer, "Ilāni/Elohim."

62. Burnett, *A Reassessment*, 62–63.

demonstrates again that אֱלֹהִים is a term with a broad range of application in the ancient Near East.

The use of אֱלֹהִים as mediators of justice also appears in 1 Sam 2:25, אִם־יֶחֱטָא אִישׁ לְאִישׁ—"if one man sins against another," וּפִלְלוֹ אֱלֹהִים "then אֱלֹהִים may mediate . . ." The Tetragrammaton appears in 1 Sam 2:25b, which Kilmer considered to be evidence that the first rendering of אֱלֹהִים must also be translated as a reference to God.[63] However, the logic does not necessarily follow. Rather, 1 Sam 2:25 shows another instance in which אֱלֹהִים and the Tetragrammaton stand together in the same verse to reference potentially different beings. The first instance of אֱלֹהִים establishes the norm of mediation for justice. The second deity is contextual to the first. In other words, if one human has a crime against another human, the אֱלֹהִים should mediate, but if a human commits wrong against YHWH, only then the אֱלֹהִים are insufficient. Kilmer's argument for the variant use of אֱלֹהִים in The Covenant Code is better supported by the appearance of אֱלֹהִים alongside the Tetragrammaton in 1 Sam, occurring as a potential separate divine entity.[64] Both examples show further evidence of the semantic range of אֱלֹהִים in the Hebrew Bible.

The significance of so many occurrences of אֱלֹהִים with such varied context in the Hebrew Bible and proto-Semitic literature is in its range of use. Modern scholarship has tended to limit the interpretation of אֱלֹהִים to either a pre-Mosaic reference to God, or a monotheistic Judean construct to stand in for the name of God. This study demonstrates a deeper complexity for the identity of the אֱלֹהִים in ancient Near Eastern literature. Translations of אֱלֹהִים in the Hebrew Bible should consider the semantic range more carefully before committing to a singular interpretation.

For a fuller understanding of the various meanings which אֱלֹהִים can represent, it is useful to consider the Semitic roots of the word. The Hebrew Bible is a collection of narrative, legal, and poetic texts compiled from various points in time, spanning anywhere from a few centuries to millennia.[65] As such, terminology in some parts of the Hebrew Bible reflect social constructs or values that differ from that same terminology used in other parts. Tracing connections between words that form similarly across time reveals how a term evolves and provides insight into its

---

63. Kilmer, "Ilāni/Elohim."

64. Firth suggested that אֱלֹהִים here can be translated as "God" but with the expectation that God acts through human judges. Firth, *1 & 2 Samuel*.

65. Theories range broadly on dating the Hebrew Bible. This will not be discussed at length in this project., but recent scholarship about indeterminacy within the Psalter is discussed in Chapter 6.

meaning in different contexts.⁶⁶ The term אֱלֹהִים is rooted in proto-Semitic literary texts and inscriptions.

The relationship between God and the proto-Semitic deity El is implicit in linguistic similarities between the Tetragrammaton and attributes of the Ugaritic deity El. It has been proposed that the Tetragrammaton is in fact a shortened version of one of El's epithets. Frank Moore Cross wrote at length, describing the linguistic rationale to explain how El's Ugaritic title "one who creates armies," *yhwê ṣĕbā'ôt*, likely provides a proto-form of the Divine Name in the Hebrew Bible.⁶⁷ Cross affirmed a pattern in numerous proto-Semitic epithets of El ascribed to God. An example of this includes the imagery of YHWH as "creator" and "father" in Deut 32:6⁶⁸. Mark Smith furthered this discussion of parallels between the Hebrew God and the Ugaritic deity, El. His scholarship noted that the word *'il* (El) appears over 500 times in texts from Ugarit with a range of meaning that spans from generic reference, to a proper noun naming the god El, to divine attribution in other proper names.⁶⁹ He concluded that in Ugaritic myth, El is conceivably the "divine patriarch par excellence,"⁷⁰ a quality that is easily transferrable to YHWH via the biblical text. The linguistic relationship between אֱלֹהִים and אֵל is largely recognized in scholarship and connects these two figures textually.

Hebrew Bible texts with linguistic or literary connections to Ugaritic are usually thought to be regionally Northern and evidence of earlier traditions or influences, since Ugarit's city center is in the Northern Levant region, and their society crumbled near the beginning of the first millennium BCE. While well-established connections between אֱלֹהִים and אֵל exist in older Northern texts and inscriptions, there is also inscriptional evidence that El was worshipped in southern regions of the Levant, and possibly even in Jerusalem. One example of this is the formulaic Phoenician construction highlighting El as creator in a similar way as Genesis

---

66. One peculiarity of working with ancient texts is the guesswork surrounding when certain texts are written, and then determining when and where they were redacted. Since the MT was compiled much later than the content it contains, this is not a precise scientific process. As a result, there will be some generalizations made about dating and influence of language.

67. Cross pointed to Exod 3:14 and its linguistic heritage to trace the morphology of the name of YHWH. Cross, *Canaanite Myth*, 68–9.

68. Cross detailed a number of parallels in the first chapter of his book. Some include the following: ' *ab* ' *adm* "father of humanity," *bny bnwt* "creature of creatures," ' *il qny* ' *arṣ* "El creator of the earth" (cf. Gen 14:19) (*KAI* 26 A III:18); Cross, *Canaanite Myth*.

69. Smith, *Origins of Biblical Monotheism*, 135–37.

70. Smith, *Origins of Biblical Monotheism*, 135.

portrays God as creator, a divine being who forms and builds the world and places things in it. The Phoenician construction, *El qônēh ʾereṣ*, parallels an inscribed fragment found in the Jewish Quarter of Jerusalem.[71] Patrick Miller reconstructed this fragment to read "El, Creator of Earth."[72] This is hardly revolutionary given the numerous parallels already discussed, but it does provide insight into how widespread the knowledge of El worship was throughout early proto-Semitic culture. Further connections that demonstrate a relationship between El and YHWH worship in the south can be found at Khirbet el-Qôm, where a text was found which describes an affiliation between the tribes of Israel and YHWH with El, and at Khirbet Beit Lei, where an inscription refers to YHWH as *ʾl ḥmn*, "El the gracious."[73] Then, there is the Kuntillet ʿAjrud inscription, a series of blessings attributing YHWH in relationship with El's known consort, Asherah.[74] These inscriptions demonstrate evidence of early connections in Israelite religious culture to its roots in earlier Semitic religious ideas.

The strongest evidence of a tradition of El-worship in the Hebrew Bible is *pre-Mosaic*.[75] The patriarchs called the deity they worshipped by the name of El, אֵל. An early example of this can be found in Gen 14:18–22, wherein veneration is shown for El, אֵל עֶלְיוֹן, by Abram, who is acknowledged to be a founding patriarch in regards to YHWH worship. This is a prime example in which El is acknowledged as a distinct deity in the earliest cultic context by a man who is later said to be Yahwistic.[76]

Throughout the Hebrew Bible text there is evidence of wide associations between the worship of El and YHWH. El, אֵל, like אֱלֹהִים appears to represent a range of meaning in the Hebrew Bible. Otto Eissfeldt

71. Avigad, "Excavations."
72. Miller, "El, The Creator of Earth."
73. Dever, "Iron Age."
74. The reference in this pottery inscription places Asherah in a possessive form—indicating that Asherah may be referring to either the goddess or a common noun. It is interesting to note here that while the inscriptions demonstrate some ambiguity about whether Asherah's consort is El or YHWH, or if they are perhaps one and the same, parts of the Hebrew Bible polemicize against Asherah (particularly in books of Kings). It may be that the authors of the Hebrew text are fighting against a cultural acceptance of the El/YHWH connection.
75. In Exodus, God reveals the identity and name of the godself to Moses. This seems to be the narrative that describes a turning point for both the identity of the Hebrew God as well as for the Hebrew people. Pre-Mosaic is a way of referring to events that are described as taking place before Moses. Though pinpointing a date for the patriarchs in Genesis is nearly impossible, twentieth-century scholarship affirmed the patriarch's worship of El in the first half of second millennium BCE. Eissfeldt, "El and Yahweh."
76. Note Josh 24:2.

categorized these into three major uses: 1) אֵל is used singularly, without polemic, to indicate God;[77] 2) אֵל is YHWH by consciousness of will claims made by the narrator;[78] and 3) אֵל is different from, and a primal superior to YHWH.[79] While the Hebrew Bible contains many polemic texts against other Canaanite deities, for example Ba'al, whose Ugaritic attributes are sometimes ascribed to YHWH in the Hebrew Bible, El remains largely unchallenged.[80] This is indicative of the friendly relationship the Israelites had with El, which is why the text takes a stand in some cases for the likeness, if not the sameness, of El and YHWH by presenting polemics against shared enemies, like Ba'al. Although texts of the Torah have been considered to bring a kind of reform to the worship of El as God,[81] there is still some ambiguity in the practical implications for worship of El/YHWH in the ancient Near East, even among Israelites.

There is a temptation in scholarship to simplify the complex relationship between אֱלֹהִים and אֵל by describing a direct evolution of reform from polytheism to monotheism.[82] However, proto-Semitic inscriptions and the text of the Hebrew Bible reflect a more diverse paradigm. Some scholars have pointed to Psalm 82 as a summary of theistic evolution. Here, however, is a good place to consider Mark Smith's proposal that monotheism and polytheism are philosophical categories imposed by modern historians on

---

77. As in Josh 22:22 wherein representatives of tribes erect an altar monument in Geliloth hal-Jordan to "El Elohim YHWH . . ." Also in Job 3:1, where in El occurs in dialogue to indicate the Hebrew God as Eloah, Elohim, and El Shaddai, and in Psalm 104, which speaks of El in parallel poetic form to introduce praise to YHWH. Eissfeldt, "El and Yahweh."

78. As in Isa 43:12, Isa 45:2, Isa 40:13, Isa 43:12. See Eissfeldt, "El and Yahweh."

79. Following Isa 14:13, a statement from outside the sphere of YHWH, a non-Israelite claim "Above the stars of El I shall raise my throne"; Ezek 28:2 "El I am; a divine seat I have in the ocean." Neither acknowledges a clear relationship between El and YHWH. Eissfeldt, "El and Yahweh."

80. It could be noted that some of El's behaviors in the Ugaritic texts are not well attested in the Hebrew Bible as an attribute of YHWH. The scarcity of such texts could be evidence of religious reform in the Israelite community. There are, for instance, more descriptions of El's drunkenness and sexuality attested at Ugarit than is attested in the Hebrew Bible. (Although there is some debate about this, as Psalm 44, for one, perhaps hints at the drunkenness of the Hebrew God!)

It may be helpful here to also recognize that there is arguably no polemic against El in the Hebrew Bible. Chalmers looked at the question of such a polemic and concluded that there may be evidence of some angst for El in Hosea 11. Clearly, though, there are more cases of comparison, accepting likenesses of the characteristics between El and YHWH, than diversion. Chalmers, "Who Is the Real El?"

81. See previous discussion on Exodus 3–6.

82. Refer to chapter one for a description of various scholars whose interpretation of Psalm 82 hinges on the assumption or importance of monotheism.

an ancient text that is probably doing something entirely different. Smith observed that YHWH is the "eventual historical winner" in the Hebrew Bible's historical record, but the journey is less clear.[83]

Modern systems of classification often force us to work within a limited scope to the exclusion of ancient cosmology and perceptions about the divine. The concerns of modern historians drive scholars to pack ancient ideologies into neat, tight-fitted containment; whereas ambiguous ancient biblical texts evidence a complex relationship between Israelites and the name of the God they worship. The complexities of the relationship between אֱלֹהִים and אֵל which have been explored in this chapter are evidence of the potential for ambiguity, especially in a mythological text. In light of this, obscure occurrences of אֱלֹהִים in the Hebrew Bible, such as is found in Psalm 82:1, anticipates a broad audience from various cultic backgrounds.

The Behavior of אֱלֹהִים in Psalm 82:1

Two verbs modify the אֱלֹהִים in v. 1. The first is נִצָּב, which is easily parsed as a *nifal* masculine singular participle from the root meaning "to stand." It is conjoined with the first instance of אֱלֹהִים. The second verb, יִשְׁפֹּט, is also easily parsed as a *qal* imperfect third person masculine singular verb from the root meaning "to judge." It appears as the final word in Psalm 82:1. The question of how these verbs function in relation to the subject of אֱלֹהִים is often tied to the debate over the identity of the אֱלֹהִים. It is difficult to perceive the context of a scene that is not clearly in line with a perceived monotheistic context.

Conceptually, the divine council scene is recognized as a place where justice takes place at the highest levels. Psalm 82 begins with a description of the subjects who stand in the divine council. While it is normal in a divine council scene to portray groups of standing beings, it is not common that those standing are in a position to have the final say in judgment. The standing beings in a council of judgment often represent those responsible for lower level order. They may, however, bring cases of importance to a high judge, who is usually portrayed as seated (discussed below). For those who attempt to replace אֱלֹהִים with the Tetragrammaton in Psalm 82:1, some contrivance of explanation is required to make sense of this divine council scene, since it would follow that YHWH is standing[84] as a lesser deity, or lower level judge in this case.

---

83. Smith, *Origins of Biblical Monotheism*, 144.

84. While the scene itself is not unusual, it is an unusual portrayal of El and the Elohim in the Hebrew Bible. Nasuti discusses this well in his work. Nasuti, *Tradition*

The presiding authority over judgment in the ancient Near East is often portrayed as seated.[85] This is evident from imagery that depicts a judge or king in a seated position.[86] The ancient Israelite community also followed in this tradition. From humble beginnings of society in Exodus, to the height of the united monarchy, the seated rulers make judgment, while their subjects often stand. An early example of this is described in Exod 18:3, where Moses sat to judge (וַיֵּשֶׁב מֹשֶׁה לִשְׁפֹּט), while his people stood (יַעֲמֹד) around him. As time passed, Moses could not keep up with all the cases brought before him, so his father-in-law advised a model that would become normative for the distribution of rulership and the formation of Israelite society from then on.

Moses became head of a tiered system of governance. Below him, a group of officials who oversaw other officials, in groups of thousands, hundreds, fifties, and tens, respectively. These levels of under-rulers judged the people and brought important cases up the line to Moses himself. Though the NRSV renders the "able men" as ones who "sit as judges" (Exod. 18:22), the Hebrew text does not include the word for sit, but instead simply states that they will judge (וְשָׁפְטוּ אֶת־הָעָם). This model becomes a standard for Israelite ruling. In the following generations of Israelite leadership, the model is extended. In Judges 4, the prophetess Deborah sat under the palm tree while Israelites came to her for judgment (v. 5) and Israel's first king, Saul, sat under a tamarisk tree in Gibeah while his servants were standing around him (1 Sam 22:6). The seated high judge is formally established in Israelite culture when King Solomon constructs a judgment room which contains a throne from which judgment is pronounced, and while it is not under a tree, the room is constructed entirely from cedar wood, symbolic of the tree-tradition (1 Kgs 7:7).[87] This same model of judgment is also described in higher cosmological terms in Dan 7:9–10. There, the throne is inhabited by a most ancient deity, עַתִּיק יוֹמִין, served by standing thousands while the highest authority is seated in judgment.

While Psalm 82 does not directly mention a seated judge, it is implied by a description of those who are standing in attendance. It may, however, also be the case there is no seated judge, or an abdication of a high judge, which might explain the lack of proper judgment. It might also be that an

---

History.

85. Some scholars have pointed to exceptions in the Hebrew Bible to defend their translation of אֱלֹהִים as YHWH. Tate, *Psalms*, 335. Tsevat, "God and the Gods."

86. Keel-Leu and Hallett, *The Symbolism of the Biblical World*, 207–08.

87. Also note Isa 16:5 in which a throne is established for the rule of right justice; Isa 28:6 describing a ruler seated in judgment; Ps 122:5 refers to thrones of judgment in the house of David; in Prov 20:8 a king sits on the throne of judgment.

unnamed being is the seated high ruler, or, more likely, it might be that "El" is the seated high ruler. What can be known from this study is that Psalm 82 describes the אֱלֹהִים as standing, and as such, they (plural or singular) may be counted as subjects or lesser rulers of the seated judge. The verbal forms and subjects they modify seem to evidence intentional ambiguity that is capable of enticing the reader to consider an ethical response.

The אֱלֹהִים Who נִצָּב

The verb נִצָּב functions in Psalm 82:1 as an attributive participle, and acts adjectivally,[88] modifying the subject it follows—אֱלֹהִים. The meaning should be taken simply as "אֱלֹהִים (are) standing in the council of El." Scholars have defended both singular and plural interpretations for the subject (as previously discussed), and the singular form of נִצָּב does not seem to pose a problem since a singular verb can represent a collective plural subject like אֱלֹהִים.[89] I will not repeat the discussion of possibilities for אֱלֹהִים here, except to say that the main interpretations fit nicely in translation, be they any of "God (is) standing in the council of El," or "judges (are) standing in the council of El," or "gods (are) standing in the council of El." All here seem to fit grammatically. Scholars who take on this subject, do so to determine what it means for a divine being to stand.

Assuming that a seated judge is present, "El" might be seen to be the highest judge. After all, the council is named for El. This leads to the question of true identity of this divine entity—"Is El the Hebrew God in this divine council scene?" If so, then there are problems for one or more interpretations which consider the אֱלֹהִים to represent God.[90] In other Hebrew Bible divine council scenes, YHWH tends to be considered the implicit, seated deity. For example, consider Job 1:6 and 2:1, and Zech. 3:1–8, in which the head of council is seated, while other beings move about in his presence.

On the other hand, if the first אֱלֹהִים is God, and the psalm represents a pre-monotheistic Israelite view of divine council, as some have suggested, then El is not God, but leads a divine council in which God stands with others as one of the אֱלֹהִים.[91] This is supported by those who would translate at least the first instance of אֱלֹהִים as representing the Hebrew God, or as the Tetragrammaton, in which case the divine council does not belong to YHWH. The challenge in this interpretation for some scholars becomes evident in v.

88. See notes on translation and explanation of the grammar above.
89. See discussion in chapter one.
90. See previous section(s) on the multiple interpretations of אֱלֹהִים.
91. This is one of the positions supported with reference to Deut. 32:8.

8 wherein the אֱלֹהִים are called upon to rise. If אֱלֹהִים are already standing, then it must be either that another figure is called upon to rise—perhaps the implicit Most High El of divine council? Or, it might be that קוּמָה in this instance is figurative, a common feature of Hebrew Bible poetry.[92] If this is true, it also supports a metaphoric reading of נִצָּב, that the standing action represents either subordinate position of authority relative to the implied seated judge(s),[93] or a representation of lack of judgment. All of this is to say that the verb נצב provides clues to the relative position and authority of the אֱלֹהִים, rather than determining the identity of אֱלֹהִים.

From these various divine council descriptions, it may be safely understood that there are different sorts of beings who maintain right of admittance into the divine council. The ambiguity of the psalmist's use of אֱלֹהִים in Ps 82:1 invites the reader to consider any or all who may be present in such a scene, and furthermore, to consider their role in matters of justice in the human realm.[94] The ambiguity in v. 1 also offers multiple insights into the divine council, where multiple deities are gathered together "standing around," waiting for a judge to act. The language in the scene heightens the significance of the final verb—יִשְׁפֹּט. Divine council exists for the sake of justice. The ambiguity leads the reader to consider an implicit ethical question: is justice actually taking place?

The verb יִשְׁפֹּט could be rendered here "to judge." This is a useful interpretation for achieving the psalmist's purpose of bringing the reader to the central meaning of the psalm. The likely meaning here is to convey a sense of judgement or justice.[95] This translation is not without precedent and fits better in this context than trying to force a simple imperfect action, even though some have tried to translate יִשְׁפֹּט to fit with their interpretation of the אֱלֹהִים, that "El," "YHWH," or judges will judge.[96]

To determine how the verb is functioning, it is useful to look intertextually. The *qal* imperfect inflection of יִשְׁפֹּט appears twenty-seven times across twenty-six verses in the Hebrew Bible. In fourteen occurrences, it

---

92. Discussed further on in this chapter.

93. And so there are translations that attempt another description, i.e. "are gathered," etc.

94. In addition to the main discussion present in this research of אֱלֹהִים as human or divine figures, there are others mentioned in the text, i.e. הַשָּׂטָן, and מַלְאָךְ. Heiser made an intensive study of the relationship between אֱלֹהִים and מַלְאָךְ in which he concluded that they are not likely the same at all. Heiser, "The Divine Council."

95. Consider 1 Kgs 7:7 where a throne room is constructed for purpose of conveying a place of judgment, where the enthroned one judges, יִשְׁפָּט־שָׁם ("where he was to pronounce judgment" NRSV).

96. See notes on translation.

forms as a *waw* consecutive. In each of these cases, the verb modifies a human subject, either named or unnamed. The syntax in these cases certainly supports a simple *qal* translation, "PN judged[97] . . . " The remaining non-*waw* consecutive forms of the verb modify divine entities, in most cases the entity is YHWH. In all cases where יִשְׁפֹּט modifies a divine subject, the mood is either jussive or indicative of an anticipatory request. Translations render "*may YHWH* judge" or, as in Kgs 7:7, "to pronounce judgement" and in Ps 82:1, "holds judgment" (NRSV).[98] The meaning of יִשְׁפֹּט is consistent with an anticipatory request, and the divine council type scene sets up the reader to anticipate a discussion about a single topic—the matter of justice in divine council.

In a similar way that ambiguity surrounding the previous verb, נִצָּב, leads the reader to consider an implicit ethical question about the effectiveness of the אֱלֹהִים, the final verb in v. 1 also renders an ambiguity of subject that encourages ethical consideration. The first half of v. 1 leads the reader to question whether the אֱלֹהִים are doing their job, and the second half of the verse directs that question toward the matter of justice.

The actions of the אֱלֹהִים in Ps 82:1 provide insight into how divine council exists and the expectations of justice. The verbs provide clues for the reader as to what they should expect in the verses that follow. They do not, however, resolve the question of identity of the אֱלֹהִים, only their role in administering justice (or not!). Scholarship is driven to try and fit the language of Psalm 82 into the context of a Psalter that centers on God, but the ambiguous language halts the process, which leads me to think about the composition of Psalm 82 in a polyphonic world. The very least that v. 1 clearly communicates is an appeal for the reader to consider implicit ethical questions about justice.

A Case for Leaving אֱלֹהִים Undesignated in Psalm 82:1

If the composer of Psalm 82 is employing a technique of intentional ambiguity in v. 1, then the reading that best fits the meaning is one in which אֱלֹהִים is untranslated so that the reader is prompted to consider the implications. A simple transliteration offers the opportunity of engagement by a reader from today's polyphonic religious culture. Even if the reader is unaware of the Hebrew language, they would be prompted to seek meaning.

---

97. Gen 19:9, Judg 3:10, 10:2–3, 12:7–9, 12:11(2x), 12:13–14, 15:20; 1 Sam 7:6, 7:15

98. Gen 16:5; Exod 5:21; Judg 11:27; 1 Sam 24:13, 24:16; 1 Kgs 7:7; Ps 9:9, 72:4, 82:1, 96:13, 98:9; Eccl 3:17; 2 Chr 1:10.

By means of ambiguity, the reader will be drawn in to assess the situation of injustice presented in the composition.

In Ps 82:1, the ambiguity of who the אֱלֹהִים represent and how they relate to matters of justice in the human realm invites the reader to take pause and think deeply about societal justice. The verses that follow feed the reader with a challenge to the status quo and a plea for change. The Torah and Psalter, at least, directly encourage mindful consideration of the text. Ambiguity becomes a method by which this may be achieved.

The use of intentional ambiguity in Psalm 82 draws the reader's attention to a situation that may or may not directly affect them—the position of the poor and weak in their society. Eben H. Scheffler stated that the very poor are often without voice, do not write poems about their desperate condition: rather their plight must be broadcast by one looking in from outside the condition of poverty.[99] Of course, we have evidence of creative prayers, poems, and songs in poverty, but Scheffler's point speaks to the inability of the poor to broadcast their plight beyond themselves and their circumstance. They require advocacy. Psalm 82 appeals to advocacy for the poor.

The audience may not experience poverty themselves, but certainly they feel the consequence of earth's shaken foundation (v. 5). The psalmist sheds light on the problem of the wicked, the experience of the voiceless poor, and the root of injustice flowing down from the elite. The reader of Psalm 82 is called upon to consider the relationship between the disadvantaged and the way that justice is or, as in this case, is not dispensed. Intentional ambiguity in v. 1 sparks a question in the reader's mind as to the situation of *justice*, which is the central topic of Psalm 82. Furthermore, if justice is not concrete enough, v. 5 demonstrates a more tactile consequence: the earth will become unstable when the demands of justice are not met.

By leaving אֱלֹהִים undesignated, a broad audience is invited and empowered to engage with a discussion about justice. In an ancient context, some would hear אֱלֹהִים as an epithet for YHWH, some would consider אֱלֹהִים a reference to multiple deities who control the cosmos, and others would consider the אֱלֹהִים as representing titles of rulership by divine right—their kings and judges. Even within the Hebrew Bible itself, there is evidence of some range of understanding about who and what the אֱלֹהִים are and how the אֱלֹהִים function(s) in different contexts. It is clear that in the ancient world, the range of use for the term אֱלֹהִים was broad and polysemous, its meaning depending on a person's religious or cultural background. The ambiguity of אֱלֹהִים in Ps 82:1 invites the reader to think about the relationship and role of gods, God, kings, and judges in matters of human justice.

---

99. Scheffler, "The Poor in the Psalms," 9.

Furthermore, in a modern context, leaving אֱלֹהִים as undesignated allows readers to engage in Ps 82:1 without the imposition of one translator's definition of the אֱלֹהִים over another's. This invites the reader to see or hear the poem in a way that is more closely aligned with the ancient audience and the purpose for which it was written. There are enough commonalities between the pluralistic culture that inhabited the ancient Near East during the time(s) Psalm 82 is thought to have been composed and the religious and ethical pluralities that inhabit today's world to make such a correlation between the readers and message of Psalm 82. In fact, the societal problems are also similar in today's world. The author of Psalm 82 captured the essence of a conversation about societal justice that extends beyond transcending culture, but also to transcend time. A translation of Psalm 82:1 should reflect the ambiguity and likewise encourage thoughtful discussion among a diverse audience.

Psalm 82:1 describes a scene of rule that takes place somewhere far away from the common person. In a council that sits in the heavens, among the stars or over the waters, the gods do as they will. For others, the scene certainly looks familiar for they have seen the inside of such a court reflected on earth, filled with select human rulers who have been invited into a council of judgment with a king or seated judge. The ambiguity in the language of v. 1 allows people from various backgrounds to access to the thematic concern of the psalm. The conclusion of v. 1 states clearly the context of the psalm: a message to the reader that they should consider what virtue of justice there is in the matter that follows.

Psalm 82:2–4: Poverty and Injustice

Psalm 82:2–4 begins a new segment of direct speech which offers a response to the narrated events of v. 1. It centers the reader on the matter most important to the composition: justice. Psalm 82:2 reveals a conflict behind the seeming innocuous scene described in the previous verse. While v. 1 describes a divine council in its element—those with authority to judge are dealing with matters of justice, v. 2 follows with an accusation. The audience is made aware by the speaker that what has been called justice is actually not justice at all. Furthermore, the lines that follow in vv. 3–4 express the injustice in detailed description. It is a list of grievances posed to the audience for consideration. The shocking reality then becomes apparent—if the ones who are meant to judge justly are misbehaving, then who remains to make sure things go right?

Coming out of the first two lines of the composition, the reader should be met with surprise at the accusation hurled in v. 2. The expectation after such a divine council scene as is described might be for the unfolding of some case or another. Likely, it would be through the details of the divine council meeting that the audience could gain awareness of exactly who the אֱלֹהִים represent, or perhaps they expected to hear a story like others common to the ancient world, where deities meet and squabble among one another. But instead, there is accusation. And, even as modern readers struggle to determine exactly who is speaking in v. 2, the ambiguity makes space for an audience to think about who is challenging the אֱלֹהִים and why.

Ps 82:2 עַד־מָתַי תִּשְׁפְּטוּ־עָוֶל וּפְנֵי רְשָׁעִים תִּשְׂאוּ־סֶלָה׃

Verse two relies on shock factor to appeal to a broad audience and cause discomfort. Commentaries often refer to the prophetic nature of the rhetorical question in v. 2. It is that confrontive nature of the question that transforms it into a challenge that not only confronts the characters in the composition, but extends by implication to anyone who listens. Those who came for a good story have now been drawn into a rhetorical challenge made against the אֱלֹהִים. Others, who came to worship, were expected to listen to a poetic narrative challenging injustice. The impact of the message, though addressed to higher beings, may be felt by an audience at all levels.

Syntactically, v. 2 is unremarkable. It begins with a rhetorical device which commonly appears in prophetic literature.[100] The question signals a message of judgment rather than a request for information. The speaker presumes authority to stand for justice.[101] In the ancient Near East, the right to care for justice is divinely inspired.[102] Social order depends on the character of the ruling class, or of a particular ruler, to bring well-being to the community through proper justice. When a judgment is challenged, it is the character of authority that comes under scrutiny, rather than a particular law or precedent.[103]

---

100. The rhetorical question, introduced by the עַד־מָתַי interrogative, often appears in laments such as Ps 6:4, 49:5, 74:10, 94:3; Exod 10:7; 1 Sam 1:14; Jer 4:14, 21; Prov 1:22.

101. Note Lev 19:15—unjust judgment is that which defers to either disadvantaged or the advantaged. Impartiality is central to a biblical ethic of justice.

102. This is laid out in more detail in Chapter 5, mainly to note that ancient Near Eastern kings claim authority to oversee justice by divine right. The same is true in the Hebrew Bible, where kings and judges rule under the authority of God.

103. This is described in more detail in TWOT, under the listing for špt. Harris, et. al., *Theological Wordbook*.

Identifying the speaker of v. 2 has been the subject of some debate among scholars.[104] The phrase עַד־מָתַי invokes protest or rebuke. The protest-question may be put from one human to another or from a deity to a human; however, in the Psalter it is often used by a human to address the deity. Goldingay proposed that עַד־מָתַי may signify in some places that a prophet is admitted into divine assembly for the purpose of addressing the court. He described the speaker in vv. 1–2 as one and the same, although also admitted the possibility of a congregation or leader reading vv. 1 and 8 as a way of framing the psalm.[105] There is no reason to think that any of the אֱלֹהִים from v. 1 are speaking in v. 2. The Hebrew formula עַד־מָתַי is common enough among human speakers. The speaker could just as easily be the narrator, continuing on from v. 1. However, since there is a shift in voice, it could be nearly anyone among those who live under the rule of the אֱלֹהִים. There could be as many as four or five speakers in the psalm as a whole.[106]

With a view toward clarifying the ethical message of Psalm 82, it is more useful to examine the meaning of the verse rather than identify possibilities for the speaker. A closer look at intertextual language tells us that the phrase עַד־מָתַי usually addresses the divine,[107] as is the case in v. 2, but it also appears to represent protest against other humans in leadership. Again, the composer incorporates language of ambiguity that allows for multiple interpretations of the authority figures as well as the respondent. Even though the overall theme of justice and its accountability is not ambiguous, the ambiguity does make space for a diverse audience. While v. 1 sets up the reader for a case of justice, v. 2 anticipates a persecution of injustice, even at the highest levels.

One of the difficulties for certain theological approaches to Psalm 82 is the temptation to protect YHWH from collusion with other אֱלֹהִים in v. 1, who are being called out for injustice. Since YHWH is the supreme deity in the Hebrew Bible, the reasonable canonical assumption is that YHWH is on

---

104. Perspectives on the speaker are heavily influenced by who the אֱלֹהִים in v. 1, discussed in the previous section.

105. Goldingay pointed out that while in the psalms, the phrase addresses God, and in other texts, it can be a human addressing another human, or even God addressing a human. "In the Psalms, "how long?" is usually a protest addressed to God (see 74:10), but elsewhere it can be a protest and implicit rebuke uttered by one human being to another (e.g., Exod 10:7; 1 Sam 1:14; 2 Sam 2:26; 1 Kgs 18:21), or by God (e.g., Exod 10:3; Num 14:27; 1 Sam 16:1)." He proposed that it is likely a prophet, who is admitted into divine assembly for the purpose of addressing the court (as in 1 Kgs 22:19–22). Goldingay, *Psalms*.

106. Gillingham's forthcoming Psalms commentary expresses the possibility of multiple voices in the psalm. Gillingham, *Psalms*.

107. Ps 6:3, 74:10, 80:4, 82:2, 90:13, and 94:3.

the right side of justice in Psalm 82. However, the continued debate about how YHWH may or may not be referenced in Ps 82:1 is further evidence that intentional ambiguity drives the composition of Psalm 82, especially given its inclusion in the Hebrew Bible Psalter.

The point of an unidentified speaker in v. 2 is an invitation to subvert authority. In tribal settings, ancient and present, a small group of elders gather together in the center of town to deliberate over important matters of their society. They are visible, so that everyone in that community may look on and watch the proceedings. The divine council reflects this ideal. This is the image painted in Psalm 82, with the אֱלֹהִים in v. 1 gathering for the sake of ensuring a just society. The challenger in v. 2 could be anyone, even from outside the circle of authority, who sees a problem and refuses to be silent. Psalm 82 recommends a model of involvement, of resistance against blind and unjust leaders. It is an invitation to break into the closed council and interrupt proceedings for the sake of justice. The composer invites participation by everyone who hears or reads this psalm. The ambiguity of the challenger's identity creates a universal script to address injustice in one's sphere.

Ps 82:3 שִׁפְטוּ־דַל וְיָתוֹם עָנִי וָרָשׁ הַצְדִּיקוּ׃
Ps 82:4 פַּלְּטוּ־דַל וְאֶבְיוֹן מִיַּד רְשָׁעִים הַצִּילוּ׃

Psalm 82:3–4 includes the densest language of poverty and the poor that exists in the Psalter, and perhaps even more dense than in any other Hebrew Bible text. A specific analysis of the language of poverty is taken up in Chapter Four, so this section will focus on other features of the verses.

These two verses are the least ambiguous in Psalm 82. If there is one clear point that the composer communicates, it is the desperate dependence of the marginalized, and by extension the earth, according to v. 5, upon right justice. The clear and straightforward nature of the rhetoric in vv. 3–4 indicates its importance. The cry for help writ in the form of lament indicates the need for someone to actively intervene on behalf of those without power. There is an implicit contrast between the active favor for the poor that is required and the deities' favor for the wicked as they fail to meet the needs of the marginalized.[108] The appeal by the speaker, addressed to the אֱלֹהִים, insists on a global consideration for the powerless. The speaker is not under any illusion that they have power to control matters. The appeal is to the אֱלֹהִים for a change before it is too late.

---

108. Tate emphasized the contrast as a way to communicate the failure of the deities in v. 1. Tate, *Psalms*, 336.

The poetic features of these verses come across by means of sound and structure. The imperatives demanding justice dance around the language of poverty. The text of the poem itself is trying to protect the vulnerable, wrapping the demands for justice, salvation and restoration, around the terms for the poor, vulnerable, and outright destitute. The language of poverty draws the reader's attention.

The expected pairings, such as אַלְמָנָה and the יָתוֹם do not appear, suggesting either an association of this psalm to ancient Near Eastern textual traditions outside Hebrew Bible norms, or an emphasis on this list as different from common Deuteronomic references. There is also evidence of wordplay through sound as the common word for poor, רָשׁ, in v. 3 is contrasted with a consonantal homonym implicating the wicked, רָשָׁע, in v. 4. The intentionality of the composition demonstrates its integrity as a text meant to deliver a message about the vulnerability of humanity before the powerful אֱלֹהִים.

Psalm 82 opens with a summons to the great assembly of the gods in the highest place. It is an exercise for the imagination; an invitation to glimpse the glory of the cosmos. But, as soon as we are there, the highest possible authority is challenged for their inability to maintain justice. They are critiqued by their own standard: caring for the poor. These all-powerful beings are known for empowering ancient rulers with doing justice by caring for the weak in society. The composition of Psalm 82 clarifies the injustice. Rather than pointing fingers at individual rulers or impotent laws, the composer goes straight to the top—the divine beings who have demanded justice from the beginning.

Verses 2–4 explicate the problem. The poor, the weak, the fatherless, the destitute, the desperate—they are captive to the wicked and suffer without help. There is ambiguity of agency. However, the matter of injustice is not ambiguous and deserves a response. The following verses strengthen the case for injustice and make a final appeal to make things right.

Psalm 82:5: The Earth Moves at the Center

The center of the poem in Psalm 82 is at v. 5. Syntactically, the verse is self-contained, a lone tricolon in a composition of bicola. This break in sequence causes a pause for the reader. It stops the flow of rhythm that has just barely begun and forces the reader to cease and consider something else before moving on to the next subject matter covered in the composition. The content of v. 5 describes an important consequence of the injustice under investigation in the human realm as well as in the divine.

Ps 82:5 לֹא יָדְעוּ וְלֹא יָבִינוּ בַּחֲשֵׁכָה יִתְהַלָּכוּ יִמּוֹטוּ כָּל־מוֹסְדֵי אָרֶץ׃

Verse 5 divides two major themes in the psalm: the affects of injustice upon the weakest of humanity (vv. 3–4) and the affects of injustice upon the divine (vv. 6–7). The ambiguous features of v. 5, i.e. the speaker and the subject, suggest that more than one single meaning may be derived. Who is the 3cp subject referenced in v. 5? Proximately, it could refer to the marginalized humans in vv. 3–4, or it could reference the wicked in whose hands these humans are caught. Or, following the potential voice of narration back to the poem's opening lines, the subject may be the אֱלֹהִים gathered in v. 1, who are accused of showing partiality to the wicked. Or, it may read in advance of the following verses, which describe the plight of the בְנֵי עֶלְיוֹן in vv. 6–7. The potential for v. 5 to contain relevance for each of the subjects in Psalm 82 suggests an intentional ambiguity of agency that allows for polysemy in order to make a point about the universal order. It invokes a question in the reader's mind about how all these players are connected. The subject(s) in v. 5 may be grounded in either of the realms explored in Psalm 82—the divine or the human.

A potential new speaker is also introduced in Ps 82:5. However, even if this is not the case, it is clear that a distinct voice emerges, different than the rhythmic list-maker of vv. 3 and 4. Verse 5 possibly marks a return to the more narrator-centered voice of v. 1. Or, it could be another reader, performing a pausal interlude. The unidentified speaker draws as much attention to this verse as any other feature. An ambiguous narrator zooms out from the focus of the previous verses, minute and detailed on the smallest, most vulnerable in the world, to the larger earth and universe. In v. 5, the subjects of the previous verses seem tiny by comparison to the foundations of the earth, and the supposed gods of vv. 6–7 are all the more writ large as the בְנֵי עֶלְיוֹן.

In the first two phrases of the tricolon, *they have neither knowledge nor understanding/they walk around in darkness,* ambiguous pronouns encourage critical receptors to ask questions like *who* has no knowledge, or *who* walks around in darkness. Up to this point, the composition of Psalm 82 has introduced multiple actors. The agency of these pronouns could refer to any of the actors. However, only two subjects have been described so far in terms of physical positioning: they are the אֱלֹהִים, who "stand" and the רְשָׁעִים, who hold the impoverished in their hands. This may be compared to the Deutero-Isaiah voice, "the nothingness of the idols that have no capacity to see or know or discern anything."[109] The subjects of v. 5b "walk," a physi-

---

109. Miller, "When the Gods Meet," 3.

cal action. The agency of one who "walks" is consistent with either of the two actors—the אֱלֹהִים or the רְשָׁעִים. Verse 5 could refer to one, or both, of these actors.[110] After all, they all seem to be on trial for injustice here, so they may be all blamed for the consequences.

The third phrase of the tricolon is meta description, *all the foundations of the earth are shaken*, and it returns the poem to the mythical paradigm of its introduction. Meta descriptions like this one also evoke ambiguity. The tension of how long will the earth hold up under the shaken and unstable foundations forces an imminent response. It is the third phrase of the tricolon in v. 5 that breaks the rhythmic bicolonic pattern of Psalm 82, and it is this line that offers the most extreme of any consequence of injustice given in the entire composition.

In case it is not enough that the poor and destitute suffer (a thing that goes against the value of every ancient Near Eastern civilization of the time), or that the בְּנֵי עֶלְיוֹן may lose their position as divine entities (a thing unimaginable in the ancient Near East), v. 5 rocks the paradigm by suggesting that the stability of the universe is at stake. The fate of the world depends on an appropriate response to the events in the psalm.

Verse 5 forces the reader to cease for a moment at the center of Psalm 82. Its disruptive rhythm and meta-descriptive content speaks to the seriousness of the injustice. Not only are the unrepresented, underrepresented, and marginalized peoples made even more vulnerable, but the whole momentum of events is causing larger repercussions in the cosmos. Robert Alter wrote of the verse, "the perversion of justice is the first step toward the apocalypse,"[111] a view that assesses the conditions described in Psalm 82:5 as an end-of-the-world event. Verse 5 is determined to provide the reader with an intense and big-picture consequence. It anticipates unfathomable ideas about gods falling toward their death presented in the following two verses, and a desperate plea for correction in v. 8.

Psalm 82:6–7: Consequence of Injustice

Just past the half-way marker in Psalm 82, the reader has already been exposed to a whirlwind of discourse about divine congregation in the heavens, the suffering of humans on earth, and the foundations of the

---

110. Scholars have been divided on this. For example, Goulder described the "*They* of v. 5" as the "*wicked* of v. 4." Goulder, *The Psalms of Asaph*, 164. On the other hand, Strawn noted that "it is most likely that it is the oppressed." Strawn, "The Poetics of Psalm 82," 28.

111. Alter, *Book of Psalms*, 292.

cosmos in the deeps. The two verses that follow continue along the theme of injustice and its consequences. Not only are the innocent and vulnerable abandoned without refuge, and the cosmos is losing its balance, but the lives and status of those upon whom humanity depends for justice, the gods, are now threatened.

Ps 82:6 אֲנִי־אָמַרְתִּי אֱלֹהִים אַתֶּם וּבְנֵי עֶלְיוֹן כֻּלְּכֶם׃

Ps 82:7 אָכֵן כְּאָדָם תְּמוּתוּן וּכְאַחַד הַשָּׂרִים תִּפֹּלוּ׃

The first-person speech that leads v. 6, אֲנִי־אָמַרְתִּי introduces yet another potential speaker into the short poem. This formula occurs only a dozen times in the Hebrew Bible. Some scholars have viewed God as a direct speaker in this verse, for example Robert Altar, who wrote in his commentary on the Psalm,

> God confesses to have been taken in by the polytheistic illusion. He imagined that these sundry gods entrusted with the administration of justice on earth would prove or justify their divine status by doing the job properly. In the end, He was sadly disappointed.[112]

Alter's reading is in line with other Hebrew Bible passages. In Exod 12:12, YHWH judges the gods of Egypt, and also in Num 33:4 YHWH judges other gods. Other scholars have denied that it is possible for an infallible deity, such as YHWH, to make the claim which follows in v. 6. Consider Marvin Tate, who stated that YHWH could never be fooled by these so-called deities.[113] John Goldingay offered another view, stating that the phrase אֲנִי־אָמַרְתִּי normally occurs as divine utterance through a human prophet.[114] Primary assumptions have read the speaker as divine, either through direct speech or by proxy through a human prophet. However, following the work of Gordon Wenham in *Psalms as Torah*, it seems that the emphatic first-person pronoun, more importantly, invites the reader to participate in the psalm as liturgy, so that the reader may enter the text at the point where the composition describes consequences for unethical behavior.[115] The impact of this revelation for the reader recommends an ethical response.

---

112. Alter, *Book of Psalms*, 292.

113. Tate, *Psalms*, 338.

114. Goldingay, *Psalms*, 559.

115. Although Wenham does not directly deal with Psalm 82, his work demonstrated that the liturgical nature of the Psalter offers a natural participatory invitation regarding ethical matters. Wenham, *Psalms as Torah*.

The ambiguity of the identity of divine entity(ies) emerges again in v. 6 as it was in v. 1. The addressee אֱלֹהִים (Ps 82:6a) is parallel with the phrase בְּנֵי עֶלְיוֹן (Ps 82:6b). In addition to the obscurity of meaning for the potential range of identity of אֱלֹהִים in v. 1, v. 6 further complicates the matter by emphasizing the connection of אֱלֹהִים with the more obscure canaanite-oriented reference to עֶלְיוֹן. Mowinckel suggested that אֱלֹהִים should be read here as "(sons of) god," following a Qumran fragment which substitutes בְּנֵי אֵל in place of אֱלֹהִים in v. 1.[116] The interconnectedness of these terms is understandable only in context of Canaanite literature and reinforces the early, mythological, proto-Israelite themes which Psalm 82 draws upon.

Among other qualities that create opportunities for discussion about the provenance of Psalm 82, the portrayal of אֱלֹהִים in vv. 6–7 is quite unique in the Hebrew Psalter, and also in the larger corpus. The phrase בְּנֵי עֶלְיוֹן does not appear anywhere else in the Hebrew Bible. The עֶלְיוֹן, however, does occur in the Hebrew Bible. For example, in Deut 32:8, the עֶלְיוֹן is a deity who divides up the land among the בְּנֵי יִשְׂרָאֵל, sons of Israel. Some read עֶלְיוֹן as a title for God who is credited with creating extant deities.[117] The apparatus in the BHS identifies some manuscripts which preserve בני אל or בני אלים in place of the בְּנֵי יִשְׂרָאֵל in Deut 32:8. Ackerman discussed a rabbinical interpretation of Israelites as gods,[118] which he then applied to a reading of Ps 82:6, to interpret the psalm as referent to the judges and elders of Israel. This reasoning led to earlier interpretations of Psalm 82 that relied on the socio-political positioning of Israel in its ancient Near Eastern setting (such as those discussed in Chapter One). However, the uniqueness of the phrase בְּנֵי עֶלְיוֹן in Psalm 82 has raised questions for scholars about the significance of these two verses as well as the placement of Psalm 82 in the Psalter.

As direct locution, the meaning of אֲנִי־אָמַרְתִּי is "I said." Occurrences of this phrase in the Hebrew Bible suggest that it introduces a counterfactual statement. Morgenstern identified a potential for interpretive concern about this phrase[119] and cited Karl Budde's analysis that אֲנִי־אָמַרְתִּי should be read as colloquial, and it potentially includes a negative nuance that is better translated with a regretful pluperfect—"I had said."[120]

A study of the phrase אֲנִי־אָמַרְתִּי in the Hebrew Bible supports the pluperfect rendering. The phrase אֲנִי־אָמַרְתִּי occurs twelve times: five times

---

116. He also placed this in context of Dt. 33:2, recommending that "holy ones" in the Hebrew Bible always refer to divine beings (footnote 132). Mowinckel, *The Psalms*, 150.

117. Rogerson and McKay, *Psalms*.

118. Ackerman, "The Rabbinic Interpretation," 186–91.

119. Morgenstern, "Mythological Background," 33.

120. Budde, "Ps 82:6f."

in the Psalter, five times in the latter prophets and twice in the writings. There are no occurrences in wisdom literature, the Torah, or in the former prophets. Seven of the twelve occurrences clearly indicate a counterfactual (Isa 38:10; Isa 49:4; Jer 5:4; Jon 2:5; Ps 30:6; Ps 31:23; Ps 116:11). Each of these is a poetic, or psalmic, text. Three occurrences are less clearly counterfactual but stand out as confessional intensifiers (Jer 10:19; Ps 41:5; 1 Chr 21:17). McKane described the use of the phrase in Jer 10:19 as one that invites the audience to participate, contextualizing Jeremiah's grief as their own, and join in the lament.[121] In the final occurrence (Ruth 4:4), the narrative suggests a subjunctive mood, which also indicates a type of counterfactual statement.

The phrase in Ps 82:6 introduces a counterfactual and also acts as an intensifier, drawing explicit attention to a wrongful scenario. The occurrence of אֲנִי־אָמַרְתִּי in Ps 82:6 easily follows the pattern in other Hebrew Bible passages and prepares the reader or audience to anticipate a counterfactual description. Therefore, "You are gods, children of the Most High, all of you ... " (v. 6) should be taken as a counterfactual statement. The subjects addressed either are not deities at all, or they should not be deities. The rhetoric then invites the audience to discern the quality of events in the psalm, as no clear resolution is offered by the composer. The reader becomes sympathetic to the first-person speaker and so is no longer an observer to the composition, but a potential actor.

The parallel occurrence of אֱלֹהִים with בְּנֵי עֶלְיוֹן has led to discussions about divine sonship and the inheritance of deities. Emmanuel Usue explored attributes of divine sonship reflecting on four prominent descriptions that occur in the Hebrew Bible, with a primary focus on Genesis 6 and Psalm 2.[122] Two of these viewpoints apply to the divine epithets in Ps 82:6. The first is that "sons of God" may be nobles, rulers, kings and leaders. This view follows Egyptian and Assyrian traditions, and also could be the case in the Ugaritic *Epic of Kirta*, in which the king is referred to as "son of El." Trotter applied this logic to his interpretation of אֱלֹהִים in Psalm 82 as divine kings, backfilling his definition to v. 1 from the parallel of בְּנֵי עֶלְיוֹן in v. 6.[123] Usue's second viewpoint was to read "sons of God" as angelic beings, spirits, godlike beings, or demons. Usue referred to Hebrew Bible correlatives in Job 2:1, 38:7; Dan 3:25, Ps 29:1, 89:7 as evidence. He also

---

121. McKane et al., *A Critical and Exegetical Commentar*.

122. Usue, "Theological-Mythological Viewpoints."

123. Trotter insisted that there is no room for ambiguity, engaging Niehr on the subject, whose interpretation he dismissed as "implausible." Trotter, "Death of the אלהים," 11

cited the Epic of Gilgamesh which supports the use of "sons of God" as a name for members of divine pantheon.[124]

Essentially, these two definitions return to the early twentieth-century dualistic paradigm that Morgenstern wrote about regarding the interpretation of Psalm 82. Usue preferred a reading of divine sonship that interprets human leaders as divine,[125] and his view is in company with Trotter, who supported a reading of the אֱלֹהִים subject as divine kings or rulers,[126] and Mowinckel, who read Psalm 82 through Deut 32:8 as a complaint against foreign powers.[127] Prinsloo, however, differed. He took a stand for a reading that supports supernatural beings, in which the אֱלֹהִים are impotent Canaanite gods compared to YHWH.[128] Also leaning toward a supernatural reading is Parker, who described Psalm 82 as "Israelite myth," and drew parallels between Psalm 82 and Genesis 6 as a referent for divine sonship.[129] Then, as noted earlier, Niehr concluded there is deliberate ambiguity at work. He defended an interpretation of divine entities in vv. 1, 6–7, but he presents a human position of agency in vv. 2–4.

> Die viel diskutierte Frage, ob in Ps 82 Götter oder Menschen angesprochen sind, ist dahingehend zu entscheiden, daß beide Gruppen gemeint sind. Dies beruht auf dem in Analogie zur Welt konzipierten Pantheon, so daß sich im menschlichen Handeln das Handeln der Götter zeigt.[130]

Niehr posited that Psalm 82 infers critique both of Canaanite rulers as well as their gods. The contrast of human agency and divine agency drags the text from heavenly heights into the social realm of humanity.

In v. 7, the consequence of losing immortality is at stake for the subjects of the indictment in the composition. The give-and-take of immortality is not unique to Psalm 82. In the Ugaritic *Epic of Aqhat*, immortality is offered to Aqhat by the divine Anat in exchange for his most prized possession. This will be further assessed in Chapter Three. While the reversal of immortality is not a common theme in ancient Near Eastern texts, it does appear elsewhere in the Hebrew Bible. Isaiah 14, which is also thought to

---

124. He also noted New Testament and Apocryphal references in Jude 6; 2 Pet 2:4; and 1 En 6–11. Usue, "Theological-Mythological," 84.

125. Usue, "Theological-Mythological," 86.

126. Trotter, "Death of the אלהים."

127. Mowinckel, *The Psalms*, 220–21.

128. Prinsloo, "Psalm 82."

129. Parker, "The Beginning of the Reign of God," 556

130. Niehr, "Gotter oder Menschen," 98.

be an early mythological text,[131] refers to the "morning star" who tried to ascend to divine heights (v. 14) to be like the gods and was instead brought low, unto death (v. 15), becoming a man (*ish*) and causing the earth to tremble in response (v. 16). Heiser called this a "taunt-song,"[132] which follows a similar speech introduction—אַתָּה אָמַרְתָּ, the second person counterpart to the first-person phrase in Ps 82:6. Likewise, the supposed deities addressed in Ps 82:6–7 are understood to have failed. They are gods, but not gods; judges, but not judges. It becomes the task of the reader to question the rights of the subject of trial in vv. 6–7.

The shaken earth, already mentioned in Psalm 82:5, suggests a fall of cosmic proportions. Like Isaiah 14, a potential divine entity becomes mortal and risks the stability of the earth. It is unclear whether Psalm 82 is saying something about the fertility or potency of the deities to pass along progeny, or if their individual ability to live is being stripped away. The consequences of the loss of immortality of the deities may also have consequences for the earth. On the subject of mythopoeia or myth-ritual models, Frazer described the fertility of a king, or ruler, as tied to the fertility of the land.[133] The בְּנֵי עֶלְיוֹן who are likely considered to have authority or rulership over some land or other may not only be in trouble themselves because of the matter of injustice, but their misbehavior threatens the provision of the land for human preservation. Furthermore, the negative consequences of injustice extend to everyone else.

The actors so far presented in the first five verses of Psalm 82 must also be considered as part of the whole composition. The use of אֱלֹהִים in v. 6 anticipates a divine subject, given earlier references in v. 1, and it may also be implied that the subject who best fits the criteria of those who do not belong among the אֱלֹהִים are the רְשָׁעִים from vv. 2–4. The רְשָׁעִים have contributed as much to the problem as the אֱלֹהִים who have permitted them to undo the fabric of the cosmos, causing the foundations of the earth to tremble. As in Isaiah 14, a subject who seeks their place among the divine may be dropped down low, which is also described in v. 7. In Psalm 82, the ambiguity acts as an inclusive element, allowing space for the audience to observe and hold accountable not only the actions of רְשָׁעִים in their society, but also to monitor the unjust actions of the אֱלֹהִים, a high authority, be they rulers, judges, or even the gods.

Another source of problematic identity in v. 7 is in the reference to הַשָּׂרִים. In the mid-twentieth century, some scholars considered the

---

131. Heiser, "The Mythological Provenance," 354–69.
132. Heiser, "The Mythological Provenance."
133. Frazer, *The Golden Bough*.

references to הַשָּׂרִים in v. 7 as representative of angels, with a particular leaning to read this alongside Genesis 6, in particular consideration for references to the Nephilim. Gaster referred to this in Psalm 82 as an example to remind scholars that just because a word comes to mean a thing, like princes coming to mean angels, cannot be a logical reason to replace an earlier tradition, like associating the princes in Ps 82:7 with the Nephilim in Genesis 6.[134] Dahood discussed the הַשָּׂרִים as evidence of a merism expression common to ancient Near Eastern literature. "' ādām . . . sārīm forms a merism denoting "all mortals."[135] This inclusive aspect of interpretation fits with the themes already explored in Psalm 82.

The reader is a silent observer, brought along through the narrative as the case for injustice unfolds, until vv. 6–7. The first-person direct speech invites the reader as a sympathetic actor. The composer anticipates passive judgment by its audience, and then invites the reader into the composition. The reader is intentionally led toward a conclusion that demands reconciliation—be it from the gods or from the reader. A response is required.

Acknowledging the ambiguity in Psalm 82 makes room for an ethical reading that engages in the human social realm. While it is not quite clear whether the subjects of vv. 6–7 are divine or human, there is a consistent acknowledgement of the perception of divine status. The composition juxtaposes human and divine extrapolations; therefore, the reader must consider a paradigm that includes both possibilities. The composer beckons the reader to consider not only the origin of the social dynamic of its subjects, but the ethical implications of their behavior. It is an ambiguous composition that invites the reader to engage and respond to the ethical situation it presents.

Psalm 82:8: Appeal for Correction

The final verse in Psalm 82 returns the reader to a scene of divine council. However, it does not mirror v. 1, with its hazy description of powerful beings residing, and possibly executing judgment, on a far away and unreachable plane. Instead, the verse confronts the אֱלֹהִים directly with a command to rise and respond. By the end of Psalm 82, the line which separates the אֱלֹהִים

---

134. Note that Gaster referred to Psalm 82 in the introductory material of his book on myth in the Hebrew Bible, but he did not explore the mythical qualities of the psalm in the body of his work, even though he looked at a large number of psalms. Gaster and Frazer, *Myth, Legend, and Custom*, ii.

135. i.e. UT, 51:vii:43 *umlk ublmk*, "either king or commoner," or Phoenician Karatepe iii:19-iv:1, *hmlk h' w' yt ' dm h'* , "that king or that man." Dahood, *Psalms II*, 270.

and the רְשָׁעִים has become very thin. The demand for justice is a powerful response to the revelations of injustice and perversion which the composition has unveiled. The v. 8 speaker is not rhetorical nor subtle like the speaker in v. 2. The response is direct. The composition questions the motives and capabilities, if not the power, of the אֱלֹהִים, and v. 8 demonstrates a response that could hail from anyone in the audience.

Ps 82:8 קוּמָה אֱלֹהִים שָׁפְטָה הָאָרֶץ כִּי־אַתָּה תִנְחַל בְּכָל־הַגּוֹיִם׃

The אֱלֹהִים is/are called upon to rise and judge the land. Verse 8 reads as a liturgical response to the matter of injustice described in the first seven verses.[136] It also beckons an audience who is familiar with Psalm 1, in which the רְשָׁעִים fail to rise (יָקֻמוּ) in judgment (1:5). The appeal in Ps 82:8 continues from v. 1 to press the matter of the divine council and the purpose of the אֱלֹהִים, their favor of the wicked, and neglect of the oppressed. Verse 8 also continues from v. 6, in which the identity of the אֱלֹהִים as divine beings is questioned. The final call to the אֱלֹהִים in v. 8 demonstrates the speaker's hope for restoration, and the cry for justice makes its appeal on the stakes of the land (הָאָרֶץ), drawing from the image in v. 5, which refers to the instability of the earth because of injustice. The cry in v. 8 suggests the possibility of a change in behavior by the אֱלֹהִים, who have been accused of behaving like the רְשָׁעִים. There is an implicit appeal to reform, to return to right judgement.

The speaker of v. 8, who cries to the אֱלֹהִים for justice anticipates the description of justice in Ps 76:10 in which the אֱלֹהִים rise to judgment, saving the oppressed when the earth was stilled (76:9), describing a scenario opposite of that in Ps 82:5. McCann noted the reversal of language in Ps 76:10 compared to Ps 1:5.[137] He did not mention Psalm 82 in his study, but certainly there is also a connection to be made. For an audience who is familiar with the Psalter, the appeal for justice in order to stabilize the land is reminiscent of references to a quiet earth, a still earth. The speaker asks the אֱלֹהִים to rise (קוּמָה), a term which has been identified as a direct opposite to the passive "standing" action of the אֱלֹהִים in v. 1 (נִצָּב) by Bovati, who argued that a judge remains in a static state during a debate, as is demonstrated by the *nifal* participle in v. 1, and rises to pronounce a verdict, as is appealed for in v. 8.[138] The speaker seeks reform, invoking the

---

136. Parker, "The Beginning of the Reign of God," 550–51.

137. McCann. "The Single Most Important Text," 114.

138. cf. Ps 76:10; Job 31:14 for examples of a rising judge; also cf. Exod 5:20, 7:15 where Moses and Aaron stand passively before Pharaoh, awaiting action or decision.

repositioning of the אֱלֹהִים from a passive state to an active one. The passivity of the אֱלֹהִים has led to an unstable earth and oppression of the poor. Reversal is sought through the appeal in v. 8 —an active אֱלֹהִים will bring a stilled earth and salvation for the oppressed.

The composer reveals in v. 8 that it is not too late for justice to be done. The poor may be helped, and the wicked may be judged. The land may be saved, and the gods may retain order. In the beginning, v. 1 described the status quo, and by v. 2, the revelation of a shocking truth that the אֱלֹהִים failed in their duty to uphold justice. On the other side of the composition, in v. 8, a silent agent has become a judge of right justice—the reader becomes a player in this drama and must respond in their virtue. Rightness in the human realm is required for order everywhere—from the lowest lows (vv. 3–4) to the highest heights (vv. 6–7). As an ethical text, Psalm 82 informs its audience about the importance of right attitudes in judgment and the importance of societal justice. Schroeder described the divine council as a symbol of agency for justice, and noted "only in the awareness that justice is dependent on the openness of society for the forces from beyond time does justice become a possibility and reality."[139] Psalm 82 levels the plane between divine and human spheres so that a human ethical response can be met.

The composition of Psalm 882 leads the audience toward a conclusion that justice is not limited to the real or metaphorical domain of divine council. A human ethical response to get involved is elicited by the composition. Verse 8 is evidence of that response, the cry of a human for right action, for justice. The cry is heard not only by the divine council, but also by human peers. The identity of the אֱלֹהִים is inconsequential, for it is a response to the oppression of the marginalized that is required. Each, divine or human, may contribute to the lifting up of a person in need. Verse 8 is an opportunity for understanding the ethical response required for justice to prevail.

Conclusion

Psalm 82 has been a particular source of discussion among biblical scholars due to its inherent complexities. It does not fit well within the Hebrew Bible Psalter, nor in the wider corpus. It is also difficult to place within an historical realm. It has many ties to ancient Near Eastern texts outside of the Hebrew Bible and Israelite culture. For this reason, along with thematic mythical elements reminiscent of other Levant-region texts, it is likely

---

Bovati, *Re-establishing Justice*, 233.
   139. Schroeder, *History, justice*, 14.

early. In the mid-twentieth century, Ackerman noted that most scholars encouraged a post-exilic date of Psalm 82. However, he leaned heavily on the Canaanite influences in the text to loosely place the psalm between the reigns of David and Josiah.[140] An early dating of Psalm 82 also fits with Albright's conclusions about psalms that seem to reflect Canaanite influences. He leaned on parallels in the *Song of Deborah* and the laments of David over Saul and Jonathan to confirm placement in either sixth–fourth centuries or eleventh–tenth centuries BCE.[141]

Given the many linguistic and thematic elements in the psalm which align with early Canaanite literature, it is likely the origination of Psalm 82 is fairly early and originally belonged to a proto-Israelite society. The fact that Psalm 82 was adopted by the Israelite community and even preserved in a post-exilic version of the Psalter speaks to its reach. The early mythological provenance of the psalm rooted the poem in an historical setting of the Levant, and the ambiguity of the composition allowed it to span across time and influence its reception in the Hebrew canon. Accepting a provenance of Psalm 82 within a proto-Israelite setting helps make sense of seemingly obscure or unorthodox references to Canaanite traditions regarding deities and divine council, but it does not limit its influence.

The text of Psalm 82 invites an audience to participate in matters that are normally held exclusive to divine council. The composer of the psalm opens a window to make visible not only the proceedings of justice, but also reveals the deep-seated iniquity that corrupts justice, even at the highest levels. This scandalous revelation invokes a response from the audience. If the *most high* will not do right for humanity, or for the earth, someone must rise to the occasion. It is the human audience whose passion is invoked. The psalmist appeals to a human ethical respondent. However, after the conclusion of Psalm 82, there is no compositional response. The final cry for divine assistance goes unanswered. The rhetorical affect will sit with the audience until they are either resolved to action or resolved to find an answer from their deity(ies).

In its early composition, Psalm 82 challenges a proto-Israelite or Canaanite audience to consider their role in caring for the oppressed and shaping justice in their world. In its later reception by an Israelite community which is redefining itself post-exile, Psalm 82 speaks to the various identities of a mixed multitude—those who returned from Babylon, those who grew up in Judah, and others who were caught in the transition of an expanding Persian Empire. Psalm 82 retains a form that resists conformity

---

140. Ackerman, "Exegetical Study" 457.
141. Albright and Lewis, *Archaeology*, 128–29.

to Persian-era Judaism. Its message extends beyond the purview of the leaders and invokes response from the crowd, at least regarding matters of justice for the poor.

Zimmermann's *Organon* model for discerning ethics in ancient biblical texts accounts for intentional ambiguity as a sign of potential ethics embedded in the text. Psalm 82 contains many literary and poetic features that lend to not only an ambiguous reading, but an ethical reading as well.

3

Mythopoeia and Myth in Psalm 82

> "The only thing necessary for the triumph of evil is for good people to do nothing." —Edmund Burke, author and philosopher

PSALM 82 IS WIDELY considered a mythical text.[1] Its style encourages the exploration of boundaries in divine and human realms, probing the roles of agency and nature of the relationship between the two aspects. As descriptions of divine rulership in literature often reflect human experience, so the mythical features of this text provide insight into the priorities of human agency by means of descriptions of the divine. This insight is evidence of implicit ethics in the text. Following Zimmermann's *Organon* model, the mythical features that reveal human priorities of the "ought" contribute to the justification of an overall ethical reading of Psalm 82.

In a mythological text, there are multiple layers to consider. Broadly, in this approach, a myth is a story that can cross realms (i.e. divine and human) as well as cross aspect (i.e. narrative and metanarrative). What this means specifically for securing a definition of myth will be sorted by first reviewing a history of approaches to myth, and then followed by a description of how portions of the Hebrew Bible have been treated as myth and how Psalm 82 fits in that category.

Psalm 82 will be read as a mythic text to see what themes surface and assess how those themes align with the overarching thesis that the composer includes intentional ambiguity, both linguistically and thematically, in order to engage a broad audience in thinking about ethics for the poor and the leaders who are failing them. Also, the mythological provenance of Psalm 82 provides support for the *Organon* model discussed in Chapter One, by which various aspects of a text contribute toward support of an ideal. In this study, we are exploring evidence of implicit ethics in Psalm 82.

---

1. The title of Morgenstern's groundbreaking thesis, *The Mythological Provenance of Psalm 82*, likely influenced this perspective.

The mythical nature of Psalm 82 provides accessibility for a broad audience to engage with the implicit ethical message of the composition. This will be explored further as Psalm 82 is considered in conversation with other ancient Near Eastern mythological texts.

In this chapter, Psalm 82 will be read alongside the *Epic of Aqhat*, a mythical literary text from Ugarit that has been noted for its inclusion of ethical ideas and has been mentioned in connection with themes in Psalm 82.[2] Both texts contain themes of justice advocacy for humans who are at the mercy of powerful deities. Both maintain a concern for keeping order for the poor. But, the difference between these two texts is great. While Psalm 82 is a short poem, the *Epic of Aqhat* is a lengthy poetic narrative. This study will attempt to reason through the connections and determine how Psalm 82 engages with ancient Near Eastern mythopoeic thought as a means of describing what is right and wrong in the world, asking also if ambiguity is a natural feature of mythopoeia. It is an exploration of mythical literature as a context for communicating ethical concerns that are shared by humanity across time and space.

Background of Scholarship on Myth

For many decades, scholars have speculated about myth. Is it a literary genre? Is it a science? Is it a story from another time and space with different cosmic rules? What makes myth so fascinating is that it developed in this world, in the same space time continuum that we inhabit today, yet myths tend to function in a seeming alternate reality.

Defining Mythic Literature

Myth is a label which often categorizes ancient narratives and poetry that tell a story which operates outside witnessed human experience. For example, a mythic story sometimes describes tangible interactions between deities and humans, a phenomenon that does not fit into a modern category of experience. Therefore, ancient myths are often received in a modern world as something other than a record of historical events. This has spurred a series of reflections on how myth should be viewed from anthropological, scientific, philosophical, literary, and religious perspectives.

---

2. Though some scholars, like Parker and Smith, have made connections between Psalm 82 and Ugaritic literature, a full comparison of the psalm with an epic has not been played out.

In the nineteenth century, predominant views described myth as a precursor to science, eventually replaced by scientific method and thought. Some thought that myth should be read as literal descriptions of the world by the ancients, ignorant of science.[3] Others believed the ancients were intentionally speculating about the world in allegorical terms for a purpose other than science.[4] Both views speculate about the origination of myth in human thought, and both views recognize ancient humans as the source of myth.

In the first view, ritual grows out of the myth because the myth is considered a literal representation of how ancients saw the world they lived in. In the second view, the ritual inspires the myth and over time the myth reminds people of an older ritual. An example of this is the burning of effigies rather than humans in some pre-modern and modern pagan religious practices. The first view, credited to E. B. Tylor, considers the ancient world as unknowledgeable and sees myth as a way of describing the world that is locked in a particular time and place.[5] The second allows for myth to supplement scientific thought, making two things possible: 1) myth can be created in any era, and 2) myth contains allegory and metaphor.

By the beginning of the twentieth century, philosophies about myth began to consider intelligent and intentional design by the ancients. Ernst Cassirer attempted to classify myth as a way of thinking about the world which is altogether incompatible with science. He believed myth to be modern and that the ideas presented were meant to be challenged.[6] In the mid-twentieth century, Henri Frankfort and his wife Henriette Antonia Frankfort furthered this idea by applying a term to describe mythic thought: 'mythopoeia'.[7]

The Frankforts wrote about mythopoeia as what they called *primitive thought* in contrast to (modern) *philosophical thought*. Whereas philosophical thinking is abstract, critical and unemotional, primitive (mythopoeic)

---

3. Segal's *Brief Introduction to Myth* gives a categorical description of premodern and modern views about myth. In this, he proposed E. B. Tylor as the originator of the view in which myth is considered a literal description by ancients of their world and its happenings. Some other followed, including Bronislaw Malinowski, and to some extent Max Müller. Segal, *Myth*.

4. i.e. Frazer, *The Golden Bough*; Lévy-Bruhl, *How Natives Think*.

5. Though Tylor (who is credited with originating this idea) was critiqued for not being able to envision an era of postmodern science, postmodernism may provide further support for Tylor's argument. Segal, *Myth*.

6. Segal, *Myth*, 38–39.

7. Frankfort and Frankfort, *Before Philosophy*.

thought is concrete, uncritical and emotional.[8] Mythopoeia imagines a world in personal relationship with the human and subject. The Frankforts describe an "I–Thou" relationship, recognizing mutual relational qualities between the earth and all its inhabitants. In contrast to modern philosophy, which they describe as detached and intellectual, mythopoeia is involved and emotional. Whereas philosophy distinguishes between the subjective and the objective, mythopoeia distinguishes between appearance and reality. An example of the I–Thou relationship is love.[9] It is emotional and connected. The Frankforts contrasted the modern scientific person who sees the world externally (as 'it') with the ancient primitive one who sees the world in a connected way (as 'thou').[10]

The Frankforts made sense of ancient Near Eastern literature that has been often casually labeled as mythic by defining the philosophical context for mythology as mythopoeia. Mythological texts are initially an expression of mythopoeic thought. Many scholars also look more specifically at the literature of the Hebrew Bible to explore the context of a mythopoeic tradition. Myth scholar Segal defended a shift from the mythopoeic to the philosophical that begins with Hebrew literature: the ancients "lived in a wholly mythopoeic world. The move from mythopoeic to philosophical thinking began with the Israelites, who fused many gods into one god and placed that god outside of nature."[11] However, Segal's argument is difficult to uphold as the idea that the Israelites sought worship of God outside of or apart from nature is unfounded. Not least of all, nature is connected with the divine in the Psalter and the prophets, where there is also evidence of mythopoeic thought.[12] This chapter looks for a connection between the Hebrew Psalter and the mythic texts of Ugarit as evidence of shared values expressed in mythopoeic thought.

A mythopoeic reading of Psalm 82 leans into the understanding that all subjects and subject matter of the poem are connected. The divine beings are not ethereal but involved. The poor and disadvantaged are affected by those who wield power over life and nature, and the land itself shares a relationship with everyone living upon her and suffers for the sake of injustice.

---

8. Frankfort and Frankfort, *Before Philosophy*, 10–11.
9. Frankfort and Frankfort, *Before Philosophy*, 12–13. Segal, *Myth*, 41.
10. Frankfort and Frankfort, *Before Philosophy*, 4.
11. Segal, *Myth*, 42. Segal's view aligns with some of the twentieth-century scholarship that attempts to interpret Psalm 82 as descriptive of a shift from monotheism to polytheism. See chapter one for more details.
12. Consider Ps 74 and Isa 27, for example.

Myth in the Hebrew Bible

Before Psalm 82 is evaluated for mythical themes, it is essential to examine the scholarship that has already been produced on the topic of myth in the Hebrew Bible. Describing Psalm 82 as mythic includes the psalm in a category of literature that has been treated broadly without adherence to any strict definition. Myth in the Hebrew Bible has been explored in numerous ways over the past century. In as much as myth has been a subject of consideration for ancient ways of thinking and storytelling, scholars have attempted to make sense of how mythic paradigms do and do not fit within the Hebrew Bible.

In the mid-twentieth century, John L. McKenzie responded to the wide acceptance of the statement that there is no myth in the Hebrew Bible.[13] To engage a new approach, McKenzie appealed to defining myth as a type of literature in which patterns may be seen to have commonalities with other mythic texts outside of the Hebrew Bible corpus, acknowledging that "there is no generally accepted definition, and the forms of expression covered by the term [myth] are too diversified to be easily brought together."[14]

Herbert Gordon May also tackled the subject of myth in the Hebrew Bible in the mid-twentieth century, defending a method that seeks to find patterns connecting stories from the Hebrew Bible to historical events in the ancient Near East as well as other literary references. May cited parallels between the story of David and Goliath as mythic representations of order and chaos in mythic literature from Ugarit and Assyria.[15] This method of reading Hebrew Bible texts with other ancient Near Eastern texts to explore themes and shared cultural values is useful for the following study of Psalm 82 and Ugaritic epic literature.

Most recently, a volume edited by Dexter E. Callender, Jr., attempted to define myth in the Hebrew Bible as it relates to the text as scripture. Callender's approach presumes myth as an "established category in the academic humanities," and the bulk of the volume is devoted to describing how scripture can be defined in such a way as to reconcile certain Hebrew Bible passages that have been identified as mythic with their role as sacred scripture.[16] This approach may be useful for religious readings of the text,

---

13. McKenzie claimed to be responding to Gunkel's view of an absence of myth in the Hebrew Bible. He drew on ideas about myth presented by Cassirer and Eliade to discuss the nature of mythology beyond the scope of genre category in order to flesh out artistic approaches to interpretation. McKenzie, *Myths and Realities*, 265.

14. McKenzie, *Myths and Realities*, 267.

15. May, "A Sociological Approach," 98–106.

16. Note that this volume does not engage with theories of myth and it does not

but it does not get to the heart of determining how and why a text fits with mythical provenance in the ancient Near East. More specific to myth in psalmody, Dirk Human's *Psalms and Mythology* volume explored various specific interpretations of mythic influence in the Hebrew Bible Psalter. This volume demonstrated that there are a variety of approaches to defining myth in the Hebrew Bible.[17]

Myth is often conceptualized as any story that contains a supernatural agent. This is related to an idea about reading parts of Genesis as myth. This is also the case in the book of Job, where a divine council meets to discuss the fate of one human. When a supernatural agent is present in the literature that cannot be explained in historical terms, the term myth seems to be applied. However, the term myth is not often (if at all) applied to Hebrew Bible texts where a prophet interacts with the supernatural (i.e. Elijah goes up in a chariot of fire, or Ezekiel's visions). This predetermination about texts that may or may not be read as mythical is a barrier to understanding the nature of myth in ancient texts. Certain biblical texts are not considered mythical even though they share commonalities with other texts. For example, the description of Isaiah, as he is approached by an otherworldly being who purifies his mouth with burning coals, carries a high sacred factor as evidence of the calling of a prophet. It is not, however, dealt with as mythical, even though it aligns with the criteria of containing a supernatural agent.

Myth is also described as participatory. A mythic text is one by means of which a reader may engage themselves in the activity of a text, an aspect that myth has in common with liturgy.[18] C. S. Lewis addressed the nature of myth, describing myth as a story that is experienced, prompting contemplation by the reader who must then participate in the action of the text. The myth is defined by its ability to affect a reader and act upon the "conscious imagination" in order to appropriate a response.[19] G. K. Chesterton also described the influence of myth in a similar way. He claimed that a mythic text invites a reader to participate in the action of the text by imagining himself or herself within the construct. Chesterton referred to myth as evidence of a search for meaning. In Chesterton's view, the myth departs from the religious leader who says "these things are" and introduces the voice of a dreamer and idealist crying out "why cannot these things be?"[20] The engagement of an audience becomes part of the process

---

include Psalm 82. Callender, *Myth and Scripture*.

17. Human, *Psalms and Mythology*.
18. This is a discussion developed in Chapter 6.
19. Lewis, *An Experiment in Criticism*, 45–47.
20. Chesterton, *The Everlasting Man*, 102.

by which meaning in a myth is shaped. Encouraging reader participation also informs the ethical shape of a myth.

Myth can also act as ritual drama. Myths can be audience-centered when they are acted out to communicate virtues for religious or cultural importance. Purtill explained a dual purpose for ancient myth in his work about mythic context in religion. Ancient myths were thought of as stories that were intended to honor the gods and heroes they portray as well as inspire their listeners, while the audience received the stories as a source for moral and religious lessons.[21] This view particularly supports the idea of reading mythic literature as a source of implicit ethics in ancient societies.

The Problem with Myth

This study seeks to further the research by exploring aspects of mythology that may be useful for interpretation and shed light on reading Psalm 82 ethically. Rather than quarantine the identity of deities in Psalm 82, this study explores the relationship between the divine and human realms in light of a concern for order and justice by caring for the poor. The nature of mythology and aspects of a mythic text are explored as a means by which both divine agency and human agency are compared and contrasted in the psalm. The study also considers how mythology can access and describe divine realms while directing implication for human agency, thus leading to the possibility of reading Psalm 82 as implicitly ethical. For this reason, mythology will serve as a means by which the agency of divine entities and human entities may be explored to determine how a mythical text may include an ethical paradigm for human consumption.

One major problem with exploring myth in Psalm 82 is that myth and the Hebrew Bible have a historically difficult relationship, and while some psalms have traditionally been identified as mythic, it is not a common interpretive approach in biblical studies. In the few recent works identifying mythology in the Hebrew Bible, Psalm 82 is rarely included and not adequately explored. By 1995, Parker had already declared "it is remarkable that Psalm 82 is not cited in various recent studies of myth in the Bible."[22] Since then, scholarship on myth has continued to exclude Psalm 82, likely due to the difficulties already noted.[23] In works that have looked more deeply at mythology particular to the Psalter, Psalm 82 is often merely referenced and it is suggested that there is room for further

21. Purtill, *J.R.R. Tolkien*.
22. Parker, "The Beginning of the Reign of God," 542.
23. Callender, *Myth and Scripture*. Human, *Psalms and Mythology*.

work to be done.[24] The way that scholars refer to myth also varies widely as does its use for interpretation. There is no clear consensus on what it means for a Hebrew Bible text to be mythic.

The term *mythological* is, itself by nature polysemous, often used in a variety of ways. John W. Rogerson, who wrote on the subject of myth in the Hebrew Bible several decades ago, pointed to the problem of scholarship that is unable to determine an all-encompassing definition of myth.[25] Current biblical scholarship seems to be talking past itself instead of directly conversing about the nature of myth or mythic texts in the Bible. Groenewald attempted to address this issue by claiming that myth is an important theological medium, the use of which has not been sufficiently worked out; he recognized the main problem as "a great deal of debate among scholars concerning a single definition of 'myth.'"[26] This has led to a variety of presumptive attitudes toward mythological texts in the Hebrew Bible, when it comes to interpretation and critique. This divergence may be demonstrated by examining two chapters in Dirk Human's recent edited volume, *Psalms and Mythology*.[27]

Flip Schutte, in "Myth as a Paradigm to Read a Text,"[28] introduced the topic of myth with a psychoanalytical flavor, describing myth as a mentality perspective or mental paradigm. He explained this paradigm as a functional backdrop against which to read the Psalms in order to discover time and culture-bound realities.[29] By this means, uncomfortable passages may be more simply explained away as metaphors bound within a particular time and culture. Schutte defended this as a way of eliminating discomfort for the reader so that they may avoid an existential crisis of faith and "well-being."[30] Myth, according Schutte, is folklore preceded by a process of imagination, *vis a vis* symbols or language that make sense to a people within a particular time. In his view, myth is a type of language which attempts to capture and express an experience of God by a human audience in a particular time and place.

Myth by this definition is not allegorical, but tautegorical, meaning myth may be only defined according to standards within a subset culture specific to the time and place of its origin. Schutte described myth as a container

24. Human, *Psalms and Mythology*.
25. Rogerson, *Myth*, 173.
26. Groenewald, "Mythology," 18.
27. Human, *Psalms and Mythology*.
28. Schutte, "Myth as a Paradigm."
29. Schutte, "Myth as a Paradigm," 2.
30. Schutte, "Myth as a Paradigm," 3–4.

for concepts of experience which may be difficult to otherwise communicate. Myth, he wrote, is essential for insight into the human psyche regarding exposure to and interaction with their religious ideals.[31] Schutte relied on Carl Jung's theories about myth as examples of human tendencies to draw on symbols that represent archetypes from the "collective universal store," by which myths are experienced rather than invented. Through Schutte's definition, myth explains the inner psychology of a time-and-culture-bound people in an expression of their particular experience of God.[32]

Schutte presented an approach that relies on consideration for a focused psychological response by a human audience in a particular time and space. This approach defends mythopoeic symbolism as a means by which ancient humans express personal and emotional experiences related to spirituality. Schutte's definition provides a way for modern audiences to remove themselves from a text labeled as mythical, disconnecting from uncomfortable language in the text, but this can hardly make sense as an approach to liturgy which is practiced across time and culture.

On the other hand, Eckart Otto, in "Myth and Hebrew Ethics in the Psalms,"[33] approached the Psalter from a mythical paradigm by extending a mythological background to include a mode by which Hebrew ethics may remain in communication with the values and normatives found in relative cultural spheres. He defined myth primarily as a genre of literature. In this way, Hebrew mythic texts may be compared to other ancient Near Eastern mythic texts to determine what values and norms they have in common. The mythical background of certain psalms gains meaning for Otto in its unique ability to legitimize Hebrew ethics.[34]

Otto noted similarities of mythic literature in the Psalter to mythic qualities in literature from neighboring cultures. For example, he compared a description of kingship, or rulership, of humans over other human beings. He examined perspectives of authority presented in the *Enuma Elish* and compared this with descriptions of human authority over creation in the Hebrew Bible. He pointed to mythic descriptions in Psalm 8 (and, by comparison, Gen 1:26–28) as an example of a mythic description as a mode of providing ethical examples of life, by means of implicit ethics. Otto included a series of further examples by the same comparative method, viewing mythical texts in

---

31. Schutte, "Myth as a Paradigm," 4.
32. Schutte, "Myth as a Paradigm," 8.
33. Otto, "Myth and Hebrew Ethics."
34. Otto, "Myth and Hebrew Ethics," 26.

comparison with one another for the purpose of identifying ethical virtues in religious or religio-mythical texts.[35]

Otto relied on an inter-literary comparison of mythic texts driven by genre categories. The connections he made between mythical literature and ethical behavior categories is helpful when assessing liturgical texts. Particularly, Otto's work helps make sense of how the Psalter can incorporate mythopoeic descriptions in order to encourage audience consideration for ethical living in response to a religious commitment. However, the classification of myth as genre can be problematic. As it has been pointed out by Rogerson and Groenwald, clearly identifying a mythical genre in the Hebrew Bible has been a difficult task.

These two approaches from Schutte and Otto represent a selection from a myriad of approaches to myth in Hebrew Bible, particularly in reference to the Psalter. They both appear in a single edited volume on a singular topic, psalms and mythology, and provide very different approaches for reading and interpreting mythical texts. Schutte's paradigm recognizes mythic elements in the Psalter as insight into an historical understanding, limited to an ancient audience. In this way, modern audiences do not need to be troubled by what Schutte refers to as theologically uncomfortable passages, since they can be relegated to a distant past perspective. Schutte's definition responds to a practical consideration for modern audiences, but it does not provide for an ethical understanding of the Psalter as practiced liturgy. Otto's approach is entirely different. The virtue in Hebrew Bible mythological texts is founded in its anthropological-literary roots. Myth, for Otto, is a specific genre of text that inherently engages in reciprocal communication with other mythic texts to communicate social virtues. Otto's approach allows mythic texts to become more broadly available, not limited to a particular time-and-culture bound system. Though the authors may agree that any conscious expression of the divine may contain mythical elements, they diverge in the application of such an expression.

This comparison demonstrates the need for clarity when discussing a mythological text such as Psalm 82. Schutte's view falls short in that it is too constricting, not allowing for the diverse polysemous perspectives that so naturally accompany mythological texts. While Otto's definition is too broad in its reach, attempting to apply one sweeping label to a diverse category of texts. Psalm 82 has been recognized for an invitation to diverse perspectives which engage in a conversant ethical narrative. Mythological aspects feature in Psalm 82 without a necessary design on its genre. A liturgical text may be inherently mythological and at the same time useful to a

---

35. Otto, "Myth and Hebrew Ethics," 29–30.

practiced liturgy. Mythological features influence expressions of religious practice and literary genre. Rather than genre or psychotherapy, mythological texts should be considered evidence of shared worldview perspectives that extend beyond the confines of time and culture.

Psalm 82 and Mythology

Scholarship has looked at the mythic roots of Psalm 82 in different ways. Myth is primarily explored in vv. 1, 6, and 7. Morgenstern's 1939 thesis introduced the concept of a mythical provenance for Psalm 82 by exploring readings that considered parallels with Hebrew Bible and apocryphal texts which dealt with cosmic references. Morgenstern's work preceded the mid-twentieth-century influence of in-depth analysis of Ugaritic literature. However, since then, there has been increased interest in understanding Psalm 82 in light of Ugaritic literary evidence.

In the early twentieth century, Morgenstern saw a connection with apocryphal literature and other writings about gods in the ancient world. His thesis sparked interest for scholars who responded to his explanation of Psalm 82 in terms of certain mythical features. Morgenstern appealed to Hebrew Bible texts such as Genesis 6 and Isaiah 14 to access parallels of divine beings falling from lofty heights to the depths of mortality as a way of interpreting the description in Ps 82:6–7 of the בְּנֵי עֶלְיוֹן who are thusly condemned.

Other scholars got on board, writing about the possible connections of Psalm 82 with west Semitic texts. As Ugaritic texts became available for literary comparison, more parallels were found to make connections between Ugaritic mythological texts and Psalm 82. Patrick Miller called Psalm 82 "one of the most overtly mythological texts in Scripture," appealing to a sense of mythopoeia and naming two primary themes: "monotheism and the place of justice in the human arena."[36]

The discovery of Ugarit in 1928–29 was remarkable due to the alignment of Ugaritic language with the style and structure of Hebrew. The literature from Ugarit was dated to the second half of the Late Bronze Age (c. 1300–1190 BCE). In an introduction to Ugaritic Language, Huehnergard noted the impact of Ugaritic upon Hebrew Bible language and literature study stating that "it is indeed difficult to overestimate the impact that the discovery of the Ugaritic texts has had on the study of the Hebrew Bible."[37] Mid-twentieth-century scholars embarked on select studies that

---

36. Miller, "When the Gods Meet," 2.
37. Huehnergard, *An Introduction to Ugaritic*, 10.

demonstrated the linguistic and literary influence of Ugaritic upon texts of the Hebrew Bible.[38]

Once connections were made between Psalm 82 and Ugaritic literature, the mythological provenance of Psalm 82 was a useful tool for dating the psalm to an early and Northern setting. However, the connection Morgenstern made between language in Psalm 82 and the motif of fallen angels was difficult to situate in early Northern Levantine literature. The recognition of an early origination of Psalm 82 caused some problems for Morgenstern's presentation of connection with Second Temple literature. In an attempt to make Morgenstern's connection, Page presented a possible parallel between the psalm and the Ugaritic Baal Cycle. However, he was unconvincing in his attempt to demonstrate early evidence of a "lost" myth of the fallen angels.[39] Meanwhile, other mythical connections became more prominent through the study of Ugaritic literature.

Rendsburg used literary comparisons of thematic concerns in Psalm 82 that connected the psalm with similar thematic concerns of mythological texts from Ugarit, which also supported an early Northern literary heritage.[40] Parker also noted the connection of Psalm 82 to early northern literature, but did not see this as necessary to its dating. He noted that the retention of early ideas does not necessarily require an early composition.[41] While there is no way to know for sure, the inclusion of linguistic and literary features that adhere to patterns in early ancient Near Eastern myth suggests an early tradition for the psalm, even if its extant form did not appear until later.

Elmer Smick defended a mythic literary heritage for Psalm 82 as evidence of its potential to reach multiple audiences.[42] Smick appealed to other Hebrew Bible poetic texts, such as Job and Isaiah, noting the tension in ongoing religious syncretism. He saw no problem with the "created reality" of gods in Hebrew Bible literature and pointed to Hebrew Bible literature that refers to kings as rulers in heaven (i.e. the kings of Babylon and Tyre, in Isaiah and Ezekiel) as evidence. Smick saw mythopoeia as a means of explanation for how ancient Israelite texts described gods as a stand-in for other rulers. He ultimately concluded that אֱלֹהִים in Psalm 82:1 are gods who rule by proxy

---

38. Brooke, "Ugarit and the Bible; Craigie, *Ugarit and the Old Testament*; Day, *The Old Testament's Utilisation*; Dietrich, et. al, *The Cuneiform Alphabetic Texts*; Fensham and Claassen, *Text and Context*; Huehnergard, *An Introduction*.

39. Page, *The Myth of Cosmic Rebellion*.

40. Rendsburg, *Northern Origin*.

41. Parker dated Psalm 82 to no later than sixth century BCE. Parker, "The Beginning of the Reign of God."

42. Smick, "Mythopoetic Language," 88–89.

through kings.[43] Smick's study affirmed Psalm 82 as mythological, but it did not fully explore the implications of divine council in the psalm.

One important aspect of Psalm 82 that beckons a consideration for mythological provenance is the reference to divine council. The divine council setting is often treated like a signal to read a text as myth, as in Job and other texts that include divine agency. However, references to divine council also indicate a strong tie to human centers of justice. Mythical narratives that feature divine council tend to explore actions that have consequences for justice and treatment of humans in the physical realm. For example, the *Enuma Elish* describes a divine council setting in which deities argue with one another and fight for control of the universe. The result is the formation of the earth and related components which make up the human realm.

James Ackerman considered a comparison of Psalm 82 with mythic texts from Sumerian, Ugaritic and Akkadian sources, in which he primarily looked for themes that confirmed ideas about divine council. Specifics are described in Chapter One. Ackerman related these descriptions to several prophetic allusions to divine council in the Hebrew Bible, focusing on covenant lawsuit motifs in the prophets.[44] His main argument was to demonstrate the lawsuit motif in Psalm 82 by way of comparing other similar mythical texts with themes in the psalm, primarily referencing the authority of a divine council and the occasional death of the deities in ancient Near Eastern mythic texts. His work made way for other comparisons of myth to Psalm 82.

Kee examined Psalm 82 as a prophetic type-scene in a study of divine council scenes. He noted a feature of divine council texts picturing members "sitting down," suggesting this implies a beginning to their meeting. He noted that "standing" is indicative of participation toward the conclusion. Kee also found that introducing a text with the common elements of a divine council type-scene prepares the reader to hear a particular kind of text. It is a tradition that invokes a judgmental scene for the audience. Through an exploration of divine council type-scenes in the Hebrew Bible,[45] Kee demonstrated

43. Smick, "Mythopoetic Language," 95–96.

44. Ackerman engaged with Cross, Huffman and Koehler in this discussion, noting shared features between mythical texts of the ancient Near East and the Hebrew Bible prophets. Ackerman, "Exegetical Study," 207–8; Cross, *Canaanite Myth*, 244; Huffmon, "The Covenant Lawsuit," 285–95; Koehler, *Deuterojesaja*.

45. i.e. 1 Kgs 22:19–23; Isa 6; Job 1–2; Psalm 82; Zechariah 3; and Dan 7:9–14. Other passages relay short events or references: Jer 23:18, 22a; Job 15:8; Ps 25:14; Ps 49:20; 73:15; Amos 8:14; Isa 14:13 and those who address multitudes of divine beings: Exod 15:11; Deut 32:8; Ps 86:4–5; 97:7,9; Deut 4:19; 17:3; Judg 5:20; Ps 148:2–3; Isa 14:13; Job 38:7; Neh 9:6; Jer 8:2; Dt 33:2–3; Zech 14:5. Others imply an event: Gen 1:26; 3:22; 11:7; Ps 29:1–2; 58:1–2; 89:6–9; Isa 24:33).

that Psalm 82 fits within this genre both in Hebrew literature and also with various literary traditions of the broader ancient Near East.[46]

Kee's contribution is a detailed analysis that connects divine council texts within the Hebrew tradition with mythological comparisons in other ancient Near Eastern literature. His work also made a strong connection between divine council texts as preparation for an ethical reading. He suggested that the tent of meeting is a reasonable human reflection of divine council, with special consideration for the description of function in Exod. 33:7–11.[47]

Parker also drew connections between thematic concerns in Psalm 82 and Ugaritic literature.[48] He considered Psalm 82 to fit as a mythical text within a genre that also included the Ugaritic Baal Cycle and the Epics of Kirta and Aqhat. He cited Rogerson's definition of myth as "a story that attempts to explain the present order, or institutions or things in the present order; a story that is tied to a cultic event,"[49] also noting that a myth could be defined as a narrative about the gods. Parker determined that Psalm 82 established the universal rule of God in a world where other gods rule or other nations claim rule by their own gods; in the scenario presented, v. 8 acts as a liturgical (cultic) response to the poetic narrative of vv. 1–7. He concluded that Ps 82:1–7 is a "genuine and thoroughly Israelite myth."[50]

While some scholars were approaching Psalm 82 by considering its features as a legal text,[51] Parker insisted on an approach that considers the psalm's roots in themes inherent to mythological texts. After making a case for a literary structure that offered a poetic narrative like those from Ugarit, he asserted that Psalm 82 could be compared to the end of the *Epic of Kirta*, in which "Kirta's son, Yassub, goes to his father, charging him with neglect of his duties and failure to give justice to the disadvantaged. He concludes his speech by calling on the king to step down and yield his throne to Yassub (KTU 1:16 VI 39–54)."[52] Parker compared the liturgical ending of Ps 82:8 to Yassub's request to take over the throne for the sake of justice. He saw both fulfilling the same function. This perspective was also

---

46. Kee, "The Heavenly Council."
47. Kee, "The Heavenly Council."
48. Parker, *The Pre-biblical Narrative Tradition*.
49. Rogerson, *Myth*, 176.
50. Parker, "The Beginning of the Reign of God," 543.
51. Ackerman, "Exegetical Study."
52. Parker, "The Beginning of the Reign of God," 545.

noted by Gordon and Dahood, who saw literary features in the Ugaritic myths that might interpret Ps 82:6–7.[53]

The motif of ruler-replacement is not uncommon in the Hebrew Bible. Parker described the scenario in 2 Samuel 15, in which Absalom seeks to displace David, as an example. In this case, Absalom pursues the displacement in an indirect way, working without the king's knowledge. Parker drew connections between this passage and the Ugaritic epic with Psalm 82, in that a case is made against the current leadership, followed by a recommendation of displacement. He also cited Deut 32:8, in which עֶלְיוֹן divides the nations and humankind among the gods, and 2 Kgs 18:33a and Judg 11:24, which assume that gods preside over boundaried nations, as evidence of Israelite understanding of the paradigms inherent to mythical texts—that the gods rule over nations as established by boundaries between them. This conceptualization by an ancient Israelite audience may be considered mythopoeic. In this case, the mythopoeia refers to Israelite understanding of divine activity which mirrors human activity. Parker's study emphasized the originality of Israel's view as represented in Psalm 82, but not its uniqueness. He saw that Psalm 82 shared commonalities with ancient Near Eastern texts that sympathized with how to respond to crisis in human government, using divine assembly as a prompt. Parker proposed that Psalm 82 is "an authentic Israelite creation, using the conventional mythical setting of the divine assembly, but modeling its plot on (accounts of) crises in human government."[54]

While many ancient Near Eastern mythical texts deal with similar subjects and motifs, Psalm 82 is unique. Its inclusion in the Psalter preserves its liturgical force as a response against injustice. Parker urged a comparison to Psalm 58 which appeals to the gods for fair judgment. He noted that while Psalm 58 anticipates the destruction of the wicked, it is a prayer of lament, while Psalm 82 poses a "critical movement of the cult: the setting to right of the world."[55] Parker's argument relies upon a mythical provenance to connect Psalm 82 not only with Ugaritic literature from the Late Bronze Age but also with other Hebrew texts, including those within the Psalter. Parker defended Psalm 82 as definitely Israelite, that is, not borrowed from another literary heritage, but also conscious of, and engaged with, neighboring cultural ideologies.

Psalm 82 portrays divine council in such a way as the tent of meeting is portrayed in the Torah. As a mythological text, the composition's

---

53. Dahood, *Psalms II*, 270. Gordon, "History of Religion," 131.
54. Parker, "The Beginning of the Reign of God," 544.
55. Parker, "The Beginning of the Reign of God," 559.

description of the divine reflects the cognitive awareness of the human community who practices the Psalter. This allows for an ethical reading of the text that speaks to a potentially diverse group of people about justice. The gathering of deities in a divine council reflects also the gathering of elders in a smaller, earthly context. The mythological provenance of Psalm 82 allows for synchrony between divine agency and human agency for the purpose of reading a text ethically.

Psalm 82 has a complicated relationship with mythological texts of the ancient Near East. Many scholars have ventured to connect the literature, but few agree on the manner of the connection and what it means for the psalm. The mythical provenance of Psalm 82 is largely unquestioned, but how the psalm connects to early Northern Levantine literature is still being discussed. The study that follows will read the psalm thematically alongside the *Epic of Aqhat* to determine how shared cultural values may have been brought forward in the poetry of Psalm 82 and how these values represent implicit ethics in the psalm, forming one "spoke" in the *Organon* wheel.

The Epic of Aqhat and Psalm 82

The mythological qualities of Psalm 82 align with ancient Near Eastern literature that is well established as mythic, particularly literature from Ugarit. Although comparisons have already been drawn between Ugaritic texts and Psalm 82, the question of divine and human agency in matters of justice has not been fully explored. The mythological features of Psalm 82 allow the poem to provide an ethical message by implicit means. The nature of poetry is such that a message may be communicated implicitly. In the case of Psalm 82, a poetic narrative describes a situation of utter despondency. The audience hears the story and knows that something is wrong, but they are not directly informed of the problem. They must participate in receiving and interpreting the message in order for meaning to take place. This study will begin by looking at ethical themes in the Ugaritic *Epic of Aqhat* to consider a method.

Scholars have noted similarities between the *Epic of Aqhat* and Psalm 82, but this has not been pressed further to see if these connections can be made more prominent. In 1969, Tsevat's article on Psalm 82 discussed the specific reference in the *Epic of Aqhat* to immortality as a hallmark of the divine. He noted that the goddess ʿAnat offered immortality to Aqhat, which is recognized and refused (2 Aqht: VI: 26–38). This perspective supported his view of reading Ps 82:1 as a setting of divine entities.[56]

56. Tsevat also cited the Gilgamesh Epic about the gods' retention of immortality

In 1978, Gordon also ventured to interpret Psalm 82 as an explanation for values presented in Ugaritic literature. He presented the *Epic of Aqhat* as an example of the wickedness of Canaanite culture: "The goddess ʿAnat hired an assassin to kill the hero Aqhat so that she could confiscate the bow that Aqhat had refused to sell her. This is not Hebrew propaganda; it is recorded in the sacred literature of Ugarit. The Hebrews consciously reacted against Canaanite values, and Psalm 82 tells us why, albeit without the specific examples with which Ugarit now provides us."[57] For Gordon, the Ugaritic literature provides a description of the kind of behavior against which the psalmist responded. Ackerman also connected the epic with Psalm 82 in a discussion about the authority of the divine council regarding the lives of vulnerable humans.[58] These comparisons attempt to build stronger connections between Ugaritic and Hebrew literature, but they do not capture a full picture of the significance of human and divine action from an ethical perspective.

An Ethical Reading of Mythological Texts

In 2008, Chloe Sun embarked on a discussion of ethics of violence in the *Epic of Aqhat* that covers basic perceptions of the literature as filtered through the reader's lens. She included a recognition of the character's perceptions of ethics by determining whether the character approves or disapproves of an action or outcome.[59] She also assessed characters' emotional states as evidence of the narrator's portrayal of their attitude toward certain behaviors.[60] This approach looked at implicit ethics in the myth, which is an aspect that can also be applied to Psalm 82.

Sun's ethical approach presumes that the hypothetical historical audience shared commonalities with the human characters in the story.[61] She explained how the structure and values of the divine family in Ugaritic narratives correspond to the structure and values of the human families in the society that received the texts.[62] Because of this, there is an invitation

---

for themselves (X:3:3–5). Tsevat, "God and the Gods."
57. Gordon, "History of Religion," 131.
58. Ackerman, "Exegetical Study," 169.
59. Sun, *The Ethics of Violence*, 15.
60. Sun, *Ethics of Violence*, 15.
61. Sun engaged John Goldingay's *Models for Interpretation* in her discussion of how to access an ancient audience. Sun, *Ethics of Violence*, 23.
62. Sun engaged Thorkild Jacobsen and Gay Robins in a discussion about the nature of mythic texts. Sun, *Ethics of Violence*, 23.

to the reader for participatory engagement with the text. The human world and the divine reflect one another, so readers can react to activities in the divine realm, while absorbing an implicit ethical message for their own society in the human realm. In Psalm 82, both human and divine realms are presented as well. Their relationship is explored by implication. Sun's point about the reflection of humanity in the actions of the deities provides insight into why scholars have had difficulty determining if the אֱלֹהִים in v. 1 represent human leaders or divine entities.

Sun evaluated previous interpretations of the Aqhat narrative as "one-dimensional, bipolar interpretations of ʿAnat's violence in the story . . ."[63] She concluded that the narrative "invites ambiguity and openness"[64] which then prompts a question for the audience's response to an author who remains reticent to make a clear moral evaluation of ʿAnat's violence in this epic. Her evaluation of the *Epic of Aqhat* is similar to my evaluation of the scholarship surrounding Psalm 82, in that a monologic reading is unsatisfactory. Sun concludes that there is an intentional effort by an author to encourage the audience to ponder the possible responses, forcing them to "wrestle with the issue and to strive to come to terms with it."[65]

Another function Sun explored is "dynamic adaptability." Since things are left unresolved, the story may adapt for succeeding generations and even to other cultural contexts for application.[66] Sun evaluated these features as an invitation to the modern reader to ponder the "inherent moral message."[67] Sun's ethical approach to consider divine and human agency in the poetic narrative of the Ugaritic *Epic of Aqhat* presents a model for reading Psalm 82 as a mythological poetic narrative with ethical implications.

There are some challenges to reading Psalm 82 in comparison with the *Epic of Aqhat*. For one thing, the epic is much longer than the psalm. Even though it is one of the shorter narrative literary pieces among the Ugaritic corpus, with three tablets it is significantly larger than eight verses of poetry. Stylistically, it is also different. Whereas Psalm 82 follows a poetic pattern in its brevity, the *Epic of Aqhat* includes more narrative description than the psalm. The epic includes a full cycle of the hero's quest-journey, including descriptions of gender and familial roles. Psalm 82 is religious liturgy that has been preserved for hundreds of years in various liturgical traditions,

---

63. Sun, *Ethics of Violence*, 27.
64. Sun, *Ethics of Violence*, 193.
65. Sun, *Ethics of Violence*, 193.
66. Sun, *Ethics of Violence*, 193.
67. Sun, *Ethics of Violence*, 194.

while the *Epic of Aqhat* was discovered only in the last century and is missing some text, including its conclusion.

While Psalm 82 and the *Epic of Aqhat* seem different, they have many similarities, and the similarities are important because they inform how an ancient society engages with mythological texts for reasons of implicit ethics. Both texts are written in languages which share a linguistic heritage. Ugaritic has been referred to as a predecessor to Hebrew. Both texts originate in an early Northern Levantine setting. Both texts share features with other early texts, for example, the book of Job. Both Psalm 82 and the *Epic of Aqhat* engage with a scenario in which human and divine agency is at stake. Both texts share a premise that caring for the vulnerable maintains order. There is a shared concern about the health of the earth. Both texts demonstrate justice-seeking agency, and both texts lend themselves toward ritual performance.

The relationship between these two texts is not immediately obvious, primarily due to their respective provenance: one from Late Bronze Age Ugarit and the other preserved in post-exilic Judea from an unspecified earlier origin. Gordon's suggestion that Psalm 82 may respond to the kind of behavior by the gods in the *Epic of Aqhat* was on track but the connection should be further explored. Considering Sun's approach to reading the *Epic of Aqhat* as ethical may be a way to explore how both texts are responding to a particular worldview that stems from a shared episteme. The shared values and aspects of these two texts will confirm that it is reasonable to read Psalm 82 primarily as ethical.

The epic begins with a glimpse into the personal life of one man who desperately wants a son. His name is Danʾel, the root of which, *dn*, associates the man with his title as judge. His wife's name is Danatiya, also linguistically related to *judge*. Danʾel is described as a hero who sits among the chieftains at the gateway of the city, whose duties include taking care of the case of the widow and defending the need of the orphan.[68]

Danʾel beseeches the gods to grant his request of a son, and he is successful. The deity Baʿal responds, moved by compassion, and intercedes on his behalf to ʾEl so that when Danʾel lays with his wife, she conceives and bears a son. The son is named Aqhat. Aqhat is expected to be the hero of the story, one who fulfills all the duties of a son. He is even given a gift from the gods to help him along—a special bow with unique properties.

The goddess ʿAnat has taken a special interest in this bow, and she wants one for herself. ʿAnat pursues Aqhat the Hero. She offers wealth and

---

68. CAT 1:17, col. V, lns. 4–8; CAT 1:19, col. I, lns. 19–25.

long life in exchange for his bow; she resorts to threatening Aqhat. When he refuses her and belittles her, ʿAnat seeks petition with ʾEl.

When ʾEl refuses to grant ʿAnat's request for a bow, she insults him with threatening language. ʾEl responds that she will do whatever it takes to get the bow as that is her nature. It is unclear whether he is telling her to steal the bow and/or kill Aqhat for it, or if he is just predicting her course of action. Either way, passively or actively, his permission is given. ʿAnat enlists the services of a mercenary, Yṭpn,[69] who strikes down Aqhat. However, the bow is still lost to her.

In the next scene, Danʾel, who has not yet heard the news about Aqhat, notices that the vegetation in their community has dried out, withering for lack of rain. His daughter, Pughat, also notices the drought. Shortly after this realization, messengers approach to bring word of Aqhat's death. The text transitions into a time of mourning. Danʾel prays to Baʿal for vengeance. He invokes Baʿal to kill the birds of prey to see if they have eaten the remains of his son, Aqhat. After first searching the birds, then the *Father of Birds*, he finds what he is looking for in the *Mother of Birds*, and buries the remains.

After seven years of mourning, Danʾel ceases. It is then that Pughat makes a request for blessing from her father to seek vengeance. She disguises herself in warrior's garb, covered by a woman's attire. She goes to the campsite of Yṭpn, and through an act of deception she lures him into a false security before exacting her revenge. The third tablet is not quite complete, and there may be a fourth tablet which has not yet been found. So, details of the ending are unclear.

Other ancient Semitic texts, such as the biblical stories of Jael and Judith, assist in the reconstruction of the missing text in the conclusion of the Aqhat tale. Much like the Hebrew Bible story of Jael, it has been assumed that Yṭpn falls asleep, drunk and sated, in the comfort of Pughat's company when he is suddenly struck and killed by her hand, his heart filled with smooth libation. Pughat stealthily slips away, her magic staying the sleepy tents,[70] and she returns home. A significant difference indicates the adaptive nature of these story-types. Whereas both stories portray a nomadic people, in *Aqhat* the nomad, a tent dweller, is the villain; while in Judges, the tent dweller is the hero. "The nomads told the story with a nomadic heroine and a villainous

---

69. *Yṭpn* is widely recognized as a PN, though the meaning and root have been difficult to pinpoint. De Moor suggested a connection to the Arabic root *ṭfn* "to die," perhaps indicating "he who causes death." This meaning would seem to fit with the character of *Yṭpn* in the narrative. Dijkstra and de Moor, "Problematic passages," 171–215.

70. Pughat's action, *ḥršm,* may indicate an association with a magic spell, but also may be related to silence. Both nuances work in this context. Margalit restored *ḥršm>ʿršm* and translated: "double bed." Margalit, *The Ugaritic poem of AQHT.*

sedentary; the sedentaries told the same story in reverse. The former found its way into the Hebrew Bible, the latter into the epic literature of Ugarit."[71] Stories were adapted as necessitated by culture.

The *Epic of Aqhat* demonstrates a complex relationship between divine and human agency in the ancient world. The ruler of divine council and justice is ʾEl. He is the father of all gods, and he is the one to whom the gods must appeal in order to act on behalf of, or against, a human. Two divine children of ʾEl appear in this narrative: the deities Baʿal and ʿAnat. There are other deities who have parts in the story, but their relationships are not made known. Another character affiliated with the divine is Ytpn, who is somehow connected with ʿAnat. The human figures in this epic are represented by an elite family of judges, or rulers: Danʾel and his wife, Danatiya, and their two children, ʿAqhat and Pughat. Other humans are implied, such as those in the villages cursed by Danʾel after his son dies.

The social relationships between the divine and human agents are mirrored. There are two fathers: ʾEl and Danʾel. Each has a son. Baʿal is the son of ʾEl, who, in this epic, demonstrates compassion and offers support to the human family. Aqhat is the son of Danʾel. He is noted for his dutifulness to his father and family. Both ʾEl and Danʾel are rulers of justice. ʾEl rules the divine council, and Danʾel is a ruler in the human realm. Both fathers also have daughters. ʿAnat is the daughter of ʾEl, who threatens her father to attain what she desires when he will not provide it himself. ʿAnat is a character of independent action. She sees what needs to be done and goes after it. Pughat is the daughter of Danʾel. She is quiet and obedient, but after some time, she also is a character of independent action. She recognizes the need for restoration in the land and in her home, and she seeks vengeance on behalf of her family.

The narrative makes clear the connections between the divine realm and its social order, and the human realm. It is also clear that the actions of divine characters, situated in the divine realm, impact those in the human realm, and the actions of humans in the human realm impact the divine. Sun suggested that the ambiguity of judgment in the *Epic of Aqhat* makes way for the reader to participate by responding each according to their own experience.[72] Interpretations that rely on blaming the deities for their wickedness ignore Baʿal's compassion, and the blatant discrimination against ʿAnat by both her divine father, ʾEl, and the human 'hero', Aqhat. Does blatant misogyny justify threatening language and violence? This is the kind of open-ended question implicitly posed to the reader through the narrative.

---

71. Margalit, *Ugaritic Poem of AQHT*, 459.
72. Sun, *Ethics of Violence*, 193.

Furthermore, the outcome of such behavior has led to the suffering of the land. Not only did the ruling authority, Danʾel, threaten to kill even the mother of all birds to find his son's remains and curse the cities and their inhabitants in the region of his son's death, but the vegetation began to dry up and wither—the ultimate consequence being the suffering of the land, which impacts all of humanity. It is in response to the threat on the land that Pughat takes action. It is when she recognizes death in the land that she completes her mourning with personal inner strength before seeking righteous revenge.

Psalm 82 also demonstrates a complex description of divine and human realms. Divine council holds the power of judgment, but they are accused of, at the very least, not protecting the poor and marginalized from the wicked. At most, they are responsible for directly violating the poor. While the *Epic of Aqhat* does not deal directly with the poor, a similar idea of powerful beings imposing themselves upon the vulnerable is explored. Psalm 82 is unique in its emphasis on the poor, but the power dynamics are relatable. The ambiguity in the poetry presents an openness to participation, calling for the reader to respond with their own experience, much like in the *Epic of Aqhat*.

ʾEl is the same figurehead referent from the Ugaritic epics, ruling divine council in Psalm 82:1. He is descriptive of the highest authority in the divine realm. When read alongside the *Epic of Aqhat*, it may be understood that the human realm also mirrors this structure. There is a human council of judges or rulers who have similar responsibilities to justice, and similar authority. This authority may be exploited by any ruler, divine or human, and the repercussions are not limited to their own realm, as is evidenced by the degradation of the earth and her failure to provide.

Interpreters of Psalm 82 have long debated over whether the אֱלֹהִים in v. 1 are rulers of the human realm or the divine. Reading the poem alongside an Ugaritic epic demonstrates that the reference is not mutually exclusive. It can be both or either. It likely changes depending on the reader and their experience at the time of participation with the text.

As in the *Epic of Aqhat*, there is an active agent of confrontation in Psalm 82. In the epic, both ʿAnat, a deity, and Pughat, a human, demonstrate strong and confrontative behaviors. In Psalm 82, it is not clear if the agent who confronts the divine council is human or divine. Again, there is an openness in the text to consider a scenario that fits within the divine realm or the human realm, or possibly both. The reader's participation with the text engages their experience with justice or injustice, which influences their understanding of the liturgy.

Finally, what is ultimately at stake in Psalm 82 is the stability of the land. The wickedness and darkness brings instability to the earth, and this is at the center of Psalm 82's poetic structure. In the *Epic of Aqhat*, the instability of the land is also the final result that invokes Pughat to rise and act on behalf of her family, and really for all of humanity, in saving the land and its vegetation from death. The restoration of the land is at stake for Pughat, and for the whole human realm. Her actions confront the divine for their negligence of order, and their behavior, which has compromised the land and its provision for the needs of humanity. The divine have ultimate power over the land, and Pughat seeks restitution; she seeks justice. At the end of Psalm 82, a similar confrontation is made to the אֱלֹהִים in v. 8, to rise up and take action. It is justice that will restore the land. It is justice that will reconcile the vulnerable in humanity with their powerful caretakers.

A Chart of Comparison: The Epic of Aqhat and Psalm 82

In order to see correlations between Psalm 82 and the epic of Aqhat, here is a chart to demonstrate where each point of connection is made. While the psalm is much shorter than the epic, it contains certain elements that follow with the pattern and thematic elements of the longer mythic text.

Epic of Aqhat[73]		Parallels in Psalm 82	
CAT 1:17, col. I, lns. 0–2	About 10 lines are missing.[74] Then, the protagonist Dan'el is introduced as "hero."[75]		
CAT 1:17, col. I, lns. 2–15	Dan'el makes a six-day ritual sacrifice to the gods.		
CAT 1:17, col. I, lns. 15–33	Ba'al has compassion for Dan'el and intercedes on his behalf to 'El.	Vv. 1, 6–7	Evidence of divine council with 'El as leader.
CAT 1:17, col. I, lns. 34–48	'El blesses Dan'el so that he and his wife will conceive.	Vv. 1, 3, 4	'El has authority over human realm

---

73. Dietrich, *KTU*.

74. The segments follow Parker's outline. Parker and Smith, *Ugaritic Narrative*, 51–52.

75. The root *ǵzr* signifies that Dan'el is a noble person.

Epic of Aqhat[73]		Parallels in Psalm 82
CAT 1:17, col. I—col. II, ln. 8	About 20 lines are missing. Parker described these as Baʿal giving a birth announcement, sharing the good news of ʾEl's blessing with Danʾel. This continues on through Col. II, line 8.[76]	
CAT 1:17, col. II, lns. 8–46	Danʾel rejoices, hosts a divine guest,[77] copulates with his wife, and they count the months of pregnancy.	
CAT 1:17, col. II, lns. 47f—col. V, ln. 2	About 10 lines are missing, as are columns III and IV. Parker reconstructed these as inclusive of the birth of Aqhat and the origins of the bow, which is referenced in the beginning of column V.[78]	

76. Parker and Smith, *Ugaritic Narrative*, 54.

77. The *kṯrt* are described as *praiseworthy daughters of the moon* (lns. 34–36), and are likely magical beings associated with childbirth.

78. Parker and Smith, *Ugaritic Narrative*, 57.

Epic of Aqhat[73]		Parallels in Psalm 82	
CAT 1:17, col. V, lns. 3–39— col. VI, ln. 4	Dan'el is described as a hero again (ln. 5), and his duties include sitting by the gateway, among chiefs on the threshing floor, taking care of the case of the widow and defending the need of the orphan. As he goes along with his duties, he notices an entourage of deities with whom he dines, attended by his wife, the lady D'anatiya. During this meal, Kothar and Khasis give Dan'el the gift of the bow and arrows. He then invites his son hunting. About 20 lines are missing between the end of column V and the beginning of column VI. During this space, the bow is given to Aqhat and this whole affair comes to 'Anat's attention.[79]	Vv. 1, 3, 4	Dan'el's duties in the human realm mirror divine council. The chieftains are responsible for caring for the needs of the poor (i.e. the orphan and widow).
CAT 1:17, col. VI, lns. 4–46	'Anat wants the bow and she attempts to bargain with Aqhat for it. She offers him immortality, a life like Ba'al and other sons of 'El (lns. 28–29). Aqhat is not tempted, he does not want more than to be human and die in his time. Furthermore, he asserts that bows are the tools of men, mocking her "will women now hunt?"[80]	Vv. 6, 7	'Anat is a divine being from among the gods who interacts with humans in the human realm. She offers immortality, which is a power of the gods, specifically Ba'al and the other sons of 'El. Immortality of the gods is a concept referenced in Psalm 82.

79. Parker and Smith, *Ugaritic Narrative*, 59.

80. This is certainly representative of a recognized division of labor in the Ugaritic society, that men did the hunting. However, note that in CAT 1:114, in the short text describing 'El's divine feast, 'Anat and Athtarta off to "hunt." The same word is used in both texts, *tṣdn* (root=ṣd).

Epic of Aqhat[73]		Parallels in Psalm 82	
CAT 1:17, col. VI, lns. 46–55f	ʿAnat heads toward ʾEl and approaches him with respect. There are about 20 lines missing, which would include ʿAnat's first speech to ʾEl denouncing Aqhat, followed by ʾEl's initial response.[81]	V. 1	ʾEl is highest authority in the divine council.
CAT 1:18, col. I, ln. 1—col. IV, ln. 1	ʿAnat responds to ʾEl with insults. He is then called "the Kind One" and "the Compassionate" when he recommends that she goes and takes what she wants. She heads toward Aqhat, and then about 20 lines are missing as well as columns II and III.	V. 1	Divine council with ʾEl at the head.
CAT 1:18, col. IV, lns. 1–42	ʿAnat summons her weapon, *yṭpn*, who she wears like a bird in her belt, and he attacks and kills Aqhat. ʿAnat weeps for Aqhat and explains that she killed him for his bow and arrows.		
CAT 1:19, col. I, lns. 0–17	There are several gaps in the text, but ʿAnat loses the bow. It is broken and falls into the water. She tries to request its return.		
CAT 1:19, col. I, lns. 18–48	A new scene begins with Danʾel, who is sitting among the chiefs at the gateway, taking care of the widow and orphan. He looks up to see dying vegetation and he and his daughter, Pughat, both weep in grief. The loss of vegetation is acknowledged as the absence of Baʾal (lns. 44–46).	Vv. 1, 3, 4, 5	Danʾel's council of chieftains are responsible for caring for the poor. This mirrors divine council. Also, the land is suffering due to the act of injustice.

81. Parker and Smith, *Ugaritic Narrative*, 63.

Epic of Aqhat[73]		Parallels in Psalm 82	
CAT 1:19, col. I, ln. 49—col. II, ln. 57	Dan'el speaks to his daughter, Pughat, whose duty is to collect dew from the fleece. He asks her to lead him around to see the land. Dan'el sees the dried vegetation and dry, cracked earth. He attempts to comfort the vegetation through embraces, kisses, and tears. Some lines are incomplete, but a messenger comes and informs them of how ʿAnat killed Aqhat. The climax is in line 42: *mt.aqht.ġzr*, Aqhat the Hero is dead. Six lines are missing, and then Dan'el raises his eyes to see birds in the clouds.	V. 5	The land suffers as a result of injustice from the gods.
CAT 1:19, col. III, lns. 0–45	Dan'el curses the birds by Baʿal. He wants to see if they have eaten the remains of Aqhat. Baʿal breaks their wings, but nothing is found, so Dan'el asks Baʿal to restore them. He makes the same request for the "Father of Birds," *Hargub*, and the "Mother of Birds," *Ṣamal*. It is in the mother that Dan'el finds the remains of his son and buries them.		
CAT 1:19, col. III, lns. 45—col. IV, ln. 7	Dan'el curses three towns near the place where Aqhat was slain.		
CAT 1:19, col. IV, lns. 8–27	Dan'el returns home and mourns for seven years, then he makes an offering to the gods.[82]		

---

82. This is evidence of a mourning ritual. In the margin next to the line that follows (ln. 23), there is a note that reads 'here one returns to the story.'

Epic of Aqhat[73]		Parallels in Psalm 82	
CAT 1:19, col. IV, lns. 28–39	Pughat speaks and asks for blessing to slay the killer of her brother, Aqhat. She is called *yd' t hlk.kbkbm* "one who knows the course of the stars" (Ln.38). Dan'el gives his blessing.	V. 2, 6, 7, 8	An agent confronts the injustice and makes a plan to reinstate order. This mirrors the confrontative prophetic language in Psalm 82.
CAT 1:19, col. IV, lns. 40–61	Pughat washes and readies herself with the clothing of a *ġzr*, hero and rouge on her skin. She includes a sword and a woman's dress on top. She enters the tents where *ytpn* resides. She drinks with him in her disguise. He brags about killing Aqhat, and she gets him drunk.	V. 2, 6, 7, 8	The human agent confronts the gods.
A missing finale . . .	It is likely that there is a fourth tablet still missing. Similar narratives recommend an ending that includes Pughat drawing her sword and killing *ytpn*, which would restore the land.[83]		While it is not a direct linguistic connection, the missing end to the story leaves the audience with vague assurance of Pughat's success. At the end of Psalm 82, there is likewise a lack of resolution.

There are nineteen points of connection between Psalm 82 and the epic of Aqhat. These connections demonstrate that there is a link between the psalm and the epic. This is evidence that there were shared concerns about justice for vulnerable humans that is connected with concerns about the health of the land. It is by means of caring for the poor and marginalized that the land retains its health. Furthermore, this is the highest duty, reserved for leaders and deities, but when it is not enacted, they may be called to account by anyone. Even by a young daughter.

Conclusion

In conclusion, Psalm 82 and the *Epic of Aqhat* originate from a region with shared linguistic and social values, and both texts demonstrate a commitment to similar ideas about justice in divine and human realms.

83. Parker and Smith, *Ugaritic Narrative*, 50.

The recognized mythological features of Psalm 82 allow for a comparison with Ugaritic mythic epic literature. Though these two texts differ in many ways, they share themes and mythopoeic qualities which provide insight into the nature of how justice was perceived in ancient Levantine culture. The most important of these qualities is a commitment to ambiguity in such a way that invites reader participation to consider ethical responses regarding justice. This becomes evidence of support for considering Psalm 82 as both mythological and ethical.

Descriptions of divine governing systems and how they fail to observe proper justice reflect a human ethical concern for justice. Human governing systems must take their cues from a divine counterpart. Mythological texts that reveal injustice and its influence on both human and divine beings also demonstrate a negative effect on the earth itself, and therefore all inhabitants are affected. The result of this type of text is an appeal to the audience to consider what ought to be by means of embedded implicit ethics. Psalm 82 follows this model.

Although myth has for a long time been an important consideration for scholarship dealing with the interpretation of Psalm 82, it has previously been applied in various ways that seek to disambiguate the psalm by revealing the nature of divine beings in v. 1. Its use has been primarily for identifying the origins of Psalm 82 and giving meaning to the divine epithets. Reading Psalm 82 alongside Ugaritic epic literature provides insight into the literary perspective of divine and human agency in the ancient Near East. Mythology is a useful lens for interpreting Psalm 82 as a text that moves between divine and human realms, crossing boundaries of divine and human agency for the purpose of exploring ethical themes.

4

Poverty Centered Language in Psalm 82

"There are people in the world so hungry that God cannot appear to them except in the form of bread." —Mahatma Gandhi, Indian political and spiritual leader

BEYOND THE MYTHOLOGICAL PROVENANCE of Psalm 82 and its encounter with divine and human realms as a mythological text, the psalm explores the relationship between those in power and those who are vulnerable in society. Psalm 82 contains considerable language about the poor and brings forward questions about the relationship between the wicked, the rulers and the vulnerable. For this reason, an interpretation should prioritize a study of ethical expectations in society regarding these roles.

While some scholarship has acknowledged ethical concerns or implications in Psalm 82, the main consideration in past scholarship has been defining aspects of the psalm that work toward a theological interpretation. Language that focuses around power and care for the poor in Psalm 82 is evidence of implicit ethics, and it is one aspect of the *Organon* model. A closer look at the linguistic and cultural significance of poverty in the Psalter demonstrates one aspect of implicit ethics. This chapter looks in depth at how ethics have been assessed in the Hebrew Bible, and, more specifically, in the Psalter. After considering how reading Psalm 82 ethically fits into the broader scholarship of ethics in the Hebrew Bible, we will look more closely at individual terms and their significance in order to explore how language of poverty functions in the psalm.

Ethics in Psalms and Hebrew Bible

For some time in the past, ethics as a category for biblical literature has been largely relegated to legal codes and law texts.[1] More recent work, however, has attempted to make sense of ethical readings in the Psalter,[2] including Gordon Wenham's defense of an ethical approach in *Psalms as Torah* in which Wenham makes the case that the Psalter is, should be, and has been used for ethical instruction.[3] This builds on Eckhart Otto's 2006 suggestion that there may be a case for ethics in the Psalms as well as in other biblical genre.[4] Though the Psalter does not classically fit within the genre of legal codes or law texts, there may be ethical instruction at work in certain psalms, if not in the entire Psalter—after all its opening chapter speaks to the central theme of meditation on Torah in order to produce an outcome of righteous behavior.[5] In recent scholarship, there has been an increasing view toward identifying ethics in the Psalter.

What any Hebrew Bible scholar means by reading the psalms ethically requires further reflection.[6] As Andrew Mein stated, "there is considerable uncertainty about what we mean when we use an expression like 'the ethics of the Hebrew Bible.' Are we interested in the beliefs of all or most ancient Israelites, the views of certain biblical authors, or indeed the ethical outlook of the whole Hebrew Bible?"[7] Mein's evaluation noted the lack of detached reflection, or even the existence of a moral philosophy, in the Hebrew Bible.[8] Diana Lipton worked from Mein's statement about uncertainty of how one deals with ethical issues in the Hebrew Bible before

---

1. Wenham observed largely disproportionate references to Deuteronomic texts over psalms discussion in Otto's *Theologische Ethik des Alten Testaments*, Rodd's *Glimpses of a Strange Land*, and Wright's *Old Testament Ethics*, which prompted him to write more thoroughly on the topic. Wenham, "Prayer and Practice," 281.

2. Mein, *Ezekiel and the Ethics of Exile*. James, *The Storied Ethics of the Thanksgiving Psalms*. Wenham, *Psalms as Torah*.

3. Wenham, *Psalms as Torah*.

4. Otto, "Myth and Hebrew Ethics."

5. McCann included an extensive discussion about behavior modeled in the Psalter in his article on righteousness, justice, and peace. McCann, "Righteousness, Justice, and Peace," 111–31.

6. The quest for how to discuss ethical intention in the Hebrew Bible text extends back several decades. Childs wrote about the lack of coherent conversation about Hebrew Bible ethics fifty years ago. Childs, *Biblical Theology*, 124.

7. Mein, *Ezekiel*, 5.

8. Mein's broader work attempted to analyze ancient Israelite ethics by looking at social order and normative practices across moral worlds. His work focused primarily on texts which describe the experience of exile. Mein, *Ezekiel*.

attempting to make her own case for ethical issues in the narrative through the ambiguity of complex characterization.[9] This continued recognition of a lack of formal ethics approaches in Hebrew Bible speaks to the nature of ethics as a discipline formalized in the western world.[10] Yet, the conversation continues to look for evidence of a moral philosophy in religious texts such as the Hebrew Bible. Psalms, as a liturgical text seems naturally suited to being harvested for moral cues.

Appealing to the Psalter for its ethical implications must include consideration for the situation of the psalms in light of Hebrew Bible instruction. Wenham made a case for the rootedness of topics such as poverty in the Torah, concluding "that God cares for the poor is a core belief of the psalmists."[11] Around the same time, Dirk Human edited a volume entitled *Psalmody and Poetry in Old Testament Ethics* which challenged traditional approaches to ethics in the Hebrew Bible and explored fundamentals of ethical concepts as they may be found or applied in various psalms.[12] In the introduction of this volume, Eckhart Otto traced the work of ethics done in Hebrew Bible scholarship and concluded with an appeal to consider how the Hebrew Bible communicates values in its ancient Near East context. He noted the contrasting behavior of Mesopotamian deities and what they required of their human constituents. He asserted that the Hebrew Bible portrays something different, where in matters of justice, God exemplifies morality. "This difference between an ancient Near Eastern and biblical concept of God in relation to moral values, which implied divine actions, was the cradle of an 'ought' in biblical ethics."[13] The volume considers various approaches to ethical concepts in light of a selection of psalms, but it did not look specifically at the language of poverty as evidence of implicit ethics.

Identifying ethical reflections in the Psalter has created some discussion about the intentionality of the text and its effect on its audience. Wenham posed two questions about the nature of ethics in the Psalter in 2007: 1) "What is different about the way ethics is taught in the Psalms from the approach elsewhere in the Old Testament?" and 2) "What distinguishes the rhetorical force of ethical teaching embedded in prayers or songs from ethics taught through law, story or wisdom?"[14] He concluded that the psalms

---

9. Lipton, "Desire for Ethics," 35.

10. Note Mein's appeal that "by contrast with the literature of ancient Greece, the discipline of 'ethics' itself is quite alien to the Hebrew Bible." Mein, *Ezekiel*, 5.

11. Wenham, *Psalms as Torah*, 116.

12. Human, *Psalmody and Poetry*.

13. Human, *Psalmody and Poetry*, 12.

14. Wenham, "Prayer and Practice," 281.

are distinct from other Hebrew Bible texts in that they are designed for reading in such a way as to be absorbed by memorization and "religious reading" so that the ethical force of the text results in shaping the reader—"in praying the Psalms," he writes, "one is actively committing oneself to following the God-approved life."[15] Thereby, the Psalter is a conduit for the intentional relay of implicit ethics.

The approach to considering ethical instruction through repetition and memorization is supported by a time-honored tradition of reciting psalms as liturgy in various religious settings. For example, eighteenth-century communities utilized songs, hymns, and biblical psalms purposefully and intentionally to train up children in practical and moral living.[16] Also, consider Augustine's commentary on the Psalter, which encourages reciting and memorizing the psalms as a form of imitating and responding to moral behavior. Kuczynski discussed this thoroughly, with reference to the influence of psalms during the Middle Ages.[17] Karl Möller also described this use by noting the influence of psalms on those who, by merely reading the psalms, commit themselves to the ethical values in the text.[18] In so doing, the reader absorbs the message embedded by the composer.

Though it has been argued that the ethical values of the text cannot necessitate influence upon its audience, the potential for influence cannot be ignored. This is not untested. In an effort to separate the intention of the text from its reader, Joshua T. James furthered work in psalms ethics by reading the particular genre of thanksgiving psalms as ethical instruction framed by storytelling to communicate the nature of ethical living. In contrast to Wenham's views, James' work excludes liturgical engagement, which he purported cannot be necessary to ethics as the mere potential of the text to allow for transformational possibility is not enough to necessitate an ethical response by its reader.[19] However, if there is such a thing as implicit ethics in the psalms, does it not follow that its potential for influence upon an audience cannot be separated from the performative intention of the psalm? This study will embrace the idea that the nature of the psalms are such that engaging the text through reading or recitation produces an ethical consideration for reader and audience and implies an intention on the part of the composer.

---

15. Wenham, "Prayer and Practice," 295.
16. Hanway, *Songs, Hymns, and Psalms*.
17. Kuczynski, *Prophetic Song*.
18. Möller, "Reading, Singing and Praying," 113.
19. James, *Storied Ethics*, 6–7.

Rather than trying to identify which psalms are ethical, this study focuses on identifying how the content of a psalm may communicate ethically. The application of ethics as a treatment for reading the Hebrew Bible is different from reading a biblical text in a way that allows it to say something about ethical behavior. Katharine Dell briefly discussed this distinction in her introduction to the volume *Ethical and Unethical in the Old Testament*, with an interest toward what the Hebrew Bible and affiliated literature "has to say about ethical behaviour through its characters, through its varying portrayals of God and humanity in mutual dialogue, and through its authors."[20] Dell's approach is central to this study. The implicit ethics of Psalm 82 is in the language, which describes what is meant by right behavior regarding the poor and marginalized.

Poverty Language in the Psalter: An Ethical Reading

Aside from broader references to wealth disparity and exploited individuals in society, one question continues to emerge: what does it mean to be poor? From a socio-economic view, poverty is subjective to societal conditions. Since the purpose of this study is to view poverty in light of ethical concerns about justice, it is possible to consider a range of meanings for "poor," as is demonstrated in the Hebrew language, which produces several terms for the poor, to be examined and discussed further on in this chapter.

Poverty often deprives a person of power. Scheffler noted that extreme poverty denies a person the right to be heard. He warned about the disconnected evaluations which take place in an academic setting.

> one must acknowledge that, in the context of academic debate, one deliberates and writes as being non-poor, as part of the elite ... really poor people only cry out, they do not write poems about poverty ... at best we can find non-poor voices who may attempt to champion for the poor, endeavoring to express desperation on their behalf, or voices pretending to be poor themselves.[21]

To write about the poor, in some way, becomes an exploitation of their condition. Certainly, even the most deprived subject has something to say: through words, song, or lack of voice even, deprivation may be

---

20. Dell, *Ethical and Unethical*, 1.

21. Scheffler's comments reflect the inherent ethical nature of Psalms regarding the poor following the "religious reading" idea proposed in Wenham's 2007 article discussed above. Scheffler, "The Poor in the Psalms."

communicated. The advocacy of the poor is an imperfect task. In this study, advocacy is discussed in terms of intentional ethics embedded by the composer of Psalm 82.

Historiographical Context of Poverty in Ancient Israel

References to poverty in the Hebrew literature point to the socio-economic reality of those who lived in the ancient Near East. Extreme poverty was not always identified as a societal problem. Early Iron Age Israelite society operated predominately at a level of subsistence. According to archaeological records, little more than basic needs for food and shelter were met, including numerous water cisterns, terraces with fertile soil for growing food, basic mud brick houses, olive trees and domesticated animal husbandry.[22] Biblical texts about these early times fall in line with the archeological data; they do not indicate a great problem of poverty. Note, for example, the democratic style of Moses' rule (Exod 4. 27–31) with focus on assembly-like gathering and equal access to authority. While the subsistence level social structure did not eradicate resource variance, it fought against extreme poverty.

Sociological advancements led societies such as early Israelite clans in movement from a subsistence level tribal system to a tiered structure monarchy, which brought all kinds of societal change. Along with a developing market economy in ancient Israel around the ninth or tenth centuries BCE, came the establishment of a local monarch. Individual family groups within larger tribal contexts gained a means to surplus wealth, sometimes by exploiting others, a practice that invoked compensatory laws, many of which can be seen in Leviticus and Deuteronomy. For example, the requirement to set aside portions of the harvest for the poor can be found in Lev 23:22 and Deut 24:19–21, which describe efforts of charity to be practiced in agriculture.[23] The monarchy could be seen as a societal advancement that brought with it a propensity for wealth disparity.

Another level to the problem of poverty that came along with the monarchy has to do with government affairs. With the jump in social evolution from tribal system and equitable group leadership to single-head

---

22. Scheffler, "The Poor in the Psalms."

23. Agriculturally based charity included three basic functions as defined by rabbinical literature: *Pe'ah* (corner) i.e. Lev 23:22: leave the corner of the land intact for the poor to harvest, untouched. *Leqet* (gleanings): leaving grain on the ground for poor/needy. Avoid going back over to clean it up. *Shikhhah* (forgetting) i.e. Dt 24:19–21: when you forget a sheaf in the field, it should be left for the sojourner/orphan/widow. See further explanation of ethical virtue derived from rabbinic understanding by Cohen, "Justice, Wealth, Taxes," 409–31.

hierarchical governance came an additional mouth to feed—the government itself. Wealth accumulation for building programs, national savings and military protection taxed the economy. Exploitation was not limited to the monarch, though he often benefited greatly from the opportunity to gain wealth internationally. In the biblical text, King Ahab was notably connected with Phoenician trading systems in a time when wealth became large scale production. Those who could sustain trade grew wealthier and those who could not lost their land. The monarch gained power of people and their land. An example of a monarch asserting this kind of authority can be found in 1 Kgs 21. Naboth's land was taken from him by the monarch. Though this sort of behavior may have begun in many cases with the king, it spread to other influential people in same society, and the outcome was a population of wealthy aristocrats and oppressed individuals. The community was then represented by stratification of classes, for example priests, governors or officials, sojourners, orphans, and widows. In a theocratic government, priests, who were also religious leaders, carried out government functions in the name of the king. Therefore, it is not surprising to see language about the dangers of exploitation in a religious text.

The biblical narrative offers a substantial critique of the monarchy in Israel concerning the collection of surplus wealth. For example, God warns the people of Israel of the dangers of seeking a king before the first notable king of Israel, Saul, is crowned. Then, during the end of Israel's United Kingdom, King Solomon's wealth is compared to that of Egypt, a primal arch-enemy of the Hebrews. The priests as government officials also come under scrutiny, often the subject of sharp criticism by the prophets and even among themselves, as can be seen in 1 Samuel regarding Eli and his sons. The received form of the Torah attempted to redress or anticipate the negative outcome of their situation by providing an equalizer so Israel's society would remain fair, just and equitable.[24] However, it is only after Israel establishes a monarch in the biblical narrative that warnings about caring for the poor come flooding in through the prophets, Torah and in the Psalter.[25] Many psalms seem to raise concerns about the poor in society, such as how and why they are poor, what can be done to protect them and how God is or should be concerned with the poor. This study explores how psalms are useful to address poverty in the ancient Near East.

Scholarship that has focused on wealth distribution has had a tendency to speak about the poor in conceptual terms, attempting to define

24. For example, the Year of Jubilee and other laws of compensation and release for indentured servants.

25. Note that the warnings come as early as in Exodus, when Moses essentially acts as an ancient Near Eastern monarch, mediating between the Israelites and their God.

their socioeconomic status. This is helpful to an historical understanding, but it does not focus on ethical behavior based on biblical instruction in its literary context. For example, categorical "economic ethics" is concerned with biblical mandates as it is interpreted in Christian theological paradigms and read in context of modern political discussions. Consider Landgraf, who focused on theological views of good and evil, including modern economic considerations when thinking about what she calls "economic ethics" in her 2007 article on property rights and justice for the poor.[26] In a similar way, Hoppe looked more closely at the literary significance of poverty in the ancient world by summarizing the context for terms translated as "poor" in English in each section of the Hebrew Bible. He intentionally avoided focusing strictly on the terminology of poverty in the Hebrew claiming that the results of such a study is restrictive and offers an incomplete picture.[27] Hoppe takes a primarily metaphorical approach to terms of poverty in the Psalter to show an ideological connection between the poor and the righteous who are defended by God.[28] While both Landgraf and Hoppe looked at the broad context of poverty in the ancient Near East as it relates to the Hebrew text, neither provided a focused look at the language of the text for implicit ethics.

Other scholarship, such as that of Wagner-Tsukamoto, begins with an economic approach. Wagner-Tsukamoto described the socioeconomic paradigm established in the ancient Near East based on a geo-political assessment and re-assessment of a scarce physical commodity—inhabitable space in the Levant. He noted the egalitarian-like democratic structure of Moses' rule in Exodus, which gave way to Joshua's democracy with firmer guidelines for hierarchy as the Israelites sought to establish for themselves a claim to a scarce fertile land occupied by another people.[29] However, once the land was obtained and settled by the Israelites, theocracy was formalized under King Saul, then David, and then Solomon, who became also a judge and religious leader (1 Kgs 3:28; 10:9). Specialization and division of labor became more involved as the king of Israel collected tribute from his people (I Kgs 4:7). The economic implications were that it was less of an inconvenience for the common person to pay tribute than to fight their own battles. Wagner-Tsukamoto's study works to understand the economics of how a nation of people who began as marginalized slaves became a nation of people with disparate

26. Landgraf, "Competing Narratives," 57–75.
27. Hoppe, *Poverty in the Bible*, 17.
28. Hoppe, *Poverty in the Bible*, 122–23.

29. He cited Josh 8:33; 9:14–15; 20:4; 23:1–2; 24:1. Wagner-Tsukamoto, "State Formation," 391–421.

levels of wealth. This information is useful to exploring the power dynamics between classes in the ancient Near East. Understanding the social structure of economics informs why there might be a need for texts, such as Psalm 82, to communicate ethical concepts. Recognizing the underlying tensions also explains how a text like Psalm 82 may be considered resistance literature, which will be explored in Chapter 7.

Textual Context of Poverty in Ancient Israel

The discussion of poverty in the ancient Near East and in the Hebrew Bible is grounded in matters of justice and ethics. Often the first place to look when considering the situation of poverty is to legal texts, such as those found in the Torah. These texts provide insight into the cultural workings of justice and requirements for social order, and they are understood in a context of judgment. Legal texts in the Hebrew Bible have inherited a concern for the poor from ancestral influence by those who came out of Mesopotamia and Egypt.[30]

As in Mesopotamia and Egypt, the legal code of the Israelites include provisions for impartial judgment and a divine directive that the poor, powerless and disadvantaged must receive proper care. Scholarship has long looked closely at legal texts and wisdom literature surrounding matters of ethics regarding the poor, but there is still work to be done in considering ethical instruction in the psalms.

Poverty Ethics in Ancient Near Eastern Texts

In the Hebrew Bible, seven words are attested to describe people of socio-economic disadvantage—עָנָו, דַּךְ, דַּל, עָנִי, יָתוֹם, רָשׁ, אֶבְיוֹן. Two additional words represent figures typically without power in the ancient world—גֵּר and אַלְמָנָה, "foreigner" and "widow." This study reflects on how these words represent poverty in the Psalter, a book with a long-standing tradition as liturgy in religious movements spanning millennia. The impact of implicit ethics in the Psalter is magnified by how that language shapes a community of worship. In order to see this more clearly, it may be helpful to first look at how poverty and justice is conceived in the broader context of the ancient Near East.

---

30. Note Fensham's survey of connection between justice and concern for the poor in Mesopotamian and Egyptian texts. Fensham, "Widow, Orphan, and the Poor," 129–39.

The discussion of Hebrew Bible terminology regarding poverty and justice is contextualized by other ancient Near Eastern texts. Writings about the poor can be found very early in the ancient Near East, dating back to Egypt's Old Kingdom Dynasty and early Mesopotamian legal codes and wisdom literature.[31] These various texts situate Semitic terminology for the poor in a cultural context that shows concern for justice as proper judgment and care for the disadvantaged in their respective communities. The language of justice and poverty is an indicator of implicit ethics in Psalm 82. This study explores the language of poverty in the broader ancient Near Eastern corpus in order to make a more clear connection between ethics and terminology of justice for the poor.

In Mesopotamia, legal codes are sanctioned by Shamash, also known as the sun god, who is affiliated with judgment and justice. The Mesopotamian word for justice corresponds with the Semitic root *špt*, which means *to rule* or *to judge*. The care for the poor and oppressed is a central theme in the matter of justice. Hammurabi's code famously attests to the nature of judgment as proper when the poor are cared for in that no partiality is shown against those who are weak and vulnerable.

As early as the second millennium BCE, Mesopotamian law ensured the security of the poor or weak against the unjust sway of those in power. This was done by ensuring divine punishment comes against those who do not show kindness to the poor or weak. Babylonian wisdom literature also shows concern for the poor, and among duties of the king were to provide for the disadvantaged, namely, the orphan and the widow.[32]

Social and economic reform was a monarch's responsibility. For example, the Code of Ur-Namma (Third Dynasty of Ur) is the oldest in existence and refers to the concern of the monarch's care for the orphan and the widow.[33] A century later, Lipit-Ishtar, king of Isin, secured credibility by claiming to have brought well-being to the people through his care.[34] These edicts of *mīšarum* (a king's just mandates) lead up to Hammurabi's code (First Dynasty of Babylon), in which the monarch also brings justice through well-being, as well as a notable focus on provision for disadvantaged peoples.[35]

---

31. While writings from Ugarit demonstrate some concern of judgment for the poor in the Epic of Aqhat, there are no clearly attested legal or wisdom texts that deal with poverty. Fensham noted this in a previous study. Fensham, "Widow, Orphan, and the Poor."

32. Fensham discussed this power dynamic in more detail. Fensham, "Widow, Orphan, and the Poor."

33. ANET, 524

34. ANET 159,161

35. ANET 164,178

In Egypt, a shift for concern over the poor can be seen in the New Kingdom Era within the writings of Amenemope during the Ramesside period, circa 1200 BCE. Before this time, references to the poor confirmed a social order which was balanced by the existence of "haves" and "have-nots." Legal texts focused on the balance of order (*ma'at*) maintained as the poor remain poor and the wealthy remain wealthy. The Ramesside period, however, is said to have been characterized by a "religion of the poor."[36] The wisdom literature writings of Amenemope describe a changing attitude about the poor. During that time Amun-Re, the sun god, was at the center of the pantheon, and there was an increased interest in caring for the poor. Giving to the poor not only promised to bring happiness and blessing, but also preserved ma'at, which in the jurisdiction of the deity Amun-Re, is affiliated with proper judgment, which may be thought of as true justice. Furthermore, the writings of Amenemope are thought to have had some influence on the Israelite Proverbs.

The Hebrew book of Proverbs has quite a bit to say about economic distribution. Several Proverbs comment on the actions and attitudes of the wealthy as well as those of the poor. Some Proverbs seem to indicate that the poor are authors of their own misfortune, but this is not always the case. For example, Prov 13:23, "the field of the poor may yield much food, but it is swept away through injustice," (NRSV) demonstrates an understanding that injustice is a pervasive keeper of poverty. Apparent contradictions in Proverbs have been addressed by scholars, with recent views trending toward anticipating concerns about injustice explored in other wisdom literature.[37]

There are many similarities between the legal codes and wisdom literature from both sides of the Levant, Egypt and Mesopotamia, and those in the Hebrew Bible. As in Mesopotamia, the Hebrew Bible also condemns the wicked for their treatment of the poor.[38] Legal texts of the Hebrew Bible uphold a similar policy and provide for punishment to those who will not uphold the virtue of gods and kings to care for the poor, and more specific correlations exist in concern for the orphan and the widow. In his 1991 article, Lohfink claimed that the phrase "widow and orphan" is likely borrowed by Israel from neighboring nations as a symbol for those who are in need.[39] Wisdom Literature in the Hebrew Bible also corresponds to Mesopotamian

---

36. Fensham, "Widow, Orphan, and the Poor."

37. One such article considers these contradictions a means by which the book of Proverbs anticipates "fundamental tensions" in a Yahwistic faith. Van Leeuwen, "Wealth and Poverty," 25–36. Also see Hatton, *Contradiction*.

38. This is one feature that is common to texts in the Psalter, as will be shown in more detail in this chapter.

39. Lohfink, "Poverty in the Laws," 34–50.

ideals that the correct way of life involves protection of the weak.[40] Egyptian writings about the poor are also especially concerned with the maintenance of right or proper judgment as true justice. However, in contrast to other ancient Near Eastern texts, which encourage followers to favor the poor in matters of judgment, Hebrew Bible legal texts demonstrate a priority for impartiality over assisting the poor.[41] Regardless, shared features between the texts from Egypt, Mesopotamia and the Hebrew Bible far outweigh their differences. These commonalities show a widespread shared cultural value in the ancient Near East for taking care of the poor in one's own community. With this in the background, we can now turn to how language about the poor is viewed in the Psalter.

Poverty Ethics in the Psalter

Hebrew terminology for the poor has some range of dispute in meaning and application. Various perspectives offer views of interpretation which range from more literal definitions of poverty to metaphorical, and also range from individual to communal poverty. Recent trends in scholarship on the subject of poverty have leaned toward socio-economic discussions of wealth distribution and charity as well as on conceptual descriptions of the poor. Some have even discussed the Psalter as a book used primarily *by* the poor.[42] Few studies have focused on individual terms and their meanings, for example, Sue Gillingham (1988)[43] and Yael Wilfand (2014),[44] which set a precedent for exploring human behavior and potential teachings about the poor. This thesis extends this method of interpretation as a means to consider implicit ethics in Psalm 82.

The emphasis on the poor in Psalm 82 has engaged scholars for many decades. For example, Fensham attempted to avoid the psalms altogether in his article on the poor in the ancient Near East, yet he could not come to discuss the Hebrew Bible without framing the context in light of Psalm 82.[45] In another approach, Dickson's *Hebrew Terminology for the Poor in Psalm 82* focused more on the structure of the poverty terms in Psalm 82 than their meanings, arguing for a recognition of the metaphorical nature

---

40. Fensham's made this comparison clearly. Fensham, "Widow, Orphan, and the Poor."
41. Fensham, "Widow, Orphan, and the Poor."
42. Groenewald, "Psalms 69:33–34," 425–41.
43. Gillingham, "The Poor in the Psalms," 15–20.
44. Ben-Shalom, *Poverty, Charity and the Image of the Poor*.
45. Fensham, "Widow, Orphan, and the Poor."

of poverty language in the psalms.[46] Groenewald briefly explored themes of divine attitudes toward the poor in Psalm 82 as a case in point for his study on Psalm 69.[47] Psalm 82 has long been a point of interest in conversations about the poor in the Hebrew Bible, albeit without significant reflection on the ethical implications.

In addition to the aforementioned terms, other words for poor in the Hebrew Bible include דַּךְ and עָנָו. These terms are sometimes overlooked due to a possible etymological connection with other words. However, since they are independently present in the Hebrew Bible and in the psalms, they will be treated here as individual. Furthermore, to include aspects of the relationship between poverty and powerlessness, I will also look at גֵּר and אַלְמָנָה, the foreigner and widow, who remain economically and socially vulnerable in the Psalter. By the time of early rabbinic writings, the vulnerability of these persons is called into question. The גֵּר, foreigner, came to be known as "proselyte," their identity centering on a religious conversion. The אַלְמָנָה also is missing from later lists of disadvantaged classes. Due to shifts in culture and legislation, the opportunity of the widow for power and position may have increased.[48] These meanings are sometimes read back into the biblical text. However, this study will show that the גֵּר of the Hebrew Bible was limited in resource and access to opportunity, often associated in the psalms with both the אַלְמָנָה and the יָתוֹם.

Gillingham's study focused more clearly on terminology of poverty in the Psalter. Her 1988 article, "The Poor in the Psalms," sought to counter the view held by Liberation Theology that poverty language in the Hebrew Bible exclusively referenced an oppressed social class. She worked through four words in the Psalter which describe the poor. Her conclusion made an appeal to recognize spiritual as well as physical poverty in the semantic range.

Gillingham's study is the most inclusive study of individual words of the poor in the Psalter. Gillingham's stated mission was to "demonstrate that the four main words in the Psalter which describe the poor cannot be classified neatly in terms of economic deprivation . . . or even in terms of a particular religious group."[49] Her study provided insight into the range in meaning for Hebrew words that represent poverty. She found that some words must signify abject poverty of an individual person without regard to moral or spiritual qualities (I.e. דַּל and אֶבְיוֹן); however, she extended the range of meaning for the psalmist who claims to be אֶבְיוֹן to refer to the

---

46. Dickson, "The Hebrew terminology," 1029–45.
47. Groenewald, "Psalms 69:33–34."
48. Wilfand Ben-Shalom, *Poverty, Charity, and the Image of the Poor*.
49. Gillingham, "Poor in the Psalms," 16.

mere threat of losing property and/or life. She defended a similar use of the term עָנִי, with an additional assertion that this term extends beyond the individual and is used to represent an entire nation. Finally, she examined the Hebrew term עָנָו, which she concluded is interchangeable with עָנִי, and perhaps even semantically related.[50] Gillingham's study demonstrated that the inclusion of such language is evidence enough to support a conversation about ethical themes. A consideration of implicit ethics in Psalm 82 is a way to explore how language about justice for the poor could encourage an audience to think about ethics in a particular way.

A more recent book, Wilfand's *Poverty, Charity and the Image of the Poor in Rabbinic Texts from the Land of Israel* attempts to get at the original semantic meaning of terms of poverty by looking at how the Rabbis defined terms for the poor. Wilfand cited a translation of summary made in the *Leviticus Rabbah* (c. fifth century CE) that addressed Hebrew terms for the poor, noting that the list is incomplete and some cultural shifts have impacted the way terms become defined. Wilfand proceeded to examine Hebrew terms individually but only treated three words (עָנִי, דַּל, and אֶבְיוֹן).[51] Wilfand's application of rabbinical interpretations of the language of poverty in the Hebrew Bible found that instructions about the poor lean toward an egalitarian economic structure. While patronage relationships existed in rabbinical times, there is evidence that the biblical idea of egalitarian relationship between classes was still active in the first–fifth centuries CE, suggesting that both the benefactor and the beneficiary were considered equally under the patronage of God. Human dependencies were an undesirable outcome.[52] Wilfand's conclusions provided insight into how Hebrew language of poverty was ethically applied in later times. He did not, however, make a case for how ethics may be considered in light of such language.

Language of the Poor

The language of poverty in the Psalter expresses the condition of the poor in an ancient world. Psalm 82 demonstrates how the poor might be conceived in relation to divine rulers responsible for justice. Five words for the

---

50. Gillingham, "Poor in the Psalms," 18.

51. Ben-Shalom noted the absence of *gēr*, *ytwm*, *'lmnh*, which are important in Exod 22:20–21, an early mention of certain powerless figures who should not be exploited. He attributed this to their shifting status in later rabbinical times. Ben-Shalom, *Poverty, Charity, and the Image of the Poor*, 30.

52. Ben-Shalom, *Poverty, Charity, and the Image of the Poor*, 276.

poor are presented in Psalm 82: דַּל, יָתוֹם, עָנִי, רָשׁ, אֶבְיוֹן.[53] Constructed within merely eight verses of poetry, Psalm 82 reflects more intensely on marginalized persons as victims by clustering a list of five distinct synonyms, six words in total, to represent disadvantaged classes. In Psalm 82, the marginalized are victims of injustice and held captive by the wicked. This is not an unusual circumstance for the poor to find themselves entrapped by the wicked, as we will see in the exploration of other psalms. However, in the unique perspective of Psalm 82, the faults of the wicked are bypassed and primary blame is set upon a higher authority: in this case, the אֱלֹהִים. It is impossible to discuss poverty in the Hebrew Bible without considering justice and its relationship to rulers and divine authority. Themes of justice and poverty are concentrated in Psalm 82.

FIVE TERMS FOR POOR IN PSALM 82:3–4

Psalm 82:3–4 features two short lists that cover a variety of persons who are unjustly subject to the whim of the wicked. Each list is packed between parallel imperatives addressed to, and/or on behalf of, the אֱלֹהִים in v. 1.

The word דַּל occurs five times in the Psalter.[54] In *HALOT*, the verbal root, דלל, is defined as "scanty, poor," with cognates in at least six different languages that indicate the same meaning.[55] Clines noted a potential linguistic relationship between דלל and דלת in Prov 22:22, "open and insecure."[56] The term appears several times throughout the Hebrew Bible referring to poor beings, people and animals, insignificant or small people, powerless and downcast people. The midrash *Leviticus Rabbah* indicates the דַּל as "one who has lost his possessions." Its root (*dll*) also refers to pruning plants to produce yield and it can refer to modest or thin sacrifices from the poor and those whose yield was less than sufficient.[57] This term for poor is the one word repeated in Ps 82:3–4. The Hebrew word דַּל sets

---

53. Even though some studies include the roots *mśkn* and *mkk*, they are not explored in this study, because only one appears in the Psalter (*mkk*) and it acts as a verb meaning "to be low" (Ps 106:43).

54. In Psalm 41:2, the ones who consider the דַּל are delivered by YHWH. Psalm 72:13 states that the דַּל are pitied by God. In Psalm 82:3 & 4, דַּל are among those who have become subject to the wicked.
Psalm 113:7 says that YHWH raises the דַּל.

55. Aramaic, דליל, means thin or sparse. Syriac, *dallīl*, means little or few. In Arabic *ḏallīl* means low and despised. In Akkadian *dallu* means miserable, and also root cognates exist in Ugaritic, *dl*, and in Phoenician. (*HALOT*)

56. Clines, *DCH*, 438.

57. Ben-Shalom, *Poverty, Charity, and the Image of the Poor*, 34.

the context for each list of the poor, the other terms in apposition: in v. 3—with the orphan, the poor and the person in want; and in v. 4—with the needy. The few references in the psalms indicate that God takes pity on the דַּל, as well as those who look after them.[58]

The word יָתוֹם occurs eight times in the Psalter.[59] *HALOT* defined the noun יָתוֹם as "orphan," or "the boy that has been made fatherless." It has cognates in five languages[60] and is attested in Hebrew inscriptions.

A יָתוֹם is one who has lost status and livelihood due to the circumstance of being fatherless. God takes on a more specific role for the יָתוֹם than with others, a role as father and protector, standing in the place of the family they lack. Another characteristic of the יָתוֹם is that they are subject to the wicked. However, it is notable that although the morality of the poor is not generally considered a prerequisite for God's grace, Ps 109:12 states that the יָתוֹם of the wicked are not to be pitied. A few verses before, in v. 9, we learn that יָתוֹם can be born out of punishment for the wicked. This does raise some questions about the nature of poverty in Hebrew Bible ethics regarding the innocence of the poor.[61] Generally, the poor are not discriminated against in the Hebrew text, rather, they seem to be prioritized for care and concern. Clines noted the invitation to show the orphan compassion in Hos 14:4, for example.[62] Also, in Psalm 109, there is complaint of wickedness so great that the psalmist is willing to compromise care for the orphan for the sake of punishing their enemies. In the psalmist's view, at least, wickedness is a category that supersedes concern for the poor, for which there is no redemption, not even for their orphaned children.[63]

---

58. Psalm 41:2, 72:13, 82:3 & 4, 113:7

59. In Psalm 10:14, YHWH gives refuge to the helpless and helps the יָתוֹם. In Ps 10:18, the psalmist prays for YHWH to do justice for the יָתוֹם. In Ps 68:5, God is a father of the יָתוֹם. In Ps 82:3, the יָתוֹם are among those who are subject to the wicked. In Ps 94:6, the wicked murder the יָתוֹם, who is listed alongside the widow (אַלְמָנָה) and the stranger (גֵּר). In Ps 109:9 it is a curse for the wicked that their children become יָתוֹם. In Ps 109:12, the יָתוֹם children of the wicked are not to be pities. In Ps 146:9, YHWH protects the יָתוֹם (and also the widow and the stranger) while bringing ruin to the way of the wicked.

60. It is included in the Aramaic Targum, and also has a similar meaning in Syriac, in Arabic, in Ugaritic, and in Phoenician. (*HALOT*)

61. Firth noted that this is a prayer of the accused, seeking *lex talionis* or that false accuser receives penalty otherwise ascribed to the psalmist. This may explain the exceptional use of the term in this case.

62. Clines, *DCH*, 342.

63. Ps 10:14, 10:18, 68:5, 82:3, 94:6, 109:9 109:12, 146:9

The word עָנִי occurs thirty times in the Psalter.⁶⁴ It is the most commonly used word for the poor in the Hebrew text. *HALOT* defines עָנִי as "without property" in a sociological sense, or "in a needy position," usually in reference to God.⁶⁵ Its use implies an oppressive or needy situation. It is possibly the most prevalent term in Hebrew with a wide range of semantic meaning, including weakness, hunger, humiliation, economic challenges, psychological challenges, and general disadvantage.⁶⁶ It is often contrasted with the word "wealthy," and sometimes contrasted with the word for "homeowner"⁶⁷ or the word for "riches."⁶⁸

In the Psalter, the עָנִי desire judgment (Ps 72:2, 4), and an appeal is made to אֱלֹהִים for justice and consideration, since they have no helper (Ps 72:12), they are in the hand of the wicked (Ps 82:3), and they are pursued

---

64. In Ps 9:13, YHWH does not forget the cries of the עֲנָיִים. In Ps 10:2, the עָנִי are pursued by the wicked. In Ps 10:9, the wicked set out to seize the עָנִי and they do seize the עָנִי and drag them away. (2x) In Ps 10:12, YHWH is called upon to remember the עֲנָיִים. In Ps 12:6, the groaning of the עֲנִיִּים causes YHWH to rise and place them in safety. In Ps 14:6, the counsel of the עָנִי is in danger of being confounded, but YHWH is a refuge for them. In Ps 18:28, the עָנִי people of are delivered as the proud are brought low by YHWH. In Ps 22:25, YHWH is described as being so good as to not despise the עֱנוּת עָנִי, nor hide his face from the psalmist. (Note the substantive use of עָנִי to emphasize the state of being). In Ps 25:16, the psalmist is lonely and עָנִי. In Ps 34:7, the psalmist cried out to YHWH as עָנִי. In Ps 35:10, YHWH delivers the עָנִי from the strong, and the עָנִי וְאֶבְיוֹן from theft. In Ps 37:14, the wicked bring down the עָנִי וְאֶבְיוֹן. In Ps 40:18, the psalmist is עָנִי וְאֶבְיוֹן. (Note the poetic use—וַאֲנִי עָנִי, "and I, I am needy.") In Ps 68:11, God provides for the עָנִי. In Ps 69:30, the psalmist is עָנִי and in pain. (Note again the וַאֲנִי עָנִי. Is this a poetic pattern?) In Psalm 70:6, the psalmist again is עָנִי וְאֶבְיוֹן. (Note again the וַאֲנִי עָנִי, "and I, I am needy.") Ps 72:2 is an appeal to God to judge the עָנִי with justice. Ps 72:4 is an appeal to God to judge the עָנִי among the people. In Ps 72:12, God delivers the עָנִי who have no helper. Ps 74:19 is an appeal to God to not forget the living עָנִי. Ps 74:21 is an appeal for God to act so that the עָנִי וְאֶבְיוֹן have reason to praise. In Ps 82:3, the עָנִי are among those in the hand of the wicked. In Ps 86:1, the psalmist asks YHWH to answer, for he is עָנִי וְאֶבְיוֹן. In Ps 88:16, the psalmist is עָנִי and close to death. (Note the "I am needy" rhetoric is reversed: עָנִי אֲנִי.) Ps 102:1 introduces the psalm as a prayer of one who is עָנִי. In Ps 109:16, the wicked pursued the עָנִי וְאֶבְיוֹן to death. In Ps 109:22, the psalmist is עָנִי וְאֶבְיוֹן. In Ps 140:12, YHWH maintains the cause of the עָנִי.

65. Note the cognate in Aramaic: עַנְיָא.

66. This is the most prevalent term for the poor in rabbinic texts, with a wide range of semantic meanings: disadvantage and weakness, hunger, humiliation, economic, psychological challenges. The root is *'nh/'nw*: material lack and humility. It seems to carry both meanings in the biblical text, although the rabbinical texts interpret the term to mean economic relative depravation almost exclusively. Ben-Shalom discusses this more thoroughly. Ben-Shalom, *Poverty, Charity, and the Image of the Poor*, 36.

67. Ben-Shalom, *Poverty, Charity, and the Image of the Poor*, 40.

68. Clines noted that synonyms of this root can also extend to "toil," "trouble," "oppression," and "wandering," and he references one possible antonym, עֹשֶׁר, as it appears to be contrasted in Si. 13:24. Clines, *DCH*, 506.

by the wicked (Ps 10:2, 9). This term often occurs in conjunction with אֶבְיוֹן, and it is used by the psalmist on several occasions to indicate self-depravation before God (Ps 25:16, 34:7, 40:18, 69:30, 70:6, 86:1, 88:16, and 109:22).[69] In the psalms, עָנִי indicates lowness.[70]

The word רָשׁ occurs only twice in the Psalter.[71] *HALOT* noted the definition for the verbal root, רוּשׁ, as "to be poor," qualifying that it is "the most neutral designation of the poor (man) in his social and economic situation." It has no known cognates and only appears a handful of times in the Hebrew Bible. One defining use is taken from Prov 13:7, where the root appears in the hithpolel participle to describe a subject who is wealthy pretending to be poor.[72] In the Psalter, occurrences are too sparse for a conclusive realization. However, רָשׁ clearly signifies a being in need and likely refers to an individual. The most descriptive use occurs in Ps. 34:11, wherein young lions suffer רָשׁ and hunger. This seems to reflect the definition of being in want, in this case for need of sustenance.[73]

The word אֶבְיוֹן occurs 23 times in the Psalter.[74] *HALOT* defined the verbal root, אבה, "to be needy." Known cognates exist in Coptic and Ugaritic,

---

69. The psalmist's status is emphasized by the use of a rhyming phrase: "אֲנִי עָנִי"—"I am needy"—with the use of the long-form first person pronoun in Psalm 40:14, 69:30, 70:6, and 88:16 (where it is reversed—עָנִי אָנִי). The term is also used in parallel poetic structure as a synonym of the psalmist in Ps. 22:25. The psalmist partners their condition as עָנִי with "lonely" in Ps. 25:16, with "in pain" in Ps. 69:30, and with "close to death" in Ps. 88:16.

70. Psalm 9:13, 10:2, 10:9, 10:12, 12:6, 14:6, 18:28, 22:25, 25:16, 34:7, 35:10, 37:14, 40:18, 68:11, 69:30, 70:6, 72:2, 72:4, 72:12, 74:19, 74:21, 82:3, 86:1, 88:16, 102:1, 109:16, 109:22, 140:12

71. In Psalm 34:11, young lions suffer רָשׁ and hunger. In Psalm 82:3, רָשׁ are among the poor who have become subject to the wicked.

72. Clines noted the opposite is also referenced in the *hithpolel* form of עשר in the same verse. Clines, *DCH*, 456.

73. Ps 34:11, Ps 82:3

74. In Ps 9:19, the אֶבְיוֹן are forgotten, in parallel form with the עֲנָוִים. In Ps 12:6, the groaning of the אֶבְיוֹן causes YHWH to rise up (אָקוּם) in order to place them in a safe place. In Ps 35:10, YHWH delivers the עָנִי וְאֶבְיוֹן from those who would rob them. In Ps 37:14, the wicked lower the עָנִי וְאֶבְיוֹן. In Ps 40:18, the psalmist claims to be עָנִי וְאֶבְיוֹן, and therefore delivered and helped by his lord. Ps 49:2 refers to extremes on a scale, wherein אֶבְיוֹן seems to be the opposite of wealthy (עָשִׁיר). In Ps 69:34, YHWH listens to the אֶבְיוֹן. In Ps 70:6, the psalmist again is עָנִי וְאֶבְיוֹן, and cries to God for help and deliverance. Ps 72:4 is an appeal to God to defend the sons of the אֶבְיוֹן. Ps 72:12 describes God's faithfulness to deliver the אֶבְיוֹן and those who have no helper. Ps 72:13 describes God's pity for the אֶבְיוֹן and salvation for the lives of the אֶבְיוֹן. Ps 74:21 is a prayer to God to give reason for the עָנִי וְאֶבְיוֹן to praise God's name. In Ps 82:4, the אֶבְיוֹן are among those subject to the wicked. In Ps 86:1, the psalmist claims to be עָנִי וְאֶבְיוֹן and asks YHWH to listen and answer for this reason. In Ps 107:41, YHWH is described as lifting the אֶבְיוֹן from distress. Ps 109:16 speaks of the wicked, among whose actions

both indicating "misery."[75] The term often appears in conjunction with עָנִי, and as with עָנִי, the word אֶבְיוֹן also occurs opposite the word for wealthy (Ps 49:2). These similarities and proximity of use suggest a closeness in meaning.[76] This term in the Hebrew represents destitution and very low social standing, "humiliated by a level of poverty from which only God can raise him."[77] Clines noted a special emphasis on divine help for the אֶבְיוֹן.[78] The root can also indicate "to be in want" and *Leviticus Rabbah* includes that the אֶבְיוֹן desires everything, furthermore concluding that the one who desires everything will forever be in want. This meaning is affirmed in the *Sifre Deuteronomy* which states that the אֶבְיוֹן as the neediest is always at the front of the line at the distribution of alms, indicating desperation.[79]

In the psalms, the אֶבְיוֹן is forgotten (Ps 9:19), they are lowered through the actions of the wicked (Ps 37:14). They cry out and are heard by God (Ps 69:34), they have no helper, except God (Ps 40:18, 70:6, 72:12). The אֶבְיוֹן is paralleled with the "brokenhearted" and "pierced of heart" in Ps 109:16 and also in 109:22. The psalmist also claims to be עָנִי וְאֶבְיוֹן in Ps 40:18, 70:6, and 86:1. While some believe this is a reference to religious oppression,[80] it has also been considered representative of a state of humility before God, and by the first century, BCE, there is evidence that the phrase עָנִי וְאֶבְיוֹן is used to

---

are forgetting to show kindness and pursuing the עָנִי וְאֶבְיוֹן to their death. The terms for poor here are in parallel with the brokenhearted. In Ps 109:22, the psalmist claims to be עָנִי וְאֶבְיוֹן and has a pierced heart. In Ps 109:31, YHWH stands at the right hand of the אֶבְיוֹן to save them from those who would put them to death. Ps 112:9 is among a long list of the goodness of the righteous in which they are described as giving freely to the אֶבְיוֹנִים. Ps 113:7 is among a list of reasons to praise YHWH, among them that YHWH lifts the אֶבְיוֹן from the refuse. Ps 132:15 describes YHWH's promise to satisfy the אֶבְיוֹן of Zion with bread. In Ps 140:12, YHWH is described as one who maintains the cause of those in need and executes justice for the אֶבְיוֹנִים.

75. In Coptic, *ebyēn* is "miserable or poor," and in Ugaritic, ' *bynt*, is "misery."

76. Note that whereas in multiple cases the terms עָנִי and אֶבְיוֹן appear in conjunction, they are separated by one line in Psalm 82.

77. Ben-Shalom, *Poverty, Charity, and the Image of the Poor*, 34.

78. Clines, *DCH*, 104.

79. Ben-Shalom, *Poverty, Charity, and the Image of the Poor*, 34–35.

80. Especially as is noted in *HALOT*.

express *Armenfrömmigkeit* in the Qumran community.[81] In the Psalter, the אֶבְיוֹן are humbled by their desperate need.[82]

The previous five terms are all contained in Ps 82:3–4.[83] Some significant features of the particular terms appearing in vv. 3–4 are that they represent varying aspects of poverty and deprivation. There are a couple of distinctions that should be recognized. First, the reference to יָתוֹם is unusual in that it is not paired with its common partner—אַלְמָנָה. Additionally, the words עָנִי and אֶבְיוֹן often appear together, as a syntagm; but in Psalm 82, they are divided. The one Hebrew term that is repeated in both verses, דַּל, is one of the rarer occurring terms in the Hebrew Psalter. Its meaning is also somewhat ambiguous in that it could refer to one who has lost what they had, or to one who never had anything. The ambiguous term leads each listing, emphasizing the poverty contained in these parallel lists.

Additional Terms for the Poor

The Hebrew Bible has seven terms for the poor commonly used. The five previously discussed are central to the main thesis of this study. However, the other terms are important to consider, as their use informs societal views of poverty and justice.

The word דַּךְ occurs only three times in the Psalter.[84] *HALOT* defined the root, דכך, as "oppressed, miserable," and a synonym of עָנִי, יָתוֹם, and אֶבְיוֹן. There are no known cognates. Clines recommended a definition of "crushed," suggesting its connection to the root דכה.[85] The metaphorical sense is retained in both readings. The דַּךְ in the psalms are not mentioned in terms of their struggle against the wicked, but in terms of their dependence

---

81. The phrase עָנִי וְאֶבְיוֹן in the Qumran Community shifted from a more literal, economic poverty, to a metaphorical poverty of spirit, as the Qumran community used the words to self-identify as a "congregation of the poor." Schiffman and VanderKam, *Encyclopedia of the Dead Sea Scrolls*, 900.

Also note Ro's analysis on the metaphorical poor in the Qumran Community. Un-Sok Ro, *Poverty, law, and Divine Justice*.

82. Ps 9:19, 12:6, 35:10, 37:14, 40:18, 49:2, 69:34, 70:6, 72:4, 72:12, 72:13, 74:21, 82:4, 86:1, 107:41, 109:16, 109:22, 109:31, 112:9, 113:7, 132:15, 140:12

83. Ps82:3 שִׁפְטוּ־דַל וְיָתוֹם עָנִי וָרָשׁ הַצְדִּיקוּ׃

Ps82:4 פַּלְּטוּ־דַל וְאֶבְיוֹן מִיַּד רְשָׁעִים הַצִּילוּ׃

84. In Ps 9:10, YHWH is a stronghold for the דַּךְ. In Ps 10:18, YHWH is called upon to do justice for the orphan and the דַּךְ. Ps 74:21 provides an instruction or request of God, that the דַּךְ should not be put to shame, rather the עָנִי וְאֶבְיוֹן should have cause to praise the name of God.

85. Clines, *DCH*, 437.

on God as a stronghold (Ps 9:10) and for justice (Ps 10:18).[86] It is only by God's help that they are not crushed under the wicked.

The word עֲנָוִים occurs twelve times in the Psalter,[87] always in plural form.[88] *HALOT* defined the noun, עָנָו, as "bowed" and did not cite any cognates, except for its appearance in the Samaritan Pentateuch. Clines described this term as "humble, meek, poor" and suggests that it is opposite "proud" or "wicked."[89] This term in its singular form is likely related to עָנִי, possibly sharing the root ענה.[90] Unlike other terms for the poor in the psalms, the עֲנָוִים seem to be often recognized as those who have been restored by the Hebrew God (Ps 9:19), whose hearts have been strengthened (Ps 10:17), they are fed in the presence of God (Ps 22:26), they are taught and led by God (Ps 25:9), they are glad when they hear praise of God and delighted in prosperity (Ps 34:3, 37:11, 69:33), they are saved when God rises to judgment (בְּקוּם־לַמִּשְׁפָּט אֱלֹהִים) in Ps 76:10, an action that is longed for by the psalmist in Ps 82:8. The עֲנָוִים are lifted as God casts down the wicked (Ps 147:6) and they are made beautiful in salvation (Ps 149:4). While other terms for the poor seek help, salvation, and care, the term עֲנָוִים appears to represent those poor who have received the reward of salvation.[91]

---

86. Ps 9:10, 10:18, 74:21

87. In Ps 9:19, the עֲנָוִים have lost hope, but it may be restored with YHWH's help. In Ps 10:17, YHWH hears the desires of the עֲנָוִים and strengthens their hearts. In Ps 22:26, the עֲנָוִים will eat and be satisfied in the presence of YHWH. In Ps 25:9, YHWH leads the עֲנָוִים and teaches them. In Ps 34:3, the עֲנָוִים are said to be glad when the psalmist boasts in YHWH. In Ps 37:11, the עֲנָוִים inherit the land and be delighted in abundant prosperity. In Ps 69:33, the עֲנָוִים see the psalmist's praise of God and are glad. Ps 76:10 describes a scene where God rises to establish judgment in saving all the עֲנָוִים in the land. In Ps 147:6, YHWH lifts the עֲנָוִים while casting down the wicked. In Ps 149:4, YHWH makes the עֲנָוִים beautiful in saving them.

88. Groenwald discussed this in contrast to the individual, singular occurrences of references to the poor, stating that עֲנָוִים represents the community of poverty. Groenewald, "Psalms 69:33–34."

89. Clines, *DCH*, 502.

90. The MT contains *Ketib Qere* notes in Ps 9:13, 19 and 10:12 that suggest an interchangeability between עָנָו and עָנִי. Gillingham discussed this in further detail and included other cases of their interchangeability in the Hebrew Bible. Gillingham, "Poor in the Psalms."

91. Ps 9:19, 10:17, 22:26, 25:9, 34:3, 37:11, 69:33, 76:10, 147:6, 149:4

Terms for Figures of Poverty

Finally, this study looks at figures of powerlessness in Hebrew: the widow and the foreigner.[92] In many ways, the אַלְמָנָה and the גֵּר are living pictures of poverty. The Hebrew Bible prophets also share a concern for these figures as societally marginalized people, victims of oppression and subject to the mercies of the ruling authority.[93] While the exact meanings of these terms have shifted throughout time, depending on societal expectations, the terms once referred to marginalized persons, and that aspects remains a part of the terminology in its history.

The word אַלְמָנָה occurs only five times in the Psalter.[94] *HALOT* defined the noun as "widow," noting direct cognates in six regional languages.[95] In the Psalter, the widow occurs most of the time alongside the יָתוֹם and the גֵּר.[96] It only appears once in the Psalter without יָתוֹם. The אַלְמָנָה is subject to the wicked and her socio-economic status is low. In Ps. 109:9, the wicked curse the psalmist, threatening his death by referring to his wife as אַלְמָנָה and his children, יְתוֹמִים. The Hebrew God is concerned for the plight of the אַלְמָנָה as well as that of the יָתוֹם and the גֵּר.[97]

The word גֵּר occurs only four times in the Psalter,[98] although it occurs in the entire Hebrew Bible more times than any other term in this study.

---

92. It is likely that in the concrete world of the ancients, the foreigner, the widow and the orphan were the relational picture of poverty in social order. Adamo discussed the socio-economic status of the poor in the Hebrew Bible as distinctive social categories. Adamo, "The Poor in the Book of Psalms," 797–815.

93. Houston, *Contending for Justice*.

94. In Ps 68:5, God is the protector of אַלְמָנוֹת (and the father of orphans). In Ps 78:64, the אַלְמָנוֹת are wives of the priests who fell in battle. In Ps 94:6, the wicked kill the אַלְמָנָה, and the גֵּר and the יְתוֹמִים. In Ps 109:9, the wicked curse the psalmist that his wife will become a אַלְמָנָה (and his children, יְתוֹמִים). In Ps 146:9, YHWH keeps the יָתוֹם וְאַלְמָנָה, and also watches over the גֵּר.

95. In Ugaritic, *'lmnt*; in Phoenician, אלמת; in Akkadian, *almattu* < **almantu*; in Aramaic and Syriac, אַרְמַלְתָּא; and in Arabic, *'armalat*.

96. Notably, the יָתוֹם is the only one of this triad that appears in the list of the poor in Psalm 82:3–4. Often in the Hebrew Bible, the term for orphan, יָתוֹם, is also joined with the term for widow, אַלְמָנָה. Widow only appears in one Psalm without being accompanied by the term for orphan. (Orphan, 4x w/o widow.) In the entire Hebrew Bible: 60x orphan and widow occur together. Orphan occurs 12 times w/o widow. Widow occurs 25x in the HB w/o orphan. Widow and orphan is a combination often mentioned. They occur together in the Torah (26x), wisdom literature (12x) and latter prophets (20x). Clines listed these three terms as synonyms in the *DCH*, and he also includes לֵוִי (Levite) among them. Clines, *DCH*, 295.

97. Ps 68:5, 78:64, 94:6, 109:9, 146:9.

98. Ps 39:13 is an appeal to YHWH to listen, because the psalmist is a גֵּר, a תּוֹשָׁב. (Note: תּוֹשָׁב only appears this one time in the Psalter, translated as alien or foreigner.)

HALOT defined the noun as a "protected citizen, stranger." The word appears to have the sense of a shelter-seeking refugee who has been displaced from their ancestral home. At least six cognate languages contain the same word with a small range of semantic meaning.[99] The status of the גֵּר has been connected with the poor in cases of charity (cf. Lev 19:10),[100] likely because they are dependent on the community for position and opportunity. The patriarch Abram considered himself a kind of displaced citizen, calling himself a גֵּר־וְתוֹשָׁב, a foreigner and traveler, when he entered the land of the Hittites (Gen 23:4).[101] Clines noted a connection between the גֵּר and one who lacks sustenance, particularly the רָשׁ and the עָנִי.[102] In the Psalter, the גֵּר is hunted and killed by the wicked, along with the אַלְמָנָה and the יְתוֹמִים; however, God watches over them (Ps 146:9). The psalmist claims to be a גֵּר in Ps 119 and a גֵּר תּוֹשָׁב in Ps 39:13. Consistent with the psalmist's frequent claims about being poor before God, this is a recognition that the land they live in belongs to God, and it is under God's instruction they live as גֵּר.[103]

In several places, the psalmist appeals to God for special consideration and relies on the argument that they are poor, whether it is עָנִי, אֶבְיוֹן or as גֵּר. This use paints a picture of a God who prioritizes the poor and needy. There is an interesting theological discussion to be had here regarding the position of the poor as near to God. Some religious movements have promoted poverty as a directive of spiritual living—consider the ascetic monk for example. But the psalmist does not seem to be in a permanent state of poverty. Certainly in the cases where the psalmist is a king claiming to be poor, it cannot be literal! It is a temporary state, an appeal of desperation.[104]

In Ps 94:6, the wicked kill the גֵּר, along with the אַלְמָנָה and the יְתוֹמִים. In Ps 119:19, the psalmist lives as a גֵּר in the land and appeals to YHWH to share the commandments. In Ps 146:9, YHWH watches over the גֵּרִים, and also upholds the אַלְמָנָה and the יְתוֹמִים.

99. Noted cognates are in Aramaic, גִּיּוֹרָא meaning proselyte, in Ugaritic, *gr*, in Phoenician, גר, in Syriac, *gayyārā* meaning adulterer, in Arabic, *jār* meaning neighbor, and in Ethiopic, *gōr*.

100. Laws regarding charity by leaving agriculture uncollected so that the poor may have something to eat.

101. *HALOT* noted that there is semantic evidence of two types of גֵּר: the גֵּר־וְתוֹשָׁב, who seeks limited citizenship and is obligated to partial acceptance of local law, and a גר צדק, who is a full proselyte.

102. Clines, *DCH*, 373.

103. Ps 39:13, 94:6, 119:19, 146:9

104. Also note Levin's discussion of King David, who is confronted by the prophet Nathan with a parable of a poor man's encounter with a rich man. Levin noted that like the poor man in the parable, "the person petitioning the Deity in prayer terms himself 'poor' in order to win attention and commitment." It does not represent the real material status of the petitioner. Levin, "The Poor in the Old Testament. 253–73.

The recognition of the Hebrew God as one who responds first to the poor is not unique to the Psalter. The Hebrew patriarch, Abraham began as a גֵּר, a foreigner in the land long before the Israelites came to dwell in it. Also, the Hebrews began as a people in service to Egypt, so desperate in their need that they groaned, וַיֵּאָנְחוּ,[105] crying out for help, וַיִּזְעָקוּ,[106] to be lifted from the poverty of their situation. It is at the very least descriptive of a biblical theme that God is concerned with the plight of the poor.

Conclusion

The Psalter contains a great number of references to the poor and disadvantaged. The psalms not only refer to communities or classes of people, but also to individuals. References to poverty imply material need as well as metaphorical. In contrast to legislation that protects the poor from injustice, and the sages who communicate indifference, the psalms engage the subject of poverty on a level of personal involvement. It is in the liturgy that a community of worship is faced with the plight of the poor. Not only that, but they are tasked by the standard that God establishes by example. In a world where humans are normally held to higher moral standards than those of the highest deities, God challenges this ethic by practicing correct behavior toward the poor as is demonstrated in nearly every psalm.

A community of worship that is shaped by the Psalter considers caring for the poor a priority. This is evident in modern reflections upon the psalms as well as in religious structures that promote teachings centered on care for the poor, including Judeo-Christian and Islamic communities. The significance of inclusive language of the poor in the psalms is the consideration for the marginalized during a time of devotion and practice of faith. Thereby concern for the poor becomes itself part of the liturgy—an act of faith that proceeds from a community of worship. The language and terminology in Psalm 82 make a strong appeal to the reader to consider an ethical response in light of discussion about the poor. By this means, the linguistic texture demonstrates one aspect of Zimmermann's *Organon* model, encouraging the reader to encounter the ethical paradigm present in the psalm. With an ethical interpretation at stake, questions of application persist—how can the poor be helped? Also, what happens when the poor are not assisted? These are questions that Psalm 82 attempts to address by presenting terminology of justice alongside terminology of the poor.

---

105. From the root אנח, to sigh or groan. (HALOT)
106. From the root זעק, to cry out as for help. (HALOT)

5

Justice Centered Language in Psalm 82

"When a poor person dies of hunger, it has not happened because God did not take care of him or her. It has happened because neither you nor I wanted to give that person what he or she needed."
—Mother Teresa, Roman Catholic nun

AT LONDON'S TRAFALGAR SQUARE, 2005, Nelson Mandela spoke on eradicating poverty in the developing world, and his speech centered on justice. He stated "overcoming poverty is not a gesture of charity. It is an act of justice."[1] This sentiment about justice and poverty echo other modern voices, for example Charles Dickens, Elizabeth Gaskell, and Martin Luther King, Jr. The point is that caring for the poor can be an act of justice.

Rhetoric about poverty often ends in rhetoric about justice and vice-versa. Advocacy of justice is often centered on the poor. Why? Because the poor are dependent upon community. They have little or nothing to offer in exchange for their need. Others in a community, when faced with the poor, must decide what is just. Champions for justice advocate on behalf of the poor because that is where the need is greatest. Therefore, discussions of poverty cannot exist without discussions of justice, and discussions of justice cannot exist without consideration of advocacy for the poor. This is also represented in religious literature of the ancient world, including the Hebrew Psalter.

The main concern for the poor in the ancient world is that they receive advocacy in judgment, and that proper judgment makes way for justice. For the purpose of this study, justice will be defined as right or proper judgment based on the language used to describe judgment as right and true in Hebrew and ancient Near Eastern linguistic cognates. Not only do the poor have a right to access equitable advocacy in judgment, but it was one of the highest mandates of divine authority in the ancient Near East

1. Mandela, "Nelson Mandela."

to ensure that such justice is upheld for the poor. Furthermore, through the Psalter, just advocacy for the poor is both the divine example and the ethical obligation of the broader worship community. Some of the areas explored in this study include lament and advocacy for the poor, with a specific view toward the Psalter as a window into the ethics of an ancient religious ideology. Identifying the language of justice in Psalm 82 bolsters support for evidence of implicit ethics in the psalm. This chapter will explore why and how justice is centralized with divine authority in the ancient Near East, then look at how scholarship has viewed justice themes in the Hebrew Bible. In conclusion, the terms for justice will be explored individually to determine how their meaning contributes to support for reading Psalm 82 as an implicitly ethical text.

Scholarship about Justice

In the mid-twentieth century, biblical scholars began to develop ideas about themes of justice in the Hebrew Bible and how the legal system may be represented. Gamper (1967),[2] and Crüsemann (1976),[3] attempted to define societal justice by making loose correlations with legal terms. In 1994, Bovati published an extensive study on legal aspects of justice in the Hebrew Bible.[4] Bovati's work engaged a structured study of legal terminology which provided a depth of information for analyzing legislative terms in Hebrew Bible texts. Bovati's work laid the groundwork for making clear connections between themes of justice and terminology for justice as a way of understanding how ancient Israelites envisioned the law. However, his work landed in the University's law library, which might explain why it is not well engaged with biblical scholarship.

In more recent years, there has been a revival in scholarship to identify social justice and define what is meant by it. For example, Moshe Weinfeld's *Social Justice in Ancient Israel and in the Ancient Near East*,[5] *Marx and the Bible* by José Miranda, 2004,[6] and Walter Houston's 2015 book *Contending for Justice*.[7] These works on justice in the Hebrew Bible provide insight into the current state of scholarship on the matter, which centers mainly on social justice as an aspect of liberation theology.

2. Gamper, *Gott als Richter*.
3. Crüsemann, "Meine Kraft," 117–21.
4. Bovati, *Re-establishing Justice*.
5. Weinfeld, *Social Justice*.
6. Miranda, *Marx and the Bible*.
7. Houston, *Contending for Justice*.

Social justice has become a term with many nuances. Exactly how and why it is useful to the study of ethical justice is somewhat unclear. This study attempts to rely more solidly on terminology and cognate language to determine what Psalm 82 is getting at by featuring language of the poor and language of justice in such a concentrated manner. That being said, some of this work coincides with views of social justice. Scholarship that references the Psalter in light of social justice is recognized below.

Weinfeld discussed a connection between Mesopotamian ideals of truth or justice and acts of mercy or loving kindness. He asserted that justice is necessitated by concern for the oppressed and poor.[8] To demonstrate this connection, he built on earlier scholarship by Gamper,[9] as well as relying on linguistic evidence, like Rabbinic Hebrew's adoption of the hendiadys "righteousness and kindness."[10] Weinfeld's study on social justice in ancient Israel focused on the act of justice as a provision of freedom for the oppressed. He stated that righteousness refers to the "freedom of the entire world from enslavement," specifically in the Psalter.[11]

Weinfeld envisioned the scenario in Psalm 82 as an act of justice wherein God, as judge, decides in favor of good people and saves them from the bad. Weinfeld based this on a reading of psalms (Psalms 7, 26, and 35) as a plea before the judge in divine court, wherein the psalmist argues for judgment on the basis of righteousness. He argued that Mesopotamian psalms extend similar pleas for judgment on the basis of justice (*mīšaram*).[12] His view of Psalm 82 is simplistic and obfuscates the matter of who is doing the judging and who is making a plea. The particular psalms he examines demonstrate a plea by the composer for justice based on righteousness, grounded in their care and concern for the poor. Those psalms justify his conclusions about the connection between mercy and justice. However, Weinfeld's study demonstrates the need for further exploration of the terms and justice situation of Psalm 82.

Houston's study of social justice, which he defined as the "elimination of oppressive action,"[13] focused on classes and wealth distribution in ancient society as evidence of a social context that informs biblical texts about justice by focusing on the relationship between authority figures and their subjects. While his work did not look closely at the Hebrew language,

---

8. Weinfeld, *Social Justice*, 7.
9. Gamper, *Gott als Richter*.
10. Weinfeld, *Social Justice*, 35.
11. Weinfeld, *Social Justice*, 15.
12. Weinfeld, *Social Justice*, 41–42.
13. Houston, *Contending for Justice*, 61.

nor at the function of economics, he concluded that the Hebrew Bible is most useful as a moral description of society.[14] For specific examples, he analyzed "moral judgments on social oppression" based on the rhetorical structure of prophetic texts, cataloguing victims, their oppressors and acts of oppression. Houston's analysis of rhetoric in the prophets revealed a level of class distinction and recognized a theme of eliminating oppressive activity. He attempted to apply this theme to Psalms and Proverbs; however, he did not mention Psalm 82, even where he addressed the Hebrew Bible's interest in *saving* (נצל) the poor, which, according to Houston, is a rhetorical connection between certain psalms and the book of Amos.[15] Overall, Houston's focus on rhetorical moral judgment against social oppression provides an example of how justice themes in the Hebrew Bible may be relevant to ethical concerns.

Recent scholarship on social justice demonstrates an interest in the connection between justice and poverty. However, language about justice should be examined beyond the scope of Liberation Theology. In her article about the poor in Psalm 82, Gillingham observed that there is a need to consider the implications of such terminology beyond the limits of Liberation Theology.[16] Through close examination of Hebrew terms for the poor and related justice efforts, it becomes apparent that the community contributing to (and utilizing) the Psalter is a society potentially represented by diverse perspectives and wealth status.

Bovati's approach considered biblical justice in terms of legislative action. He began his study on justice by breaking down legal terms as they relate to contentions for justice in Hebrew Bible texts. The book contains two parts. Part one centers on a description of the *rîb*, a word describing a legislative-style court case.[17] Part two centers on the word *mišpāṭ*, which relates more directly to this study as a Hebrew term for justice.[18]

Bovati's terminology study is broad, and focuses on formulas, describing how terms fit together in various texts to demonstrate the roles, attitudes and characterization of participants in legal or justice matters. His work is useful to this study in that his findings of structure and use for the terms that appear in Psalm 82 support the conclusions of this study. His analysis of how language patterns fit a legal context made way for a more detailed discussion

---

14. Houston, *Contending for Justice*, 18–51.
15. Houston, *Contending for Justice*, 142.
16. Gillingham, "Poor in the Psalms."
17. Bovati, *Re-establishing Justice*, 30–31.
18. Bovati, *Re-establishing Justice*, 168–69.

of justice language as ethics in the Psalter. Bovati's conclusions are engaged below in the study of the language of justice.

In the previous chapter, the study of terms for the poor demonstrated several classifications for people in need, implying the existence of the wealthy and imagining multiple levels of disparity in the liturgical community. This chapter focuses on terminology of justice as it relates to legislative concepts as implicit ethics. In Psalm 82, justice is necessary for everyone to survive. Justice achieves stability not only for humanity, but for the earth itself. Reading terms of justice as legislative supports the text's engagement with implicit ethics.

Context of Justice in Ancient Israel

Justice as a central ideal is prevalent in the ancient Near East and prolific in the Hebrew Bible. The mission to do "justice and righteousness" is a pervasive message that can be traced back to Israel's roots. Gen 18:19 notes Abraham for his distinctive duty of acting on behalf of YHWH in order to do justice (משפט) and righteousness (צדקה). While the divine mandate began with Abraham, it became the central concern for Israel's monarchs.[19] This also reflected the ancient Mesopotamian tradition of a king charged by divine right with the duty to establish *kittam u mīšaram* (truth and uprightness),[20] which involved granting freedom for the oppressed.[21] There is also a similar idea in Egypt with the concept of *ma' at*.[22] The hieroglyphic symbol for *ma'at* represents straightness, and is correlate to the Semitic root *yšr*, which means *straight* or *right*, which also describes proper judgment. The connection between terms in these various languages demonstrates the possibilities of shared ideologies for justice advocacy.

Justice and righteousness is essential in the ancient Near East, and it is a matter of great importance to Israel, as evidenced by the prophets for whom justice and righteousness are virtues upon which kings and nations are judged.[23] Furthermore, justice is greatly connected in the ancient world with the relief of oppression.[24] While topics of justice range across a variety of

---

19. See following verses for support. In all but two, the phrase צְדָקָה וּמִשְׁפָּט acts as a syntagm: 2 Sam 8:15; 1 Kgs 10:9; Isa 9:6; 16:5; Jer 22:3, 15; 23:5; 33:15; Ps 72:1–2; Prov 16:12.

20. This can be seen in the Code of Hammurabi (V:20).

21. Weinfeld, *Social Justice*, 11.

22. Epzstein, *Social Justice*, 45–46.

23. Isa 5:7; Jer 4:2; Mic 6:8.

24. Jer 7:5–6; Zech 7:9–10; Jer 22:3–4; Mic 3:9–12; Jer 45:9–10; Isa 32:1.

social issues (i.e. marriage, child bearing, land ownership, etcetera), this study is concerned primarily with the matter of justice for the poor and oppressed in society's care. A ruler in the ancient Near East carried many responsibilities of justice, but his obligation to the poor was significant.

The following sections will review the context of justice in the ancient Near East. Literature provides insight into attitudes about justice in the ancient world. Ancient Near Eastern texts from Assyria, Egypt, and the Levant may be compared with Hebrew Bible texts as a comparison of cultural values for justice in social order. Three aspects are explored in this study: how justice is administered, how it is held accountable, and how advocacy works.

Justice Administration

There are three main recognized jurisdictions in the ancient Near East for the purpose of administering justice: the elders at the gates of the city, the king or ruling judge, and the priests who are extensions of the king.[25] The role of the king was central to society, but a king was not always the central ruler of ancient Israel. Therefore, the Hebrew Bible describes a progression from earlier forms of judgment advocacy and leadership that eventually lead to the establishment of a king over the Israelites.

Before the monarchy, tribal systems relegated judgment to the elders as society's justice advocates. The idea that all members of a society have access to a right relationship is at the heart of justice. The elders at the city gates, which may be the oldest and most broadly accessed level of judgment, encouraged this right relationship by offering access to judgment for anyone who could approach them. Once a monarchy was established, however, justice became the divine directive of the king, in line with broader ancient Near East ideology. The authority of the king was also directed to priests, who were, by extension, representatives of the king's authority.[26]

Council of Elders

A council of elders as judge is the most longstanding tradition reflected in ancient society. Earliest forms of judgment stemmed primarily from

---

25. Bovati discussed this in detail as a means of analyzing the Hebrew *rib*. Bovati, *Re-establishing Justice*, 176.

26. Even though this was the prevalent model in the ancient Near Easter, biblical texts, such as in Deuteronomy, often criticize a centralized authority.

a group of elders in a given community who ruled at the city gates.[27] The role of these elders was to receive complaints and discuss the merits of a dispute. What officials did about these disputes formed what became legislation.[28] The verdict is judgment. While heads of state held the power of jurisdiction, it is important to note established venues for commoners to seek justice. The elders at the city gate may have remained as a function of society, even when a king was in power, to ensure access to justice for people far removed from the king's court.

The concept of the council as a place of justice advocacy even reaches beyond the confines of humanity and into divine realms. In Exodus 2, the recipient of complaint is הָאֱלֹהִים, which could reasonably be considered a divine version of the elders at the gates of the city (v. 23). In v. 24, the groans are heard, and (an) אֱלֹהִים remembered a covenant with the Israelite patriarchs of Genesis. The expression of divine council in the Hebrew Bible echoes the experience of the people in their own communal setting.

A council of elders was responsible for judgment and accountable to justice. The divine council is a common motif in ancient Near Eastern cognate literature,[29] and it reflects a divine model of group concern for justice. While the council of elders were an early form of governance, their impact lasted, and the city gates became a recognized place for matters of judgment.[30] The concept of a divine council mirrors this human center for justice.

Kings and Judges

A monarch ruling by divine authority is another longstanding tradition of ancient societies. Biblical narratives describe a transitionary evolution of government from familial, or tribal, to monarchical. While elders continued throughout history to be important to the cause of legislation and justice, more formal systems of judgment arose. The ancient Near Eastern monarch was assigned the task of doing justice. This is referred to in Mesopotamia as *mīšarum*, and in Egypt as *ma' at*. Texts from Mesopotamia and Egypt, which are discussed in more detail below, confirm that the role of the king is to enact justice for the sake of the well-being of people under their rule, by making right or proper judgments. The Hebrew Bible also describes the duties of a monarch as maintaining justice. The famous story of King Solomon

27. Deut 22:15, Josh 20:4, Prov 31:23, Job 29:7
28. Hart, *The Concept of Law*.
29. The gathering of deities in Ugaritic *Epic of Aqhat* and in the Babylonian *Enuma Elish*, etc.
30. in Deut 22:15, Josh 20:4, etc.

judging between two women who lay claim to the same child demonstrates the kingly duty of judgment, with explicit affirmation in 1 Kgs 3:28 that the role of the king is to "do justice" (לַעֲשׂוֹת מִשְׁפָּט:).

The Hebrew Bible engages in critique of how justice is carried out by assessing whether it is done right. As a people who began as slaves, the Israelites' journey is one that confronts injustice and even critiques its own leadership for improper judgment when necessary. Before Israel named and recognized a formal king, ruling judges brought judgments with similar monarchical authority (in fact they were named judges, because that was their primary role in leadership). Those judges were measured by their ability to do justice by maintaining right judgment. Some judged properly, or righteously, and others failed to do so, allowing wickedness and corruption to have the advantage over the marginalized. The Hebrew Bible critiqued the abilities of the judges to rule and found that they were inadequate. It is the failure of the judges to judge rightly that led to Israel's demand for a king like their neighbors (1 Sam 8). Once a king was in place, his rule was seen as absolute, empowered by the deity. The king was the primary administrator of justice in the ancient world and his jurisdiction defined best in legal and historical texts.

Seeking justice meant appealing to an administrator of justice for judgment. "A complaint is a request for intervention directed to a *judge*, who does justice by giving aid to the unjustly oppressed."[31] Complaints in the ancient Near East generally took the form of an invocation or cry that may be heard by a judge. Consider the cry of the Israelites in Exod 2:23–24 in which the Israelite slaves groan under the burden of their oppression and their cry for help rise to the אֱלֹהִים. This is the model of complaint that begins a trial of justice. In the model described by Exodus 2, the Israelites are marginalized, and they have no advocate for justice before the monarch of Egypt. They must depend on unknown assistance. The deity produces an advocate for them, the Egyptian-Hebrew Moses, who approaches the king and fights for justice on behalf of the Israelite slaves. This narrative described one of the earliest and least formal process of complaint to deal with injustice and reconciliation, but it provides the model for justice advocacy going forward in the historiographical descriptions of Israel's development as a people and a nation. When a cry of injustice arises, it receives attention.

---

31. Bovati, *Re-establishing Justice*, 323.

Justice Accountability

Responding to appeals for justice established the well-being of a society.[32] In addition to the involvement of a ruling authority and the person making a complaint, there was a third party involved to ensure proper justice. Prophets often help keep the rulers accountable to a just process. Prophets were often seen as revolutionaries for social and economic reform. The Hebrew Bible indicates that the main purpose of a prophet was to advocate for justice.[33] It is the voice of the prophet that is persistent in promoting social well-being and holding the ruler accountable to justice. Psalm 82 is often read as a prophetic text. Considering an ethical interpretation is in line with justice motifs in Hebrew prophets.

Prophets acted as a source for accountability, advocating on behalf of the poor, seeking to correct wrongful judgments by a ruling authority. Some prophets even worked closely with the monarch. For example, King David and the Prophet Nathan. The Hebrew Bible narrative in 2 Sam 12 describes the prophet as an envoy of YHWH who admonishes the monarch for unjust behavior. The prophet speaks on behalf of the marginalized victim(s), as in the case of 2 Sam 12, where the victims include a widow and an unborn (fatherless) child. The prophet urges the king to confess his involvement. Prophets who work in relationship with their monarch serve an important function to hold the king accountable to justice.

Other prophets did not work directly with their monarch but challenged injustice broadly, calling out iniquitous actions of people and rulers who compromised wellness in their land and acted against their god.[34] Often, these critiques fell more specifically on upper classes and rulers, those who had power to sway justice against the marginalized. For example, Isaiah critiqued oppression, specifically with upper classes in view (Isa 1, 3, 5, and 10). Ezekiel also addressed the ruling class, including specific references to ruling kings (Ezek 32 and 34). Micah 3 critiqued the exploitation of people in both rural and urban settings. Jeremiah addressed the king (Jer 22) and officials and priests (Jer 34). The prophets also critique people as a whole

---

32. Mesopotamian texts indicate the intention of legal codes is to ensure widespread peace, and Bovati's analysis of the Hebrew Bible lawsuit, or rîb, confirmed that justice promotes societal equanimity. Bovati, *Re-establishing Justice*, 19.

33. See Silver for a description of economic conditions in the ancient Near East and the prophets' response in the social world. Silver, *Prophets and Markets*.

34. In *Contending for Justice*, Houston focused on the role of the prophets to cry out on behalf of injustice. Houston, *Contending for Justice*.

(Jer 5, 7, 34, and Ezekiel), as well as individuals who failed to protect the cause of the marginalized in their society.[35]

Prophets were advocates for justice, commissioned by divine right, whether serving directly under the king or crying out from the periphery. The right to advocate for justice is not merely the purview of the weak and disadvantaged, but advocates for justice rise up among ruling classes as well as from the perimeter.

Justice Advocacy

Early descriptions of rulers whose concern was justice included a promise to eliminate *cries for justice*. The welfare and wholeness of society was the greatest mission of a ruling authority in the ancient world, yet textual evidence demonstrates that complaints of injustice persisted throughout the ancient Near East. The Hebrew Bible's account alone provides insight into the struggles of an entire marginalized people living in the greater Mediterranean world; however, it also describes their struggle to maintain order and care for the marginalized among their own.

Mesopotamian kings founded what it means to establish justice by ridding the world of evil, eliminating violence and enmity, until there are no more cries for justice. The prologue to the laws of Ur-Namma of Ur, dated to ca. 2100 BCE, includes a self-description in which the monarch claims to have established justice in the land when he "eliminated enmity, violence, and cries for justice."[36] A similar claim is made in a tablet dated more than a century later. The prologue to the laws of Lipit-Ishtar of Isin, dated to 1930 BCE, includes a self-description in which the monarch promises "to establish justice in the land, to eliminate cries for justice, to eradicate the enmity and armed violence, to bring well-being to the lands of Sumer and Akkad."[37] Furthermore, and most commonly cited, is the prologue to the laws of Hammurabi of Babylon, dated to ca. 1750 BCE, in which the monarch refers to himself as a shepherd (similar to Lipit-Ishtar and also similar to several of the Hebrew Bible psalms). The laws of Hammurabi provide the most detailed and well-preserved prologue account, and while it does not contain specific language about eliminating the cries for justice, Hammurabi

---

35. Consider also Jer 5:28, which calls out the people for failing to allow judgment for the orphan.

36. Laws of Ur-Namma in two sources: Nippur tablet, col. iv, lines 162–168; Sippar tablet, col. ii, lines 30–39. Hoffner and Michalowski, *Law Collections*.

37. Laws of Lipit-Ishtar, col. i, lines 20–37. Hoffner and Michalowski, *Law Collections*, 25.

claims to "make justice prevail in the land, to abolish the wicked and the evil, to prevent the strong from oppressing the weak, to rise like the sun-god Shamash[38] over all humankind, (and) to illuminate the land."[39] In the epilogue, Hammurabi affirms that he brought obedience to the world, and he "established truth and justice as the declaration of the land . . . enhanced the well-being of the people."[40] Establishing justice was an act sovereign to rulers and held accountable by divine right.

In the Hebrew Bible, Isa 5:7 acknowledges the Mesopotamian view of justice achieved by the elimination of cries for justice. The composer points out the injustice by using similar sounding words for the comparison, which could easily be confused by someone not paying close attention. In the poetic verse, God expects justice and righteousness, מִשְׁפָּט and צְדָקָה, and instead sees מִשְׂפָּח and צְעָקָה, bloodshed and a cry [for justice], The composition draws attention to the seeming lack of distinction between the antithetical behaviors. This is a clear example of a prophet's critique of justice. The book of Job also presents the desperate nature of seeking help by crying out for help. In Job 30:28, the poet is in a state of depression when he makes his way to the assembly to cry out. His appeal is for a just response to suffering. Psalm 82 demonstrates intentional composition of a cry for justice that expounds on the desperate situation of the poor, of the disadvantaged, in such a community. The elimination of cries for justice may be the goal of complete justice, but cries for justice often seem to go unanswered. At least, the literature suggests that even where injustice is addressed, cries for justice do not cease.

The Egyptian King, or Pharaoh, is also seen as an administrator of justice. The Ramisside writings discussed in the previous section point to the importance of justice by caring for the poor as a way of keeping right order, called *ma' at*. In the Hebrew Bible, when Moses and Aaron stand in the presence of the Egyptian king in Exod 5:20 and 7:15, they are taking up a formal attitude of appearance in court, as in a hearing for justice.[41] The response of the Pharaoh to deny that appeal calls into question his ability to uphold *ma' at*, at least according to the account in Exodus.

The text repeatedly points out the hardness in the heart of Pharaoh when he spurns the cries of the slaves to go free. There are three Hebrew

---

38. Shamash is typically associated with divine judgment.

39. Laws of Hammurabi, col. i, lines 27–49. Hoffner and Michalowski, *Law Collections*, 76–77.

40. Laws of Hammurabi, col. v, lines 14–24. Hoffner and Michalowski, *Law Collections*, 80–81.

41. Bovati affirmed this perspective as a model for one type of lawsuit represented in the Hebrew Bible. Bovati, *Re-establishing Justice*, 234.

verbs used to describe the hardening of Pharaoh's heart. The first is from the root קשׁה, meaning "difficult, or hard."[42] The second word is from the root חזק, meaning "strong," which may indicate a hardening or strengthening of Pharaoh's resolve.[43] And, the third is from the root כבד, meaning "heavy."[44] These verbs are used in parallel to describe Pharaoh's inability to let the slaves go. Some scholars have speculated that the hardening of Pharaoh's heart has to do with a kind of heart illness, in which his chest seized up and restricted his activity, even his ability to lead.[45] However, when considering matters of justice, which is essential to the narrative in question, another explanation comes to light.

In Egyptian religion, the Egyptian king is judged at the end of his life to determine whether or not he kept *ma'at* by upholding justice in the land during his rule. Their heart is thought to be weighed by Osiris, the Egyptian god of the underworld, against a feather of light. A heart that weighs lighter than the feather witnessed that the king succeeded in upholding *ma' at* during his reign. A heavy heart, however, indicated failure. It is possible that the references in Exodus to Pharaoh's heart being made strong (like a rock) or heavy is a critique by the writers of Exodus, testifying against the king's ability to uphold justice on their behalf. This further explains the significance of proper justice in an ancient Near Eastern setting.

The relationship between ancient Israelites and their ancient Near Eastern neighbors is the subject of much discussion in scholarship. This will not be tackled in this project as a primary concern, except to say that the influence of larger national powers in Mesopotamia and in Egypt is evident in the Hebrew Bible. The focus of this study on the Psalter fleshes out modes and ideas of societal justice and how these concepts contributed not only to the shaping of Israel's history but to shaping their religion as well. By looking at the language of justice in the Psalter, this study forms conclusions about matters of justice as an ethical exploration. Given the importance of justice in ancient Near Eastern communities, the emphasis on justice language in Psalm 82 represents a significant indicator of implicit ethics.

More specifically, Psalm 82 contains several elements discussed in this section that pertain to justice literature. Psalm 82 has been identified as a prophetic psalm in that it speaks to the issue of a ruling authority which fails to care properly for the poor. The composer advocates for justice in the manner

42. Ex 7:3
43. Ex 7:13, 8:15, 9:35, 10:27 (*yhwh* is subject), 14:8 (*yhwh* is subject)
44. Ex 8:11 (causative), 9:7
45. This is based on a 2009 study of the mummified remains of Egyptian kings, wherein heart specialists determined that some of the monarchs suffered from atherosclerosis, a disease that hardens the walls of the arteries around the heart.

of a prophet, critiquing the ruling authority of failing to uphold justice. This is done by the identification of authorities responsible for judgment, followed by a complaint in the form of a cry for justice on behalf of the poor and marginalized and a request for true justice restored. The psalm then concludes with an appeal for judgment in Ps 82:8, where the ruling authority is asked to stand and restore justice. Psalm 82 has wide ethical appeal in association with the specific language of justice in the ancient Near East. This strengthens the case for reading Psalm 82 as an implicitly ethical text. The language of justice in Psalm 82 is the subject of the detailed study below.

Language of Justice

The approach of this study on justice as ethical is linguistic and literary. By looking at the words used to demand advocacy for the poor in Psalm 82, this study focuses on the intent for justice in the psalm. The words in this study are present in the grammar of Ps 82:3–4 as imperative directives, which is one aspect of implicit ethics in biblical texts.[46] Psalm 82 intends to correct a matter of injustice by asserting right judgment, or justice, on behalf of the marginalized.

The previous chapter looked at the situation of poverty in the ancient Near East and how ancient legislative texts attempted to protect the status of the poor. The Psalter demonstrates that concern for the poor in psalms accessed as liturgical texts. This extends the practice of care for the poor as a just act beyond the wishes of a deity or the duties of a king. The liturgical use of the Psalter presents the matter of justice to a population of worship, extending concern for the poor to human ethical practice.[47] The following analysis of language of justice strengthens that position.

While acts of justice are the primary duty of a ruling authority, by means of the poetic nature of Psalm 82 and its inclusion in the Psalter for liturgical use, the responsibility to act justly extends beyond governing agency and into the broader community. The audience of the psalm participates by means of the openness of the language, which invites engagement. As the psalm is spoken, sung or read, it demands consideration for an ethical response.

There are four imperatives, terms for justice that wrap around the terms for poverty in Ps 82:3–4. They are word sets, two by two, that are commonly witnessed in pairs throughout the Hebrew Bible. In v. 3, the

---

46. Zimmermann, *The Logic of Love*.

47. The Psalter as liturgy useful for ethical teaching is discussed at length by G. Wenham. Wenham, *Psalms as Torah*.

word pair is from the roots affiliated with justice and righteousness: שפט and צדק;[48] and in v. 4, the word pair is from roots more commonly associated with freedom and salvation: פלט and נצל.[49] These word pairings are common to affirmations and critiques of justice in the Hebrew Bible. Psalm 82 is no exception.

Judgment and Righteousness (Psalm 82:3)

The concept of justice is rooted in righteous judgment in the Hebrew Bible. While justice can theoretically exist independent of judgment, the idea of "righteous judgment" is promoted in the text in three ways: 1) Judgment, שפט, can be unjust.[50] As will be demonstrated in the study below, divine intervention is sometimes requested in response to a perceived unjust judgment, 2) God is often appealed to and described as the one who offers not only שפט but offers it uprightly, and 3) those who practice the liturgy of Psalm 82 also take part in affirming right judgment.

In Ps 82:3, the form of the verb שפט is Qal Imperative. *HALOT* includes a lengthy discussion of definition for the verbal root שפט. Its cognates include Akkadian (*šapāṭ/tu(m)*), Ugaritic (*tpṭ*), Amorite (*špṭ*), and Arabic (*safuṭa*), with meanings ranging from to rule, judge or exercise authority, to obtaining justice and administer justice. The verbal root occurs more times in the Psalter than in any other HB book, with the highest concentration in the Asaph psalms (seven occurrences), more than half of those in Psalm 82. The root occurs 32x in the Psalter,[51] approximately

---

48. See earlier discussions of צְדָקָה וּמִשְׁפָּט in this chapter.

49. This parallelism relates to Weinfeld's theories that language of justice in psalms largely refers to freedom of the oppressed. Weinfeld, *Social Justice*, 15.

50. Also consider delayed judgment as an act of injustice (as with the legal maxim: "justice delayed is justice denied"). cf. Mic 6:8, etc.

51. Ps 2:10 issues a warning of wisdom to those who שפט (parallel with מֶלֶךְ). In Ps 7:9, the psalmist appeals to YHWH (who dyn) to שפט him with righteousness and integrity. In Ps 7:12, God is one who שפט righteously. In Ps 9:5, YHWH שפט for the psalmist sitting on a throne (with *tsdk*). In Ps 9:9, YHWH שפט the world and people (with *tsdk* and *yšr*). In Ps 9:20, the psalmist appeals to YHWH to rise up (*qwm*) and שפט the nations. In Ps 10:18, the psalmist appeals to YHWH to judge the orphan and the *dkk* as the earth is terrorized. In Ps 26:1, the psalmist (*dwd*) appeals to YHWH to שפט him for his integrity. In Ps 35:24, the psalmist appeals to YHWH to שפט him because of YHWH's righteousness. In Ps 37:33, YHWH will not abandon the righteous when they are brought to שפט. In Ps 43:1, the psalmist appeals to God to שפט him. In Ps 50:6, God is שפט in righteousness. In Ps 51:6, the psalmist has sinned against God and שפט is justified. In Ps 58:2, right שפט is questioned. Ps 58:12 describes a possibility of a God who שפט on earth. In Ps 67:4, God judges the people rightly. Ps 72:4 is a prayer to God for the king to שפט the rights of the poor and help the oppressed. In Ps 75:3, a

one-sixth of all occurrences in the Hebrew Bible. This is significant because it indicates a prevalent theme in the psalms.

The term שפט is also often compared with another Hebrew term meaning "to judge"—דין. HALOT includes cognates in Ugaritic (*dn*), Akkadian (*d(i)ānu*), Ethiopic, and OS Arabic, to indicate making a case for judgment, or to execute judgment.[52] Clines included a possible definition of "vindicate" or "defend the rights of," which fits as well in the context of Psalm 82.[53] The verbal root דין, appears 20x in the Hebrew Bible and 8x in the Psalter with a similar meaning and use. Both terms can be useful when identifying texts that deal with justice. The שפט verb is common enough that its meaning is clearly tied to acts of right judgment. The appeal in Psalm 82 indicates a clear imperative for ethical action; however, the specifics of carrying out that action is subjective. Each person must consider an individual responsibility. While the range of meanings is broad, for the sake of clarity, I will use *justice* to stand in for שפט in the following analysis.

In the Psalter, YHWH administers *justice* (Ps 7:9; 9:5, 9; 26:1; 35:24; 96:13; 98:9; 148:11), YHWH is called upon to oversee *justice* for the righteous (Ps 37:33), and YHWH is also called upon to save the oppressed, the needy, the orphan and the poor from justice that would lead to death (Ps 109:31). Those who practice *justice* are also called upon to praise YHWH (Ps 148:11). Requests for deliverance from *justice* indicates that sometimes an action of *justice* is unjust.[54] The Psalter affirms a relationship between YHWH and *justice*.

---

first person speaker (poss. God, v.1) offers to judge rightly. In Ps 75:8, God שפט, abasing one and lifting another. In Ps 82:1, God or gods שפט / divine council שפט. In Ps 82:2, the psalmist asks how long שפט will favor the wicked. In Ps 82:3, the psalmist demands that שפט be done for the poor. In Ps 82:8, God/gods called upon to rise (*qwm*) and ש פט the earth. In Ps 94:2, the psalmist appeals to the one who שפט over the earth to lift himself up. In Ps 96:13, YHWH is coming to שפט the earth, and to שפט the people with truth. (X2) In Ps 98:9, YHWH is coming to שפט the earth, and to שפט the people rightly. (X2) In Ps 109:7, the wicked testify against the psalmist in a place of שפט. In Ps 109:31, YHWH saves the needy from those who שפט his soul. In Ps 141:6, the wicked will be שפט. In Ps 148:11, the ones who are שפט over the earth are called upon to praise YHWH. Re: Ps 10:18—Some syntactical problems include the uncertainty of *bl*. Following Craigie, *špt* is parallel with '*rts*. Craigie, *Ugarit*, 123. Is it possible for *bl* to indicate both meanings as a play on words—affirming the former and denying the latter concepts? The translation would be something like: to do justice for the orphan and the weak (certainly) still longer; as men do terror (no) longer, upon the earth.

52. Note the parallel occurrence in Isa 10:2. Bovati also argued for the recognition of אָב as "judge" in the Hebrew Bible, parallel to שפט and דין. This would indicate a progression of titles as societal roles expanded in monarchical Israel. Bovati, *Re-establishing Justice*, 173–4.

53. Clines, *DCH*, 530–36.

54. Bovati discussed the aspects of salvation in escaping a judge. He looked at Ps

The act of *justice* requires wisdom (Ps 2:10) and is qualified by uprightness, צדק, in several psalms.⁵⁵ In some cases, אֱלֹהִים is/are called upon to enact *justice*, or is described as the bringer of *justice* (Ps 7:12, 43:1, 50:6, 58:12, 67:4, 75:1–3, 75:8, 82:8). The אֱלֹהִים is/are also called upon by the psalmist to enact *justice* when the psalmist has sinned (Ps 51:6). The Israelite monarch demonstrates *justice* on behalf of the rights of the poor and oppressed in Ps 72:4. The act of *justice* is often connected to an appeal for compassion on behalf of the poor.⁵⁶ The wicked also practice *justice* when testifying against the psalmist in Ps 109:7. The wicked also practice a form of *justice* in Ps 141:6. Some who practice *justice* favor the wicked in Ps 82:2. This demonstrates that an act of *justice* can be corrupt (in which the English forms *injustice*).⁵⁷ It is the quality of *justice* that distinguishes the wicked from the righteous in the Psalter. The אֱלֹהִים, when seen as an administrator of *justice* in Psalm 82, is accountable to uphold its virtue.

Justice is not condemning, but it is active. While there is a link between justice and innocence, it takes a defensive posture. Bovati and Weinfeld both discussed this aspect of advocacy, noting that judgment in the Hebrew Bible is primarily a defensive action and hardly ever condemns.⁵⁸ "The verb שפט is linked—as a synonym or by association—to verbs that mean to defend, to save and the like; indeed, precisely because the defense action often has as its object the category of the downtrodden, it is often turned into the equivalent of a gesture of compassion."⁵⁹ Those who cry out for judgment often include the innocent and the poor and/or humble. As discussed previously, a cry for justice expects a just response. The absence,

---

109:31 and Job 23:7, 9:15, stating that "judgment—at least implicitly—has the threatening force of a sanction." His findings affirm that there is an aspect of unpredictability when requesting justice. Bovati, *Re-establishing Justice*, 206 ftnt 91.

55. There are eight references specific to upright judgment in the Psalter (Ps. 7:9, 9:5, 9:9, 35:24, 50:6, 58:2, 96:13, 98:9).

56. Bovati came to the same conclusion in his study which analyzes the Hebrew *ryb* to determine that "The verb špt is linked—as a synonym or by association—to verbs that mean to defend, to save and the like; indeed, precisely because the defense action often has as its object the category of the downtrodden, it is often turned into the equivalent of a gesture of compassion." He demonstrated this specifically by presenting examples in the following psalms: Ps 72:2, 4, 12–14 and Ps 83:2–4. Bovati, *Re-establishing Justice*, 203.

57. The Hebrew root שפט may simply refer to either justice or injustice. Like other biblical Hebrew terms that can mean both a word and its opposite, שפט is defined by its context.

58. It is possible, however, that the verb שפט has a more condemning voice in the prophets. Note Bovati's argument about Ezekiel 34:17, 20, 22; 44:2. Bovati, *Re-establishing Justice*, 55, 203, 06. Weinfeld, *Social Justice*.

59. Bovati, *Re-establishing Justice*, 203.

or postponement, of judgment is injustice. Isa 10:2 provides an example of an oppressive judge who writes statutes which result in turning away justice for the poor by robbing them of judgment. This act of injustice has more to do with delayed judgment than with wrongful judgment. As an example of active justice, Ps. 72:1–4 describes God as one who delivers the poor by judging in righteousness. Justice requires an active defense.

In Psalm 82, justice is not correctly served. Justice is handled by those who give priority to the wicked. In vv. 3 and 4, the composition offers a clear solution. The situation of justice will be corrected by proper care for the poor. It is the poor and vulnerable who should be prioritized. This is the ethical message. A similar theme is found in Ps 58:2. The psalmist questions the rights of those who remain silent in truth and offer justice improperly or unfairly. The composition describes the unjust judge as one who makes way for wickedness and violence. Violence and corruption of the earth is also implied in Psalm 58 (as it is in Psalm 82). In both psalms, אֱלֹהִים is called upon to correct the matter (Ps 82:8; Ps 58:7).

There are multiple occurrences of the verb שׁפט in Psalm 82. It is central to the theme and the greater narrative of the composition. Considering its appearances in vv. 1, 2, 3, 8 and corresponding lexical definitions, it is important to consider the range of meaning of the term and its ethical implications. In v. 1, it is a reference to exercise judgment, in vv. 2–3, it is used to condemn the אֱלֹהִים for negligence in judgment, and in v. 8, *HALOT* notes the potential for ambiguity in two meanings: it is used meaning both to judge in a narrow sense and to rule in a wider capacity. The range of meanings and their implications for understanding justice engages the audience to decide what is just and what is their response to injustice.

In Ps 82:3, the form of the verb צדק is hifil imperative. *HALOT*'s definition includes cognates in Amorite and Canaanite (*ṣaduq*), Egyptian Aramaic (*ṣdq*), Ethiopic (*ṣadqa*), Arabic (*ṣadaqa*), with a meaning of just, sincere, right, and truthful. In the hifil, its meaning reflects maintaining the rights or declaring innocence. Clines described condemnation as the opposite of צדק.[60]

The verbal root appears mostly in the book of Job (17x), which, like Psalm 82, includes mythological themes and is introduced with a divine council scene. The root occurs once in the Asaph Psalms and 4x in the Psalter,[61] compared with a total of forty-one occurrences in the Hebrew Bible. In every occurrence in the Psalter, the verb צדק is accompanied by

---

60. Clines, *DCH*, 80.

61. In Ps 19:10, YHWH's judgment is צדק. In Ps 51:6, God is צדק in his words and in justice. In Ps 82:3, the psalmist appeals for צדק and justice on behalf of the poor and lowly. In Ps 143:2, YHWH should not judge because there is no living צדק.

שפט. Justice is an essential aspect of צדק, and it is often a virtue attributed to the deity.

The act of judgment often occurs as an intervention "in defense of someone who is *tsaddîq*, whose rights have been threatened or injured by a *rāšā*."[62] The occurrence of צדק as an adjective qualifies שפט to signify proper judgment, or justice. As a verb, its use is significant to ethical considerations, as it explicates justice as true or right. McCann defends "righteousness" (as well as justice and peace) as central to the theology of the Psalter.[63] Its frequent occurrence in the Psalter suggests its importance to the virtue of order and well-being in society.[64]

Freedom and Salvation (Psalm 82:4)

The words for justice occurring in Ps 82:4 often occur paired elsewhere in the Hebrew Bible. Their meaning is synonymous: to save or set free, though each is nuanced. The first, פלט, indicates wellness, and the second, נצל, indicates freedom for humans. The latter is especially significant to Israelite history because it occurs many times in Exodus to advocate for, and represent, the freedom of slaves from Egypt.

Both terms are significant in assuring the remembrance of Hebrew origins as a people who were delivered out of slavery. Not only is this a theme throughout the Asaph Psalms, but it is a major ethical concern in the Hebrew Bible—freedom and salvation for the oppressed.

In Ps 82:4, the form of the verb פלט occurs in the Piel Imperative. HALOT's definition includes cognates in Aramaic, Ethiopic (*falaṭa*), Ugaritic (*plṭ*), and Akkadian (*šūzubu*, to save; *balāṭu*, to get well, be in good health; *bulluṭu*, to let live, make healthy). It is also linguistically connected to root *mlt* (to flee), which insinuates saving or sparing a human life. The verbal root appears only once in the Asaph Psalms, 19x in the Psalter of 27 total appearances in all of the Hebrew Bible.[65] In the Psalter, the verb occurs nearly

---

62. Bovati, *Re-establishing Justice*, 202.
63. McCann, "Righteousness, Justice, and Peace."
64. See Schmid's focus on righteousness in universal world order. Schmid, "Creation, Righteousness, and Salvation."
65. In Sam 22:2, 44, YHWH gives פלט to the psalmist. In Isa 5:29, pursuers fight as lions, they פלט (carry victims off) so that no one can נצל. [Note the lion connection to Ps 7:3]. Mic 6:14 describes a destitution in which people will try and escape hunger by פלט and even what is פלט will be taken. In Job 21:10, prosperous cattle פלט (deliver?) their calves and are never bereft. In Job 23:7, with the help of an upright person, a judge would פלט (Acquit?). In Ps 17:13, the psalmist appeals to YHWH to פלט his soul from the wicked. In Ps 18:3, YHWH is פלט and provides refuge. In Ps 18:44, YHWH פלט the

JUSTICE CENTERED LANGUAGE IN PSALM 82   157

as many times in the imperative as in any other form. There is a special emphasis on survival and movement away from danger.⁶⁶

The verb פלט is not always used in a positive way. For example, the psalmist appeals for punishment by right of פלט in Ps 56:8. An example of this use can also be seen in Isaiah, where pursuers punish their victims by an act of פלט. However, פלט is synonymous with *rîb* defense (intervention on behalf of . . .) in Ps 43:1,⁶⁷ and is parallel with שפט in Ps 43:1, 82:4. Bovati explained this as an example of a common defense model for a Hebrew *rîb* defense.⁶⁸ This also sheds light on its use in Ps 37:40, where פלט is "parallel with *'zr* as a means of assisting a defense in judgment."⁶⁹ The act of being free can be positive or negative depending on the circumstance. It is likely that this is why Ps 82:4 clarifies the object from which the poor should be made free—the hand of the wicked.

In Ps 82:4, the form of the verb נצל is in the Hifil Imperative. *HALOT*'s definition includes cognates in Arabic (*naṣala*), Ethiopic (*naṣala*), Ammonite (*hṣl' l*), Egyptian Aramaic (הצול), meaning to extract, to draw out. The root appears 3x in the Asaph Psalms, 45x in the Psalter,⁷⁰ and 213x in

---

psalmist from dispute with people.
In Ps 18:49, YHWH פלט the psalmist from enemies. In Ps 22:5, ancestors were פלט by El because of their trust. In Ps 22:9, YHWH will פלט those who commit their cause to the godself. In Ps 31:2, the psalmist appeals to YHWH to פלט him because of YHWH's righteousness. Ps 32:7 describes a place of refuge in which there are prayers? (רן) of פלט. In Ps 37:40, YHWH פלט פלט (Piel Impf 3ms twice) those who take refuge in him. In Ps 40:18, for the psalmist, who is עָנִי וְאֶבְיוֹן, YHWH is פלט. In Ps 43:1, the psalmist appeals to God for פלט from the deceitful and unjust. In Ps 56:8, following v.7 description of those who would take the psalmist's soul, he appeals to God to פלט them for their iniquity. (Note the unusual phrasing in this verse.) In Ps 70:6, the psalmist is עָנִי וְאֶבְיוֹן, and needs YHWH to come quickly as helper and פלט. In Ps 71:2, the psalmist appeals to God's righteousness to פלט. In Ps 71:4, the psalmist appeals to God to פלט from the hand of the wicked. In Ps 82:4, the psalmist appeals for פלט on behalf of the poor and needy. In Ps 91:14, presumably God speaks - those who love God and know the name of God will be פלט. In Ps 144:2, YHWH is blessed as פלט in whom the psalmist may take refuge.

66. The same root appears to sometimes indicate giving birth, and Clines suggests a possible synonym that means "to breed." Clines, *DCH*, 690–92.

67. Bovati, *Re-establishing Justice*, 43.

68. Bovati, *Re-establishing Justice*, 43–44.

69. Bovati, *Re-establishing Justice*. 43–44.

70. In Ps 7:2 the psalmist applies for refuge in YHWH, asking for נצל. In Ps 7:3, pursuers as a lion, tear out the soul of the psalmist who has no one to נצל. Ps 18:1 describes the psalmist as one whom YHWH has נצל. In Ps 18:18, the psalmist claims to be נצל from a mighty enemy and those who hated him, by YHWH. In Ps 18:49, the psalmist is נצל from one who is violent. In Ps 22:9, YHWH נצל those in whom he delights. In Ps 22:21, the psalmist appeals to YHWH to נצל his soul from the sword, from the dog. In Ps 25:20, the psalmist appeals for נצל, parallel with refuge and guard.

the Hebrew Bible. The verbal root appears more than twice as many times in the Psalter as in any other Hebrew Bible text, most of which are in the imperative form, demanding action. This term identifies with a significant theme of salvation that persists throughout Hebrew Bible poetry and narrative. Clines suggested a range of meanings that include rescue, recovery, redemption, etc.; all of which convey an urgent need for assistance.[71] As a hifil, the causative emphasis indicates the involvement of an authoritative and/or powerful being. In the Psalter, appeals for rescue address the deity. The inclusion of נצל in Psalm 82 invokes an invitation to connect the psalm with other texts wherein there is a demand for salvation from some perilous situation for safety.

The verb נצל, like its counterpart, פלט, is synonymous with *rib* defense (intervention on behalf of . . .) in Is 19:20[72] and is parallel with שפט in Ps 72:12, 82:4, and Num 35:24–25 to indicate "judge and save."[73] This is a common intervention in the Hebrew Bible text in response to the complaint

---

In Ps 31:2, the psalmist appeals to be heard, and quickly נצל. In Ps 31:6, the psalmist appeals for נצל from enemies and pursuers. In Ps 33:16, נצל appears in the negative—a king not נצל by a great army. In Ps 33:19, the psalmist appeals to נצל his soul from death. In Ps 34:5, YHWH נצל the psalmist from all fears. In Ps 34:18, the righteous will be נצל from all their troubles. In Ps 34:20, YHWH נצל the righteous. In Ps 35:10, YHWH is praised for uniqueness in נצל the poor. In Ps 39:9, the psalmist appeals to be נצל from all transgression. In Ps 40:14, a prayer to YHWH to נצל the psalmist, and to be quick. In Ps 50:22, those who forget God will have no one to נצל them. In Ps 51:16, an appeal to God from נצל blood guilt. In Ps 54:9, YHWH נצל from every trouble. In Ps 56:14, God נצל the psalmist's soul. In Ps 59:2, there is an appeal by the psalmist to God to נצל from his enemies. In Ps 69:15, the psalmist appeals for נצל from sinking, from enemies, and from the deep waters. In Ps 70:2, there is an appeal to God for נצל. In Ps 71:2, because of righteousness, YHWH should נצל. In Ps 71:11, there is no one to נצל for a person whom God has forsaken. In Ps 72:12, God נצל the poor and needy when they call. In Ps 79:9, the psalmist appeals to God to נצל and forgive. In Ps 82:4, the psalmist appeals for נצל for the poor, needy, etc. In Ps 86:13, the psalmist praises YHWH for נצל his soul from *sheol*. In Ps 91:3, those who dwell in YHWH/s house will be נצל from the snare and from death. In Ps 97:10, YHWH נצל the faithful from the wicked. In Ps 106:43, YHWH נצל the ancestors many times. In Ps 107:6, YHWH נצל those who cried out in their distress. In Ps 109:21, the psalmist appeals on the basis of YHWH's faithfulness for נצל. In Ps 119:43, the psalmist appeals to God to not נצל the word of truth. In Ps 119:170, the psalmist appeals for נצל according to truth. In Ps 120:2, the psalmist appeals for YHWH to נצל him from lying lips. In Ps 142:7, the psalmist appeals to YHWH for נצל from enemies who are too strong. In Ps 143:9, the psalmist appeals to YHWH to נצל from enemies, as he seeks refuge. In Ps 144:7, the psalmist appeals to YHWH to נצל him from mighty waters and from the hand of foreigners. In Ps 144:11, the psalmist appeals to YHWH to נצל him from the hand of foreigners who lie and are false.

71. Clines, *DCH*, 741–44.
72. Bovati, *Re-establishing Justice*, 43.
73. Bovati, *Re-establishing Justice*, 204.

form of "a cry is heard," as found in Neh 9:28, Exod 3:7–8, Ps 18, Ps 107:6, and Is 19:20 wherein the subject is oppressed Israel, and in Ps 72:12–13, where the subject is the poor.[74] Also, in Ps 79:9, נצל is parallel with "helper" as a means of communicating assistance to the defense of judgment.[75] In the prophets, נצל appears to be an action by God to save people, or even a portion of people, from oppression. Notably, in Amos 3:12, the term is used to describe an act of salvation in which only a remnant survives.[76]

The word pairings for actions of justice in Ps 82:3–4 stand out as thematic of divine justice throughout the Hebrew Bible. In the Psalter, these demands echo a familiar expectation of just acts by god and king in the broader ancient Near East. They also echo the prophets continuing advocacy for social and economic reform. In the Psalter, these terms become solidified in a community of worship. Psalm 82 sounds the bell of justice which reminds listeners of prophetic advocacies, of historical interventions, and divine attitudes toward protection of the poor.

Conclusion

Rhetoric about justice that acts on behalf of the poor is not limited to Israelite heritage. It is the purview of the ancient Near Eastern king. Legislative texts center on the divine right of the monarch to ensure that society is fair, and rulings are just. These ideals are reflected in Hebrew Bible texts. Making provision for the poor and caring for the weak is a priority. However, justice is not often upheld well by a king or the council of elders. Prophetic literature shows a critique against wrongful justice efforts of the ruling classes, and in some cases, confronts the monarch directly. The Psalter contains texts of a prophetic nature as well, asserting language of justice that provides advocacy and defense for the poor, emphasizing the corruption of the powerful who take advantage of them. Justice language in the Hebrew Bible is often associated with acts of advocacy for the poor and advocacy of justice.

The Psalter affirms the duties and responsibilities of the ancient Near Eastern monarch, bringing to light matters of justice in a liturgical context, which, as discussed earlier, distributes ethical themes among a broad audience. While many explorations of social justice in the Psalter focus on legislative

---

74. Bovati, *Re-establishing Justice*, 324–25.

75. Bovati, *Re-establishing Justice*, 337.

76. See Houston's treatment of Amos as rhetorical commentary on social justice. He noted that נצל appears in Amos where other synonyms for salvation are expected. Houston, *Contending for Justice*, 72.

justice, limiting the responsibilities of ethics to the role of the monarch,[77] those in the community of worship who recite and practice the liturgy of the psalms subsume the ethical responsibilities therein for themselves.[78] The nature of the Psalter as liturgical is a conduit by which the ethical responsibilities of the authority is redistributed to the broader community, especially where it is clear that the authority figures or presumed administrators of justice are corrupt. Then, those who practice the liturgy of the Psalter become accountable to the text and to their community. Right justice described in Psalm 82 offers an aspect of support for reading the psalm as implicitly ethical according to Zimmermann's *Organon* model.

Inclusion of justice advocacy language in the Psalter implies that all members of society who hear and recite a psalm become active participants in its message.[79] The invitation to participate in the complaint and appeal for justice in Psalm 82 is available to everyone. Unambiguous assertions of just action on behalf of the marginalized are sharply contrasted with ambiguous language elsewhere in Psalm 82. While ambiguity in the psalm makes way for a wide readership, the emphasis on justice makes a universal appeal to care for the poor. The language of justice offers up an ethical critique of leadership and power structures which, through the composition, becomes accessible beyond the limits of society's entitled and elite. The psalm does not conform to hegemonic portrayals that esteem leaders without question. Instead, Psalm 82 encourages readers to engage critically with an evaluation of justice. This is why the text may also be considered resistance literature as it is received in a Second Temple compilation.

---

77. Grant, *The King as Exemplar*. Houston, *Contending for Justice*, 149. J. Clinton McCann, "Righteousness, Justice, and Peace." Mein, *Ezekiel*.

78. Wenham, *Psalms as Torah*.

79. Wenham, *Psalms as Torah*.

6

Psalm 82 and Psalmic Hermeneutics

"The most powerful movement of feeling with a liturgy is the prayer which seeks for nothing special, but is a yearning to escape from the limitations of our own weakness and an invocation of all Good to enter and abide with us." —Mary Ann Evans, A.K.A. George Eliot, novelist and poet

THE PREVIOUS CHAPTERS HAVE demonstrated an awareness of the linguistic and conceptual connections between Psalm 82 and broader ancient Near Eastern concerns for justice advocacy of the marginalized. What does this mean for how Psalm 82 should be understood in light of psalmic hermeneutics? Before this thesis continues its exploration of the compositional quality of Psalm 82, we step back to look at the broader hermeneutic implications of such a focused study. This chapter will explore how Psalm 82 may function as liturgy and an ethical composition by looking at indeterminacy within the Psalter and how a formative liturgical practice may impact the reader of psalms, such as Psalm 82, in which such a practice opens readers to a significant ethical message.

Indeterminacy of Psalms and the Psalter

Given the social historical setting of the Psalter as a collection of poems formed within a relatively small ancient Near Eastern social context, it is not surprising that many psalms address and model advocacy for the marginalized. Putting the canonical Psalter aside to examine the efficacy of a single psalm encourages the examination of psalms as individual texts in order to gain a better understanding of the composition's ethical impact. This approach provides insight into how a reader may be influenced by such a text wherever, or whenever, the reader is situated.

The interpretation of an individual psalm is complex. There are multiple facets to consider. Traditional academic approaches to psalms have varied significantly, as is reflected in the variety of approaches to interpreting Psalm 82 which were discussed in Chapter One. In past scholarship, the Psalter has been approached as a book of songs, it has been considered as a collection of collections, or books, and it has also been read as an evolving collection of individual poems. This section will explore means by which a single psalm may be read independently as a poetic composition, as we have done in this thesis with Psalm 82.

Past scholarship has attempted to situate Psalm 82 in various historical or theological contexts in order to make sense of certain aspects, aiming to find particular meaning. These attempts have limited the scope of reading for the psalm, not allowing the composition to speak openly and fully on its own merit. Psalmic hermeneutics must take seriously reading a psalm as a discrete poetic text in order to discover what message emerges from a text-internal dynamic of the psalm. When reading Psalm 82 as such an independent poetic composition, an ethical tenor emerges.

Historically, psalms interpretation scholarship has focused on form-critical approaches. Notable contributions include Hermann Gunkel's description of psalms as praise[1] and Westermann's proposal to further clarify the distinctions of praise and lament in the Psalter.[2] These approaches have shaped the way meaning is sought in the psalms. One problem with this approach occurs when a psalm does not fit neatly into pre-conceived categories. An example of this is Nasuti's determination that Psalm 82 does not fit into a clear and recognized tradition-history category.[3] The danger of forcing such conventions upon a text is that the meaning of a text may become discounted, obliged to fill a pre-conceived shape, rather than speak for itself in a full reading. It is understandable to try and avoid a reading that may be controversial, contradictory, or confrontive, but it is worse to discount a composition for the sake of conforming it to an established ideal. There are many approaches that may be followed in psalms interpretation, but this thesis has moved beyond the question of how Psalm 82 fits into the Psalter and explores its content independently.

In recent years, psalms scholarship has tended to view the Psalter as a single unit, made up of smaller sections, or books, that can be arranged on the basis of particular criteria. For example, Gerald H. Wilson argued for the arrangement of the Psalter as a meaningful editorial contribution to categorize

---

1. Gunkel, *The Psalms*.
2. Westermann, *Praise and Lament in the Psalms*.
3. Nasuti, *Tradition History*. Also see chapter one for a more in depth discussion.

psalms.⁴ In more recent scholarship, Frank-Lothar Hossfeld and Erich Zenger painted a complex image of the Psalter's origins. In the 2005 Hermeneia commentary, they proposed that the history of the shape of the Psalter can best be compared to the origins of the Pentateuch. They asserted that the Psalter is a collection of partial Psalters brought together across a large span of time.⁵ While the shape of the Psalter is not part of this thesis, how the Psalter is conceived shapes the way scholars have read individual psalms.

Another trend in psalms scholarship is the classification of psalms based on genre categories. One such classification is that of the nominal *Elohistic Psalter*, a system of classification which has been attractive to scholars drawn to relatable theories like the Documentary Hypothesis. The *Elohistic Psalter* demonstrates a neat attempt to justify the multiple occurrences of אֱלֹהִים in various psalms. However, recent scholarship has increasingly questioned the value of such a category for interpreting psalms. For example, Hossfeld and Zenger wrote an article that provides an in-depth analysis of some of the particulars of the *Elohistic Psalter* theory, which will not be repeated here. They called the classification into question. Their skepticism was revealed in what they referred to as "the 'dogma' of a so-called Elohistic redaction."⁶ Their conclusion appealed for broader considerations for how אֱלֹהִים occurs in the Pentateuch, especially in Genesis.⁷ This thesis has responded to such an appeal by considering a different, broader semantic range of אֱלֹהִים, especially in how it occurs in the Psalter. The approach taken in this thesis may contribute to the address of some particular concerns, like the number of "exceptions" in the *Elohistic Psalter* where the tetragrammaton occurs.

There have been many other theories and contributions to classifying psalms which are explained in a number of Psalms commentaries. As approaches to interpretation moved away from historical-critical settings, they continued to confine psalms to acceptable literary traditions. In *Interpreting the Psalms: An Exegetical Handbook*, Mark D. Futato argued that the composition of certain psalms encourage them to be read and understood in certain classifications of genre. Futato grouped psalms according to textual features, so that some psalms are seen as *hymns*, others as *laments*, others as *psalms of confidence*, and so on. His view demonstrates one method of reading and classifying psalms according to a definitive set

---

4. Wilson, *The Editing of the Hebrew Psalter*.
5. Hossfeld and Zenger, *Psalms 2*.
6. Hossfeld and Zenger, "The So-Called Elohistic Psalter," 37.
7. Hossfeld and Zenger, "The So-Called Elohistic Psalter," 51.

of features.[8] However, it should be noted here that the history of psalms reception is not a primary concern of this thesis. For the purpose of this chapter, what follows is a brief discussion of how and why a psalm, such as Psalm 82, should be examined individually as an ethical text. This will be explored in terms of psalmic indeterminacy as a means of reading a psalm as an independent poetic composition.

Current scholarship has accepted that individual psalms may be considered indeterminate, a term used to describe a psalm as an individual unit which may be read independent of the Psalter.[9] Indeterminacy of the psalms indicates that it is unnecessary to bind a psalm to a particular historical setting, or even to a pre-determined literary genre. An example of how this can be useful to psalmic hermeneutics was described by Patrick D. Miller in *Interpreting the Psalms*. Miller explored how psalms are best read without a specific adherence to a *Sitz im Leben*, especially when considering the liturgical influence of a psalm.[10] Miller's work anticipates a discussion of indeterminacy by alluding to the diachronous nature of liturgical texts. He contended that the continued use of psalms in communal liturgy demonstrates an openness to reading a psalm in light of one's own experience. Miller proposed that reading a psalm in a liturgical fashion allows the psalm to transcend its heritage.[11] The result of Miller's proposal is that psalms may address expressions of human experience in a social context other than the one in which it was originally composed, allowing the text-internal dynamic to emerge on its own merit. This thesis follows in reading Psalm 82 as a complete and discrete poem by means of which an ethical message materializes.

David J. A. Clines explored modes of indeterminacy in biblical scholarship more broadly, but he found an application in the psalms that compliments Miller's advocacy for a context-oriented reading. Clines sought to expand a consideration of what is meant by a word or phrase by defining what *cannot* be meant by that word or phrase.[12] For a fuller discussion of the role of indeterminacy in perceived meaning of a text, turn to his chapter *Varieties of Indeterminacy*, where the author presents a multitude of scenarios where biblical texts seem to convey various meanings.[13] Clines' contribution in this article is to present various approaches to discovering

8. Futato, *Interpreting the Psalms*, 139–182.
9. Grant, "Determining the Indeterminate," 3–14.
10. Miller, *Interpreting the Psalms*, 22–23.
11. Miller. *Interpreting the Psalms*, 22.
12. Clines, "Varieties of Indeterminacies."
13. Clines, "Varieties of Indeterminacies."

meaning in a biblical text, while not insisting on determined modes of meaning for interpretation. Overall, he contended that what may be determinate or indeterminate is subjective to the reader. Clines' article does more to explain the problem of determinacy than to unlock a clear method of indeterminacy. However, in psalms scholarship, Clines suggested that indeterminacy can provide a means by which a psalm may be imagined as read by or presented in a particular social group. The example he described is a reading of Psalm 2 where a marginalized people he called "Moabite" may be making an appeal for freedom from the Israelite king, their captor.[14] This he referred to as context-dependent commentary.

The significance of this approach is in what is not revealed in the composition. As Clines pointed out, the term "Moabite" is never used. However, when imagining this psalm used in an ancient context, historical information fills in the gaps of what a reader might have expected in an ancient setting. The indeterminacy of the psalm, which is to say, certain information that is not revealed, makes way for a reader in another time period to place themselves or their people, or their "captors," in the psalm. Conceptual indeterminacy not only allows a text, like Psalm 82, to be read with consideration of context regardless of its tradition-history or its canonical placement, but it encourages active participation in a present context.

While the term "indeterminacy" is recent in regard to psalmic hermeneutics, the approach considered in Clines' article is not. More than a decade earlier, Meir Sternberg described a process of "gap filling" as a technique by which the reader fills the gaps of understanding based on an understood context.[15] Sternberg supported the holding of alternative readings for interpretation, which is often the result of compositional ambiguity. It should be noted that indeterminacy is not the same as ambiguity. Whereas indeterminacy in the psalms opens the text to contextual interpretations that vary depending on time and personal experience, ambiguity is limited by the composition. The composition of a text controls the range of possible ambiguity, a subject which will be more specifically examined in the next chapter.

Jamie A. Grant took on the question of how indeterminacy provides hermeneutical access to interpreting psalms as liturgy.[16] Grant discussed the merits of an historical setting as largely relegated to scholarly tradition with a recent trend toward acknowledging uncertainty. This trend has revealed an opportunity to consider indeterminacy in psalms. "This indeterminacy should be embraced hermeneutically and never removed by

---

14. Clines, "Varieties of Indeterminacies," 134–35.
15. Sternberg, *Poetics*.
16. Grant, "Determining the Indeterminate."

over-confident claims of historical certainty."[17] Grant's argument provides support for prioritizing an independent ethical reading of Psalm 82, which has been explored in this thesis.

The poetic expressions of individual psalms can reflect an individual experience. Psalmic indeterminacy invites the reader of Psalm 82 to participate in the psalm within their own context. The indeterminacy of psalms encourages an acceptance of each composition as a true unique expression of their composer(s). Grant's recent analysis of psalmic laments focused on the reality of human experience and expression in psalmic poetry.

> The indeterminacy of the psalms means that we are, in a sense, obliged as readers to accept the poets' assessment of their own reality. They are privileged with information that we do not have and our position as 'reader' is to experience that which they have experienced through their poetic expressions of joy and despair. Part of the 'implied contract' between poet and reader is not to query what lies behind the text, but rather to accept that their words are in fact (an) honest and appropriate response to the realities that they faced.[18]

The hermeneutic value of accepting a poetic composition as an authentic expression by the composer is that the ethical expression can then be repeated in an entirely different time period with a similar appeal. For example, returning to Clines' Psalm 2 reading, where he imagined a Moabite perspective, in another social context, may reflect the perspective of another captive or victimized people. The context-dependent indeterminate reading allows for the psalm to apply in various situations with a sense of "fill in the blank" victim and "fill in the blank" captor.[19]

Indeterminacy of psalms is a methodology for psalmic hermeneutics that supports an independent evaluation of Psalm 82 with consideration to any particular contexts where the composition might have been used or received. It was made clear in Chapter One that scholars have had a difficult time binding Psalm 82 to a particular tradition history or historical compositional tradition. The current scholarly trend toward indeterminacy within the Psalter opens the door to an independent evaluation of Psalm 82 as a composition with intentional ambiguous features in the text that allows for its admittance into various settings across time. The liturgical use of these psalms opens these texts to a wide range of readers and social contexts.

17. Grant, "Determining the Indeterminate," 13.
18. Grant. "The Hermeneutics of Humanity," 190.
19. This also works in concert with the cross-cultural and cross-temporal effect of ethical values in mythological texts as discussed in chapter three.

Chapters 2, 3, 4, and 5 of this thesis have explored multiple facets of the psalm's composition and ancient Near Eastern literary heritage. So far, we have examined the socio-linguistic context of poverty and justice, and the *mythoi* relative to the potential social origins of the composition. These facets contribute to understanding the virtues reflected in Psalm 82 as they may have been read in an ancient *cultus*. The ethical implications of the composition itself cannot be untied from the narratives of human experience and the socio-linguistic connections that link them. Psalm 82 is firmly connected with the experience of oppression and elitism of the gods or rulers in the ancient world. Conceptually, oppression and elitism are universal to humanity. Such a message is arguably intended to relate a moral appeal across a wide range of time and space. The psalmic hermeneutic of indeterminacy opens the psalm to allow for implicit ethics to materialize within the reader's own context, especially given a liturgical application.

In practice, the liturgical function of such a psalm is more useful than a determined setting as a means for a theological hermeneutic. Liturgy is a ritual performance that brings the psalm into the experience of a community who encounters it in their practice. The liturgy contributes to shaping the person as they experience the expression of the poet's composition. For this reason, literary and poetic features of Psalm 82 become important in making out what meanings may be extracted by a reader (of the text) or an audience (of the spoken performance).

In 2014, Brent A. Strawn made a case for revisiting Psalm 82 as an independent poem, stating "the poetry of Psalm 82 . . . is manifestly *present*."[20] He strongly contended against exacting an historical placement for Psalm 82 as a means of interpretation, stating that "most treatments of Psalm 82 have gone awry precisely in their underestimation of the psalm's nature as poetry . . . scholars have typically been obsessed with the psalm's presumed fit in the (reconstructed) *sic* historical development of Israelite religion."[21] As an example, Strawn directly confronted Ackerman's attempts to reconstruct a *Sitz im Leben* as an unwarranted and misleading presumption. By rejecting these approaches to interpretation, Strawn's argument for considering Psalm 82 as an independent poetic composition fits well with hermeneutics of indeterminacy and with the approach taken in this thesis.

Strawn's appeal for Psalm 82's poetic provenance as the key to interpretation is fueled by his claim that scholars have attempted to force particular readings upon the psalm in order to "extract a confession" and

---

20. Strawn, *The Poetics of Psalm 82*, 46.
21. Strawn, *The Poetics of Psalm 82*, 23.

find out what the psalm "really means."²² Strawn described scholarship as ignoring the poetic function of Psalm 82, stating that "the continuing variation (quite wide at many points) *sic* among scholarly interpretations demonstrates the uncertain nature of the 'assured results' of (overly) *sic* historicized approaches."²³ On the other hand, an unbound reading of Psalm 82 allows for Strawn to pursue his interpretation of the psalm based on its poetic quality. Strawn's article focused on interpreting v. 5, but his argument supported a poetic reading of Psalm 82 that requires reflection on the variance of meaning and the influence of language about the poor and matters of injustice upon the reader.

This thesis has sought to address concerns which Strawn brought to light by focusing on Psalm 82 as an independent poem, but instead of focusing solely on poetic features, we have explored the text-internal dynamics of Psalm 82 in order to read the text fully and allow an ethical message to emerge. This opens up possibilities for other such approaches. Given indeterminacy as an hermeneutic method, psalms may be read wholly within their context, so long as the text is allowed to speak for itself without being harnessed to an historical setting where it is not necessary.

In the first several chapters, this thesis has examined the meaning and use of language in Psalm 82 as it may have impacted ancient Near Eastern readers in their conceptual sphere of existence. The next section of this chapter will briefly look into how the language and poetics of Psalm 82 may influence a modern reader ethically, with particular focus on the use of Psalm 82 in liturgy.

Why Should We Read Liturgical Psalms Ethically?

The study of linguistic and cultural connections between Psalm 82 and other ancient Near Eastern literature demonstrates commonalities of virtue in the ancient world. Religious liturgy was not exclusive to the ancient Israelites, but they clearly adopted the practice as an essential part of their *cultus*. The Psalter is a container for songs and prayers that get at the substance of an Israelite practice of worship. Psalm 82 must be considered important to the liturgical function because it is included in the Hebrew Psalter.

Gordon Wenham's *Psalms as Torah* is based on the premise that the Psalter is a collection of psalms which encourage implicit responses as much as they encourage participation. His argument relied on the use of speech act theory to demonstrate the relationship between performance and action

22. Strawn, *The Poetics of Psalm 82*, 23, 46.
23. Strawn, *The Poetics of Psalm 82*, 46.

on the part of the reader. He asserted that an agenda is set by the leader of prayers or songs in a community that establishes the virtue of what is being prayed or sung. The congregant's collective response, often an "amen," affirms the teaching.[24] It is the same for the psalms. Each psalm may become useful in a liturgical setting to act as a prayer or song to require a response of agreement from the congregation. Wenham's book offers an exploratory look at the psalms for potential as a source of biblical ethics that has yet to be drawn on sufficiently in the field of psalmic hermeneutics.

Wenham opened his study with a focus on how psalms are received in various historical and literary settings, beginning with how psalms are referenced in other Hebrew Bible texts as well as in early Christianity. After summarizing how psalms have been useful throughout the years,[25] he concluded that psalms were used in worship, during and in place of sacrifices, during and before battles, and for moral appeals. By the fourth century, psalms were used by Christians for worship, and it was a practice to memorize psalms for recitation.[26] After his review on critical scholarship of the psalms, he clarified that for a study of ethics of psalms, it is the use of the psalms in the cult that gives shape to ethical formation.[27] This brings the ethical nature of psalms in alignment with theories of indeterminacy. We may conclude that ethical readings of the psalms do not depend on tradition-history conclusions, nor does critical scholarship depend on the shape of the Psalter.

Wenham contended that psalms were meant to be memorized and that this was, in part, how a psalm shaped a person. He described how important memorization was to early human societies by presenting evidence that ancient scribes were trained to memorize compositions as well as write them down. He provided epistolary evidence that classical Greek scholars memorized epic poetry, and there was a recognized practice of memorization and related music.[28] He noted three features that support his assumption that psalms were meant to be memorized: "(1) the poetic form of the psalms, (2) musical accompaniment, and (3) thematic macrostructures."[29] By means of form, structure, and clues to musical influence, Wenham concluded that psalms were memorized and sung as religious texts for the purpose of

---

24. Wenham, *Psalms as Torah*, 3–4.
25. Wenham followed Holladay's research. Holladay, *The Psalms*.
26. Wenham, *Psalms as Torah*, 11–26.
27. Wenham, *Psalms as Torah*, 40.
28. Wenham, *Psalms as Torah*, 44.
29. Wenham, *Psalms as Torah*, 49–50.

"enculturation" by dissemination.[30] This argument is important to understanding why and how psalmic liturgy can shape a person ethically.

Wenham also made a connection between prayer and ethics. His main discussion relied on the participation of the reader in the message conveyed by the psalm. Wenham dedicated much of his argument to recognizing the performance element of reciting psalms. It is through participation that psalms are influential in ethical formation, and this is the basis for Wenham's appeal to read psalms as ethical.[31] He discussed gaps in the poetry as a means of invitation to the reader as a participant to fill in the gaps, or in some cases, where the poetry is unclear (or perhaps ambiguous), the reader would puzzle connections and meaning based on experience.[32] While Wenham did not use the term "indeterminacy," he did mention that it is unnecessary to be concerned for a precise *Sitz im Leben*. This description comes close to the earlier discussion of context-dependent indeterminacy by Clines.[33]

Wenham's work looked at what psalms may mean ethically in their received form rather than considering them bound to an historical setting. His presentation relies on a view of the Psalter as a book which opens with an instructional text (Ps. 1), and contains psalms praising the law. Wenham provided several examples of psalms that encourage meditation on the law. He also noted an alignment of psalmic virtues with Judeo-Christian values,[34] especially in Psalm 119, which is the main focus of his discussion about the conceptual nature of law in the Psalter.[35] He also gave several examples where psalms align with Torah passages and concepts about ethical matters, like the decalogue,[36] matters of violence,[37] retribution,[38] and exploitation.[39] He also detailed a number of examples where narrative law from the Torah appears to be reflected in various psalms. This, Wenham stated, is a

---

30. Wenham, *Psalms as Torah*, 56. See also Hye Lee, "The Psalter."
31. Wenham, *Psalms as Torah*, 76.
32. Wenham, *Psalms as Torah*, 62.
33. In the previous section of this chapter.
34. This is explored even more fully in Wenham's chapter 10, with the New Testament's use of psalms for moral appeal. Wenham, *Psalms as Torah*, 181–82.
35. Wenham, *Psalms as Torah*, 77–78.
36. Wenham, *Psalms as Torah*, 98–99.
37. Wenham, *Psalms as Torah*, 110–11.
38. Wenham, *Psalms as Torah*, 112–13.
39. Wenham, *Psalms as Torah*, 115–16.

"poetic reformulation of the Pentateuch's grand narrative,"[40] which supports an overall biblical ethic to live a righteous life.

Wenham went on to explore terminology of the wicked and the righteous in psalms to describe good and bad behavior. His study revealed concrete examples of how psalms might shape a person ethically as they recite, sing, or memorize psalms. The unpleasant image of the wicked is meant to deter the reciter of the psalms from imitating them, whereas the reverse applies to the descriptions of the righteous, which are intended to encourage righteous behavior. This is underlined by the parallels drawn between God's attitudes and actions and those of the righteous.[41]

Wenham referred to righteous virtues as sympathetic to those of modern readers, with a focus on kindness, honesty, and reliability.[42] In special consideration for the exceptional, Wenham also addressed psalms of lament. Especially where certain psalms seem to prioritize a retaliatory or vengeful response, psalms can seem unvirtuous. However, Wenham appealed to the ethical inflection of prayer in these "imprecatory psalms," where the underlying premise is a complete trust in God's sovereignty and the result is a model by the psalmist to "trust in God to vindicate them rather than take revenge themselves."[43] This may be evidence of an implicit ethic that supports both the liturgical function of the Psalter as well as an instruction about dependence on God.

Wenham's presentation of the psalms as indeterminate in such a way as can be useful for conveying ethics by memorization and recitation supports this thesis in its view of Psalm 82 as an ethical composition that entices those who read it as liturgy to wrestle with the text and its meaning. Wenham did not bring Psalm 82 into his study, but his presentation of the many psalms which deal with language about poverty, justice, and righteousness suggests that there is more work to be done in bringing individual psalms into a discussion about ethical "oughts." The performative features of a practiced liturgy encourage a reader to engage fully with the text. The significance of the text-internal dynamics in the psalm comes to bear upon the person when the words of the text flow through the mouth of the reader. When the psalm is read as liturgy, the meaning is formative in the reader.

The implications of ethical teaching by means of functional liturgy are implicit. This might explain the apparent lack of scholarship on psalms and ethics, which Wenham noted in his book, listing recent works on

---

40. Wenham, *Psalms as Torah*, 137.
41. Wenham, *Psalms as Torah*, 165.
42. Wenham, *Psalms as Torah*, 167.
43. Wenham, *Psalms as Torah*, 179. See also Firth, *Surrendering Retribution*.

biblical ethics that did not feature the psalms as a main source of ethics, even where liturgy was considered.[44] The Psalter, however, has a long history of being used as liturgy. Historical evidence paints a picture describing how psalms were sung and recited in an ancient setting. Second Temple Period Judah and Jewish Synagogue practices record the use of psalms in everyday prayers as well as particular psalms on special occasions.[45] Many psalms are included in a similar religious use today. *The Book of Common Prayer*, for example, moves through the Psalter according to a liturgical calendar. Constituents of faith are encouraged to read through the Psalter each year. The practice of reading psalms and repetition of the pattern works as a form of enculturation.

There is a connection between liturgy and ethics that is discovered by practice. D. E. Saliers described this link as not causal, but "conceptual and intrinsic."[46] The act of praying or singing psalms forges in a person the belief in its meaning—*lex orandi, lex credendi*—what is said (is) what is believed. Saliers's description lines up with Wenham's biblical study, making sense of a practice of prayer that intends to shape a person. Ethics are formed in a person as a result of the practice as ritual. Reading and praying psalms results in a practice of belief.

Saliers also recognized that there is a link between the ethics shaped through the practice of liturgy and the narratives that emerge from human experience. He believed the former depends upon the latter. An understanding of the implicit ethics formed in a person by the liturgy is made complete by the person's awareness of social narratives, by means of which, "a picture of the moral good and associated ideas are expressed."[47] More than expressing a religious duty, participating in the performance of liturgy shapes the person who practices. Saliers described the practice of liturgy as primary to demonstrating the development of one's own character.

The ritual of performing psalms as liturgy reorients the participant to accept the implicit ethics in their present world view.[48] This can also be applied from an external perspective in order to gain insight into multiple and complex connections between what Saliers referred to as liturgy and the moral life.[49] By understanding the social narratives, or what Saliers called, the *mythoi* of a community, the poetics of a psalm reveals how it

---

44. Wenham, *Psalms as Torah*, 5–6.
45. Wenham, *Psalms as Torah*, 6.
46. Saliers, *Liturgy and Ethics*, 174.
47. Saliers, *Liturgy and Ethics*, 175.
48. Saliers, *Liturgy and Ethics*, 179.
49. Saliers, *Liturgy and Ethics*, 174–75, 187.

may function ethically for a particular social group. For Psalm 82, the connections inherent to a relative ancient Near Eastern mythical narrative was explored in Chapter Three. Since ancient Ugaritic texts have long been considered in connection with particular Hebrew Bible passages, the conceptual and thematic commonalities between the *Epic of Aqhat* and Psalm 82 support Saliers' statement that "there is an internal, *conceptual* link between liturgy and ethics."[50]

It is not only the understanding of the liturgy that shapes a person, but the act of renewal by repetition. Stephen Platten described the influence of liturgy as mimesis, a term used by both Plato and Aristotle in regard to how nature is reflected. In Platten's description, mimesis is the means by which a person must be influenced by a scriptural liturgy. There is an implicit engagement in the performance of liturgy that involves a person so that even the refusal to participate implies a level of engagement (or disengagement, as could be the case).[51] Platten determined that the performance of liturgy not only renews the person, but in the process, the text is also renewed by the practice of its reading.[52] It is approached anew and re-asserted as fresh each time it is read. The performance of a text not only shapes the person, but it shapes the practice. By the process of mimesis, the text renews and is renewed by the reader. Platten compared this to the popularity of Handel's *Messiah* at Christmas and other traditions, stating, "such texts do not become worn by repetition, but instead, "re-inhabited" by rehearsal, owned by those who perform them through mimesis."[53] The inclusion of Psalm 82 in early Israelite practices, its inclusion in the Hebrew Psalter, and its inclusion in modern liturgies suggest the composition is influential for ethical formation.

Conclusion

A presumption of indeterminacy in the Psalter supports and encourages reading Psalm 82 as an independent ethical composition. It acknowledges a practice of reading individual psalms and considering a context-dependent message that does not rely on a determined *Sitz im Leben*. This manner of psalmic hermeneutic informs how the message of a psalm shapes its reader through formational liturgy.

---

50. Saliers, *Liturgy and Ethics*, 174.
51. Platten, *Animating Liturgy*, 105–109.
52. Platten, *Animating Liturgy*, 110.
53. Platten, *Animating Liturgy*, 111.

The influence of a formal liturgy upon its practitioner is an infusion of implicit ethics. The specific nature of the ethical influence may be determined by the language of a psalm, its social orientation, or its cultural allusions. In the case of Psalm 82, its mythological provenance, for example, gives insight into its social orientation and its cultural affectation. The language of the composition demonstrates a text-internal dynamic that focuses on ethical themes such as righteousness and justice. Particular ambiguities in the text complement an indeterminate reading that relies on and validates the context of the reader.

Psalm 82 may be read in a formative liturgical practice to reaffirm ethical values about corruption in leadership and the importance of caring for the marginalized. Following hermeneutic methods presented in this chapter, Psalm 82 may be read in light of its possible origins in an early Northern Levantine cultic setting, it may also be read in consideration of ethical influences in the Second Temple Judaic setting of its compilation, and it may be considered an ethics-shaping psalm in a modern liturgical practice. The indeterminate nature of psalms makes it possible to consider the ethical message of a psalm and also explore that ethical influence throughout its heritage, rather than binding the psalm to a particular time and location without consideration of its continued effectiveness.

7

Ambiguity as Means for Resistance

"History is written by the rich, and so the poor get blamed for everything."
—Jeffrey D. Sachs, economist

AMBIGUITY IN PSALM 82 allows the reader to accept some of the difficulties in the text and focus more clearly on the socio-ethical situation: the relationship between the poor, the wicked, justice, and its oversight. Deliberate ambiguity reveals non-ambiguous phrases. Whereas ambiguity is often linguistically playful, unambiguous language sits in somber contrast. Ambiguity invites an audience to participate in the text from different perspectives, while unambiguous phrases settle the audience with implicit ethical morality. The contrast between ambiguous phrases and unambiguous phrases contributes to the way an audience is influenced by the text. In Psalm 82, the introduction invites a diverse audience, and then points them toward a clear ethic of concern for the poor.

Ambiguity in the Hebrew Bible

There is a rising interest in ambiguity in the Hebrew Bible. Recent reflections include ambiguity studies of Hebrew Bible narrative texts in Genesis[1] and Samuel.[2] There have also been studies in Hebrew Bible poetry, including Proverbs,[3] Ecclesiastes,[4] and Isaiah.[5] Some of these focus on reading a text ambiguously, like Heard and Miller, while others focus on identifying compositional ambiguity, for example, Firth. This thesis is interested in

---

1. Heard, *Dynamics of Diselection.*
2. Firth and Grant, *Words & the Word.*
3. Miller, "Open Proverbs.
4. Ingram, *Ambiguity in Ecclesiastes.*
5. Kim, *Ambiguity, Tension, and Multiplicity.*

identifying compositional ambiguity as a means by which a diverse audience may gain access to the ethical message of Psalm 82.

While ambiguity lends itself to a reader-oriented approach,[6] ambiguous interpretation methods must come alongside a warning about distinguishing ambiguity from an interpretation free-for-all that may allow reader response to shape the meaning of the text arbitrarily. Caution is appropriate, especially when what is at stake for broadening the possibilities of acceptable interpretation is the value of the text. When the means by which the text shapes the reader becomes secondary to how the reader shapes the text, there is a danger of a text losing its authority. For this reason, it is important to define terminology carefully when considering the interpretation of literature in the Hebrew Bible.

Although scholars have mentioned ambiguity as a possible way of reading to resolve discrepancies in Psalm 82,[7] this has not been well explored. However, with its inclusive language and implicit ethical themes, Psalm 82 is a candidate for a case study in ambiguity. The evidence for this is posed not only by the content of the psalm, but also in the scholarship. The literary features of the psalm, including poetry and myth, are features that often contain ambiguity. The language, syntax, and grammar of Psalm 82 is arranged in such a way that causes the receiver of the text to pause and reflect—one certain outcome of ambiguous language. Furthermore, Zimmermann's study of implicit ethics in biblical texts made the connection between ambiguous language and implicit ethics.[8] These are signs that ambiguity is at work in the psalm. Add to this the fact that scholars have defended multiple interpretations, even when following the same evidence and source material. Ambiguity is at play in Psalm 82 and warrants exploration.

The ambiguity of Psalm 82 allows the reader to access the ethical message of the psalm more easily. The composition contains language of epic proportions, which was explored in more detail in Chapter Two. Psalm 82 portrays divine council in the heavens and the foundations of the earth in the deeps. These metanarrative references are grandiose for any human respondent. The inclusion of ambiguous language in the composition grants access to readers who would normally be left out of such a discussion. Intentional ambiguity invites the reader to engage with the text and its meaning across time and culture. The implication of this is that ambiguity is a vehicle for bringing the reader to visit and respond to the ethical message.

6. "The concept of ambiguity lends itself very readily to a reader-oriented approach to literature which permits, even requires, the reader to determine meaning." Sternberg, *The Poetics of Biblical Narrative*.

7. Nasuti, *Tradition History*. Niehr, "Gotter oder Menschen."

8. Zimmermann, *The Logic of Love*.

Intentional ambiguity is the idea that a composition is constructed in such a way that allows for multiple readings or multiple ways to understand a text. There is a difference between a composition that is vague and a composition that is ambiguous. Simone de Beauvoir demonstrated that the difference between a vague composition and an ambiguous one has to do with the integrity of a text and its reception as trustworthy.[9] Psalm 82 is received in the Psalter and its continued use in liturgy is evident. Psalm 82 will be evaluated as ambiguous at the compositional level first, followed by an exploration about how the inclusion of an ambiguous text in the Hebrew Bible Psalter may indicate evidence of resistance literature.

What Is Ambiguity?

For this study, William Empson's *Types of Ambiguity* is considered in order to define the range of meaning for ambiguity and evaluate Psalm 82 as an intentionally ambiguous text.[10] Furthermore, only four of Empson's seven types will be examined as applicable to the psalm.[11] Empson's evaluations were originally applied to poetic texts. His book demonstrated ambiguous features in poetry and poetic narratives which may also apply to certain psalms.

William Empson outlined seven types of ambiguity in poetic literature that progress upon one another to anticipate meaning.[12] Empson claimed that ambiguity in poetry forces the reader to hold onto meanings which follow certain assumptions so that once a reader determines the context, its strength grows and solidifies in their mind. He argued for shades of meaning that became more congruent for the reader as their interpretation builds upon the strength of each determination.

Of Empson's seven types, four are useful for identifying ambiguity in an ancient text:

1. details are effective in multiple ways,
2. multiple possibilities exist within a single resolution,
3. simultaneous use of unconnected meanings,
4. alternative meanings combine to clarify intention.

9. de Beauvoir, *The Ethics of Ambiguity*.
10. Empson, *Seven Types of Ambiguity*.
11. Firth determined that only five of Empson's seven types are applicable to ancient literature, such as Hebrew Bible texts. Although these five align with qualities in Psalm 82 to provide evidence of ambiguity in the composition, only four relate to the composition of the psalm. Firth and Grant, *Words & the Word*.
12. Empson, *Seven Types*.

Empson's first defining point of ambiguity was to identify text that provides room for "alternative reactions to the same piece of language,"[13] in which one word, or group of words, carries multiple meanings for the purpose of engaging a diverse audience and exciting the text. This use of ambiguity plays on the anticipation of the reader, causing surprise elements which lead to assessment and reassessment of words, phrases, and their situation. The impact on the reader is that they will pause to reflect on the quality of the text and its significance. This is apparent in the history of scholarship on Psalm 82. The diverse reactions to the psalm is evidence of intentional ambiguity in the way of Empson's first definition.

In Psalm 82, v. 1 offers an opening scene of divine council with an obscured use of the deific title and name אֱלֹהִים, which has a range of meaning in the Hebrew Bible.[14] While אֱלֹהִים is usually straight forward in definition, identified by its contextual use, Ps 82:1 uses the term in multiple ways in a single sentence that obscures its meaning. The purpose of this inclusion in the introductory lines may serve to draw attention to the psalm for the purpose of assessing and reassessing its *raison d'etre*. The result is an invitation for audience participation in determining its significance in the psalm.

The second type of ambiguity "occurs when two or more meanings are resolved into one."[15] This event opens a range of possibilities and then leads to a singular conclusion, inviting the reader to focus on a narrow question about what is being said. While Psalm 82 builds several doorways into the text, drawing on scene setting typologies of family, Hebrew Bible prophetic texts, Canaanite mythology, and Northern Israelite cultic traditions, at the heart of the psalm is a clear focus on accountability for justice. The central message in the psalm challenges the innocence of those who would allow a marginalized population to suffer at the hands of the wicked (or are themselves wicked) without recognizing the effect this may have on their own existence. The inclusion of ambiguity invites an audience of people from different backgrounds and unites them with a singular focus on concern for the poor.

Empson's third type of ambiguity "occurs when two ideas, which are connected only by being both relevant in the context, can be given in one word simultaneously."[16] The use of אֱלֹהִים in multiple ways in Ps 82:1 could be explained by this description of intentional ambiguity. Given that scholars have struggled to make a clear and consistent translation, it could

---

13. Empson, *Seven Types*, 1.
14. See discussion in chapter two.
15. Empson, *Seven Types*, 48.
16. Empson, *Seven Types*, 102.

be that the composition is playing on אֱלֹהִים as both God and gods in order to bring the audience to halt. This disorients a reader who is in pursuit of a quick resolution. The use of one word in more than one way forces the reader to hold together seemingly unconnected values until a meaning may be extracted.

The composition of Psalm 82 juxtaposes the action (or inaction) of authority figures with the behavior of the wicked and vulnerability of the poor. Interpreting Ps 82:1 as ambiguous invites the audience to examine the relationship between the אֱלֹהִים and the wicked, and between the אֱלֹהִים and the poor. This leads to a consideration of ethics and the implicit responsibility of the reader to respond.

The fourth type of ambiguity in composition happens when "two or more meanings of a statement do not agree among themselves, but combine to make clear a more complicated state of mind in the author."[17] This approach presents words that proffer multiple alternative meanings in order to develop a more complex idea in the mind of the reader.

Alternative meanings are prevalent throughout most of Psalm 82. The terms in v. 1 which describe divine council allow for multiple contradictory readings. For example, the identity of the אֱלֹהִים refers to traditions within Yahwhism and also invokes imagery from other ancient Near Eastern literary traditions. Also, in vv. 5–7, the text references terms which draw from multiple traditions and meanings.

Verse 5 presents a subject whose sight or understanding is clouded. The pronoun could refer to the אֱלֹהִים in v. 1, or the poor in vv. 3–4, or the רְשָׁעִים in v. 4. The implications of this ambiguity in Psalm 82 invokes the audience to consider complicated relationships between wickedness, rulers and the vulnerable in one's social order.

Verses 6 and 7 identify powerful beings, deities, who are at risk of losing access to immortality. It is unclear in these verses who exactly the בְּנֵי עֶלְיוֹן represent. Some have speculated that this is a reference to Genesis 6.[18] Others speculate that this is a reference to the Israelites themselves.[19] The divine council imagery and the ambiguity of deific terms in Psalm 82 force the reader to consider potential contradictory ideas and pause on the significance of the text.

Beyond the composition of Psalm 82, the compilation of the psalm and its inclusion in the Psalter also insinuates a potential for multiple

17. Empson, *Seven Types*, 133.
18. Morgenstern, "Mythological Background."
19. Particularly those who follow a more historical reading of the psalm. See chapter one for a more detailed discussion.

perspectives about divine entities in the Second Temple Period. Psalm 82 is placed among psalms that are increasingly aware of monotheistic attitudes of ancient Israelites. Many scholars have attempted to make sense of the apparent contradiction implied in Psalm 82 by attempting to justify a singular possible reading. However, after decades of justifying multiple "singular readings," it has become clear that something unique is going on in Psalm 82. Furthermore, even a few scholars have noted the possibility of deliberate ambiguity making way for this more detailed exploration.[20]

How Does an Intentional Ambiguous Text Shape Ethics?

With some amount of confidence, we can affirm that Psalm 82 contains intentional ambiguity. So, what does this mean for interpretation? This study deals primarily with how intentional ambiguity in Psalm 82 shapes an ethical reading. For that, Zimmermann's *Organon* model for determining ethics is key, for which he states that ambiguity is one textual feature that is evidence of implicit ethics in an ancient text.[21] Ambiguity is an effective conduit for implicit ethics because it makes way for reader participation by encouraging pausal reflection by the reader, drawing the reader's attention to the central message, and inviting a diverse community to engage with the text.

In an assessment of intentional ambiguity established in the book of Job, Lindsay Wilson determined that ambiguity does two things for the reader: 1) it causes pausal reflection, and 2) it conflates the central meaning of the text.[22] Wilson's assessment centered on how the composition influences the reader's focus on the meaning of the biblical text. Applying this assessment to Psalm 82 as a means by which a reader is influenced ethically builds on Wilson's proposition to consider intentional ambiguity as a means by which an implicit ethical message is made apparent to the reader. Not only is the central meaning more directly accessible by means of intentional ambiguity in the composition, but the ethical nature of the message is brought forward.

Pausal reflection is an important aspect of engaging with biblical text. It is particularly encouraged in the Psalter. Psalm 1 contextualizes the psalms that follow by describing a standard of meditation. This affirms themes in Torah about constancy and thoughtfulness.[23] Intentional ambiguity in

20. Nasuti, *Tradition History*. Niehr, "Gotter oder Menschen."
21. Zimmermann, *The Logic of Love*, 33f.
22. Wilson, "Educating Calvin About Elihu."
23. Deut. 11:19ff and 6:7ff.

Psalm 82 is a compositional technique that encourages the reader to reflect in a similar way, impressing upon the reader a need for mindful consideration of the psalm. Intentional ambiguity causes a reader to pause in order to think about what a text is saying. This is exactly what is happening in Ps 82:1. As discussed in Chapter One, many scholars have noted a peculiarity about Psalm 82 that requires attention. Identifying exactly what is peculiar and how to make sense of the psalm has become a matter of significant discussion across a broad span of time. This pause has generated discussion over the meaning of terms and phrases in the psalm. Pausal reflection drives a reader toward discerning the central message.

Accepting Psalm 82 as ambiguous encourages readers to wrestle with the meaning of the text every time they come to it. Simone de Beauvoir, in her book *Ethics of Ambiguity*, put it this way: "to say (a text) is ambiguous is to assert that its meaning is never fixed, that it must be constantly won."[24] Ambiguity is in play along several points in Psalm 82,[25] begging for consideration and a thoughtful response each time it is approached. Furthermore, the message must be won by every audience member according to their perspective. Wilson's examination identified two key results of compositional intentional ambiguity, but there is a third to consider. An ambiguous text appeals to a broad audience.

The significance of intentional ambiguity in Ps 82:1 is its ability to draw in an audience inclusive of people with diverse religious and social backgrounds to consider together what ethical morality they have in common. When a diverse audience participates, there is potential for a rich and meaningful contribution for a discussion of justice at multiple levels of society. Psalm 82 invites multiple perspectives to engage with the text. The multiple possibilities for interpretation of terms in Psalm 82 (אֱלֹהִים, for example), allows people from various backgrounds and religious realities to access the message of the psalm. Ambiguity encourages inclusion.

It is through ambiguous features in the composition of Psalm 82 that the central ethical message comes across with an ethical observation about right justice as a means of stabilizing order in creation. This is not only for the sake of the earth, but also for those endowed with power, and also for the poor or powerless. Engaging with Psalm 82 as an ambiguous text forces the reader to consider the implicit ethics. The message of how justice is carried out is not a singular message for a monolithic religious or socio-cultural group, but it extends to a broad audience. Multiple readers are invited to

---

24. de Beauvoir, *The Ethics of Ambiguity*.
25. This is detailed in the textual study found in chapter two.

consider ethics in the psalm and reflect on this insight of personal and communal practices of justice.

The invitational nature of intentional ambiguity in the composition of Psalm 82 is significant. It provides insight into the community which accessed the Psalter in its formation. The ambiguous introduction in v. 1 is interested in engaging an audience at many levels, inclusive of those who may not fit some profiles of a Second Temple Period Israelite. The ambiguity recognizes a diverse community of believers who are likely working out their ethical position regarding those among them who are outsiders, those who are poor from disability, or without family. Psalm 82 invokes an ethical message that is available not only to the religious or social elite but extends the consideration of that ethic to the very people whose lives are impacted by the injustice addressed in the psalm. In this way, Psalm 82 forms a resistant text, not willing to conform to a hegemonic standard. Its inclusion in the compilation of the Psalter is possible evidence of resistance literature in the Hebrew Bible.

Resistance Literature

In the aftermath of a political or military struggle, another struggle takes place for the narrative—how the event will be remembered to future generations. Winston Churchill is noted for pointing out that history is written by the victor. His modern claim nudged exploration into the stories of the colonized, the voices of whom so often become subdued in political conflict. The ongoing effort to unearth literary evidence of the personality and struggle of those whose culture has been absorbed into larger colonial structures has resulted in an attempt to uncover evidence of resistance literature.

Efforts to collect and publish resistance literature have produced sympathy and a response toward marginalized people in the modern world. However, in ancient literature, whose constituents are long deceased, it can be difficult to recognize the influence of a minority group or marginalized perspective upon the elite authority structures preserved in the literary tradition. A resistance literature text is one that fits into the master narrative of its own society but contains ambiguous features which allow for multiple messages to seep through. The Psalter may be considered a master narrative, compiled in the Second Temple Period.

Scholars have identified elements in Hebrew Bible narratives that are considered subversive retellings of imperialistic regional traditions[26] and

---

26. For example, consider the polemic nature of parts of the Hebrew Genesis when compared to the Babylonian Genesis. Furthermore, this paper will present the works of

internal critiques.[27] However, this concept has not been well applied to the Psalter. The Hebrew Bible Psalter is considered a Second Temple Era compilation, during a time when the ancient Israelite community was re-forming and reshaping religious and ethnic identity post-exile. It is in this context that resistance literature takes shape within the liturgy. This study identifies features in the Psalter which may be seen as markers in the composition for resistance literature, with specific focus on Psalm 82. I will begin with an outline of literary approaches to resistance literature, then summarize efforts to identify resistance literature in the Hebrew Bible and more specifically in the Psalter.

Ghassan Kanafānī was possibly the first westerner to reference literature as resistant to colonial oppression. In 1966, he distinguished literature written "under occupation" from that written in "exile."[28] Twenty years later, Barbara Harlow incorporated Kanafānī's study in her book, entitled *Resistance Literature* (1987).[29] Harlow described the importance of an historical struggle for the cultural and literary record of events during imperial expansion. She concluded that influence over the literary record was no less crucial than the armed struggle. In other words, the pen is at least as mighty as the sword. Harlow focused on written poetry and narrative which demanded attention for the social rights of colonized people in Africa, Central and South America, and Asia; however, she did not address the more subtle forms of resistance literature which had emerged in oral tradition via folklore and religious liturgy.

Another scholar was working at the same time on subversive rhetoric as a means of political resistance. James C. Scott recognized two major forms: the public and the disguised resistance. Using the term "hidden transcripts," Scott described resistant responses to dominate public rhetoric encoded in a society's master narrative.[30] He noted the ability of marginalized groups to engage in an ideological struggle within public rhetoric by means of veiled discourse.[31] In its more elaborate forms, resistance can also be communicated by ambiguous, polysemic elements inserted into

---

Niditch, Seibert, Mason, and others.

27. i.e. critiques of the Solomonic monarchy.

28. Kanafānī focused on literature from occupied Palestine. Ghassān Kanafānī, *Adab al-muqawamah fī Filasṭīn al-muḥtallah*, 11.

29. Harlow is credited with pioneering postcolonial studies in literature by western approaches. Harlow, *Resistance Literature*.

30. Master narrative is a term credited to Frederick Jameson by Harlow. Harlow, *Resistance*, 104.

31. This is achieved by the use of euphemism, metaphor and linguistic tricks as a form of literary resistance. Scott, *Domination and the Arts of Resistance*.

public discourse in such a way that does not directly oppose the public narrative approved by the dominant political force.[32] Scott demonstrated that resistance literature engages spheres of the master narrative with a subversive message by proper means, but it is hidden in a way that it cannot be treated as an open challenge by dominant entities. Examples of this are plentiful: trickster narratives, double-entendre, etcetera. Many of these literary features also emerge from influence of an oral tradition, so language and literacy play a part in resistance literature.

In 1993, Kamau Braithwaite wrote about the dependency of national language on the development of the indigenous oral culture. For example, he described the effects of native speakers in the Congo upon imperial English, Spanish, and French speech patterns. Literate expressions rely on oral traditions. While reading is individual and isolated from influence, oral tradition is participatory. It is a form of communication that influences both speaker and audience, where meaning resides in the continuum of information and feedback between the two parties.[33] When resistance discourse is embedded within public liturgies, for example, ambiguities in the message draw the attention of multiple receptors in a blended audience. Brathwaite's contribution is important when considering how a practiced liturgy, such as a psalm, may be read and received by its audience.

Braithwaite's approach was accessed by LaRose Parris as a useful tool for identifying the influence and strength of trickster tales, slave-songs, and other oral traditions that express the culture and collective humanity of those under the rule of colonial authority.[34] Parris and Braithwaite emphasized the effect of oral tradition upon written literature that would evolve as part of the master narrative in a society.[35] As a result, oral tradition from the margins seeped into the language unchallenged, even when the tradition subverted the hegemony. These subversive styles of resistance literature are read as satire, parody, irony, magic, indeterminacy, open-endedness, ambiguity, individuality, double-entendre, and others.[36]

When it comes to ancient texts, like those in the Hebrew Bible, the task of identifying third world voices can be a bit more difficult. However, biblical scholars have also been looking at subversion in folklore and biblical

32. Scott, *Hidden Transcripts*.
33. Brathwaite, *Roots*, 273.
34. LaRose, *Being Apart*.
35. "It was in language that the slave was perhaps most successfully imprisoned by his master; and it was in his (mis-)use of it that he perhaps most effectively rebelled. Within the folk tradition language was (and is) a creative act in itself; the word was held to contain a secret power." Brathwaite, *Roots*.
36. Gates, *The Signifying Monkey*, 6.

narratives since the twentieth century. Susan Niditch, for example, wrote a volume on the use of trickster narratives and biblical folklore.[37] She encouraged biblical scholars to engage with literary theories of traditional lore as a way of understanding aspects of the Hebrew Bible that are culturally shaped.[38] Niditch distinguished between versions of a narrative by temporal means, but a similar appeal could be made for distinct polyphonic resonance in Hebrew Bible literature. Literary features such as word play, exaggeration, double-entendre, and ambiguity may demonstrate the influence and advocacy for a marginal perspective even within master narratives of a society. This is evidence of resistance literature.

Literary qualities of resistance literature are also found in covertly subversive texts. Rex Mason identified subversion in biblical literature as that in which a literary presentation of ideas are targeted at "select inner circles of those who wield power and hold positions of responsibility in the 'court.'"[39] His book, *Propaganda and Subversion in the Old Testament*, dealt with the subtleties of resistance literature as subversive propaganda woven into the literature of the elite, identifying the covert nature of subversive literature. A few years later, Daniel Smith-Christopher applied Scott's work on disguised resistance to examine evidence of resistance attitudes embedded specifically in post-exilic biblical writings. His work made way for consideration of polyphonic resonance in Hebrew Bible texts that counter elite perspectives in the Second Temple Period.[40]

This study suggests that Psalm 82 is an example of a liturgical text that fits with several of the criteria raised by scholars in their assessment of resistance literature. This consideration contributes to addressing questions about how such a psalm retained its early mythological ideologies in a post-exilic compilation. This view raises questions about the social-political world in post-exilic Judah. The situation may be described as a time of resettling Israelite and Jewish identity during Persian imperialism and the subsequent colonial spread of Hellenism from the West. The impact of this correlation of Psalm 82 as resistance literature in this changing world is the realization of a liturgical text that both fits the master narrative of Jewish society while also representing non-hegemonic views from within that same society.

---

37. Niditch, *Oral World*.
38. Niditch, *Oral World*, xiv.
39. Mason, *Propaganda and Subversion*, 172.
40. Smith-Christopher, *Biblical Theology of Exile*.

Reading Psalm 82 as Resistance Literature

Psalm 82 is a pre-exilic psalm with origins suggestive of an early northern mythological provenance. Yet its resilience in being included among the psalms of a post-exilic Jewish community speaks to its polysemy. Psalm 82 contains several compositional features common to resistance literature which has been assessed by twentieth and twenty-first-century scholarship. For this study, these include intentional ambiguity and intentional covert subversion.

Ambiguity is a key factor of resistance literature.[41] Ariel Dorfman's 1983 book, *The Emperor's Old Clothes*, presented subversive themes evident in fiction produced by colonial sources. Dorfman provided numerous examples of intentional ambiguity as a key factor of subversive literature,[42] in which Roland Barthes' *Writing Degree Zero* is referenced as further support for the identification of intentional ambiguity as a means of presenting comparisons to an audience for subconscious processing. Barthes explained that ambiguity serves to assist readers in getting at the central message. Apparent contradictions may be waved away in an ambiguous text, and the reader must face the implicit ethics in the text, without regard for their personal status.[43] Ambiguity is the means by which a third world message is represented unchallenged within an imperial narrative.

Psalm 82 contains several accounts of ambiguity. To summarize from earlier in this chapter, in v. 1, the term אֱלֹהִים occurs multiple times in such a way that the grammar provides for more than one translation and interpretation of the verse. Subsequent verses also contain ambiguity. v. 2 asserts a challenge from an unidentified speaker to a recipient whose identity is clouded by the ambiguity in v. 1. Verse 5 refers to an ambiguous third person plural subject who could be defined by at least two possibilities previously raised in the psalm, the אֱלֹהִים in v. 1, or the רְשָׁעִים in v. 4. Verses 6 and 7 refer to primordial cosmic events and include a *hapex legomeno* phrase: בְּנֵי עֶלְיוֹן. And, finally, v. 8 reiterates the use of אֱלֹהִים, mirroring v. 1 without

---

41. Parris, *Being Apart*; Scott, *Hidden Transcripts*; Seibert, *Subversive Scribes*.

42. Dorfman assessed Babar the Elephant, a 1931 cartoon character whose natural state is revealed as inadequate when confronted by the proper etiquette of the imperial state or developed countries. Dorfman explained that the truth of conformity which exists for all colonized people is mirrored in the experience of Babar, and "if the truth were not inserted into Babar the Elephant's evolution, albeit hidden and bastardized, then the child (reader) would not be able to correlate the fictional process settling in his brain with the real process pleading to be understood." Dorfman, *The Empire's Old Clothes*, 27.

43. Barthes, *Writing Degree Zero*.

further clarity for the grammar.[44] Intentional ambiguity weaves a resistant message into a hegemonic literary tradition.

Psalm 82 contains intentional ambiguity that allows for polysemy in order to represent marginalized people who fall outside hegemonic structures of authority in post-exilic Israel. It is by means of intentional ambiguity that Psalm 82 prioritizes defense of the poor and marginalized, which is the focus of vv. 3–4. By means of a liturgical text, an ethical message that advocates for the powerless is practiced in the society at large. This aspect of psalms as ethical with specific regard to liturgy is a connection that Wenham made in *Psalms as Torah*. Wenham made a strong case to support ethical considerations of psalms based on their use in liturgy, both in the ancient world and in the modern age.[45] Liturgy is an ideal mode of communicating resistance ideologies. It is poetic and relies on oral tradition.

In addition to ambiguity, polysemy also makes way for covert messages in the text. In 2006, Eric Seibert published his study of subversion in 1 Kgs 1–11. Seibert's monograph engaged a thorough discussion of various approaches to interpreting Hebrew Bible texts as subversive. He distinguished between concealed and conspicuous subversion in biblical narrative. Furthermore, he described how to identify intentional subversion based on six criteria which will be examined as a heuristic by which to read Psalm 82 as resistant. These criteria are explored in this section: 1) "over-the-top" rhetoric, 2) accounts of evaluative ambiguity, 3) negative descriptions that seem to undermine overarching virtues, 4) problematic phrases which are expected to be criticized, 5) contradictory readings that cannot easily be explained, and 6) suspicion of subversion in the text.[46]

Seibert's first criterion is "over-the-top" or "over-stressed" rhetoric that is meant to grab the attention of an audience.[47] Ps 82:3–4 is the most dense list of synonyms for the poor or marginalized in all of the Hebrew Bible. The exaggerated list of synonyms emphasizes the composition's concern for minority voices. While this is not necessarily evidence of a marginalized voice, it is at least evidence of advocacy of a minority perspective.[48]

---

44. The details of these ambiguities were explored previously in chapter two. For more diverse views on literary and linguistic features in Psalm 82, see Morgenstern, "Mythological Background"; Ackerman (1966), Miller (1986), Prinsloo (1995), Parker (1995), Trotter (2012), et. al. These have been previously discussed in chapter one.

45. Wenham, *Psalms as Torah*. 3–5

46. Seibert, *Subversive Scribes*.

47. Seibert, *Subversive Scribes*, 86–88.

48. Minority voices arise from those who are indirectly involved in a conflict between two major parties. The technical term, "third world" refers to a voice that is "other than" major imperialistic or elitist voices. Of course, the modern use of third

The second criterion is "multiple instances of evaluative ambiguity" where a central figure is presented in more than one light. As an example, Seibert referenced a narrative where a central figure in the text is seen as both favorable and unfavorable in evaluation.[49] This is similarly evidenced by the multiple readings or translations of Ps 82:1 and the potential roles and identities of the אֱלֹהִים.

The third criterion for covert subversion in a biblical text is its "unchallenged inclusion of corrosive elements," or ideas in the text which seem to undermine the dominant purpose or meaning of the text without any effort to neutralize deleterious effects.[50] This is best illustrated in Psalm 82's denial of a strict monotheism, something that is defended by Judaism during the Second Temple Period. The fourth criterion can also be met by the counter-monotheistic view that Psalm 82 presents. Seibert established the fourth criteria as a "presentation of potentially problematic conduct criticized elsewhere in the Hebrew Bible."[51] Psalm 82 suggests a polytheistic or henotheistic belief system that aligns better with early, pre-exilic Israelite religion. However, it is retained in contrast as part of the practicing liturgy in post-exilic Israel.[52]

The fifth criterion is a "lack of more compelling explanations for mutually contradictory readings," in which Seibert suggested that irony (i.e. clashes of style or conflicts of belief, etc.) may be at work in some texts as an act of covert subversion.[53] Psalm 82 has been established as a difficult text filled with contradictory readings and interpretations for nearly a century, beginning with Morgenstern's thesis on the subject in 1939.[54] In fact, the psalm has been received as a Buddhist text by a scholar who considered a reading of Psalm 82 alongside the *Mūlasavarvāstvādavinaya* (MSV). The MSV describes Buddha as a teacher of deities who lectured deities in a heavenly sphere. Duncan Derrett, a scholar of eastern texts, viewed Psalm 82 as evidence of Buddhist ideologies in the Hebrew Bible.[55] Derrett's reading is testimonial to the polysemous qualities in Psalm 82 that have allowed

---

world has additional socio-economic implications. This is not being addressed here as anything more than a recognition of voices other than those involved in a major conflict. cf. Sauvy, who used the term this way (1952) and Debray (1970). Sauvy, "Trois Mondes, Une Planéte."

49. Seibert, *Subversive Scribes*, 88–89.
50. Seibert, *Subversive Scribes*, 89.
51. Seibert, *Subversive Scribes*, 89–90.
52. Mostly considered to be monotheistic, or at best dualistic, in nature.
53. Seibert, *Subversive Scribes*, 90–91.
54. Morgenstern, "Mythological Background."
55. Derrett, "An Ancient Buddhist Representation of Psalm 82," 65–67.

the text to survive from its inception in an early, proto-Israelite setting, be adopted into a post-exilic canon, and remain useful to a broad spectrum of religious liturgies two thousand years later.

Seibert's final criterion is "scholarly suspicion that intentional subversion is present."[56] Twentieth-century scholars have been reluctant to accept mainstream translations of Psalm 82. Nasuti, for one, in a thorough study of the Asaph psalms determined that Psalm 82 is exceptional to the group and exceptional in the Psalter, and perhaps in the whole of the Hebrew Bible.[57] Both he and Niehr suggested that intentional ambiguity is at play in the psalm which disturbs a clear and unnuanced reading of the composition.[58]

Intentional ambiguity and covert meanings in Psalm 82 suggest commonalities with resistance literature. The message of Psalm 82 relies on an ethical paradigm prominent in early ancient Near Eastern religious and legal texts—to care for the poor as part of honor to the deity. In post-exilic Israel, priorities of political identity which centered on preserving ethnic purity were emergent, and Psalm 82 is evidence of oppositional voices who sought to remind Israel of a counter ethical priority. The appeal of the psalm is its reach across boundaries of status, a suitable medium for an implicit ethical message.

Resistant Voices in Persian-Era Judah

Psalm 82 is an example of polyphony in Second Temple Israel. Hardly affirming elitist attitudes of a ruling class in Judah, who sought the exile of inhabitants from the land, Psalm 82 advocates instead for inclusion of the poor and outcast. While these sentiments were likely established in an earlier, pre-exilic Levant setting, echoes are retained in the post-exilic Psalter as evidence of an audience that may respond to a polysemic composition. It is also evidence of resistance literature.

Schreiner's 2018 study of subversion in the Psalter sets a precedent for reading a liturgical psalm as resistance literature. Schreiner examined Psalm 132 as a "post-exilic expansion of a pre-exilic psalm,"[59] in which there is evidence of "disguised verbal resistance" in the form of double entendre. He drew from Scott's description of hidden readings as covert subversion as a kind of resistance literature, noting the complexities of liturgical literature as a means of embedding a hidden message as the liturgy

56. Seibert, *Subversive Scribes*, 91–92.
57. Nasuti, *Tradition History*.
58. Niehr, "Gotter oder Menschen."
59. Schreiner, "Double Entendre," 20–33.

evolved from an early compositional form to a later reception. It is in the state of revision that a psalm adapted to the social realities of those who practice the liturgy. This process is part of oral transmission. Once it becomes a written tradition, the thoughts and attitudes were confined and brought forward from that particular moment.[60] Schreiner demonstrated that Psalm 132 may be read as resistance literature against hegemonic influences of the Second Temple Period.[61] He emphasized the compilation of the Psalter in its literary form. It is reasonable to extend Schreiner's reading of Psalm 132 as resistance literature in post-exilic Israel to other psalms, such as Psalm 82, which contain relevant features.

Post-exilic Judah was inhabited by a diverse group of people. According to Ezra–Nehemiah, Jewish identity was being defined in an exclusive way that promoted a drastic ethnic cleansing threatening to exile many inhabitants of the region.[62] There is, however, evidence in Nehemiah of an active opposition against the building of a wall and casting out of inhabitants who did not meet ethnic requirements of post-exilic Judaism. In Nehemiah 6:10–14, the prophetess Noadiah, who is considered to be a leader among Israel's last prophets, is described as engaged in political activism against Nehemiah's efforts. Some scholars suggest that she was an advocate for the poor and marginalized among the inhabitants of Israel in that time. While the Septuagint recommends that these efforts are those of false prophets, the canonical text makes no such distinction. Wilda Gafney offered a compelling argument to recommend that Noadiah is an influential leader and the last true prophet of Israel. "I suggest that [Noadiah] was opposed to [Nehemiah's] policies, which included breaking apart families and leaving women and their children as persons without status or identity, with neither shelter nor sustenance."[63] At the very least, this is evidence of a diverse group of people living in Judah during the Second Temple Period, which included an active opposition to the hegemonic leadership.

Psalm 82 is just the kind of text that could address multiple groups with a singular message of hope and advocacy. The message of Psalm 82,

---

60. Schniedewind described how the continual use of a psalm in community leads to constant revision and updating over time, until it becomes fixed in some written form, which also agrees with Lord's assessment of oral tradition. Lord, *The Singer of Tales*. Schniedewind, *Society and the Promise to David*, 45.

61. Schreiner, "Double Entendre."

62. Smith-Christopher discussed this as a means of social response to the trauma of the exile experience upon Persian Era Jews. His work draws attention to the fact that the texts of Ezra–Nehemiah offer a resistance literature against Persian political and societal influences. Smith-Christopher, *A Biblical Theology of Exile*.

63. Gafney, *Daughters of Miriam*, 111–12.

which stands in judgment of a leadership who would fail to advocate on behalf of the marginalized, clearly opposes the kind of ethnic cleansing which is promoted in Ezra–Nehemiah. The fact that the biblical narrative also describes an active movement which opposes the hegemony of that society confirms the presence of polyphony among the people of Israel in the Second Temple Period. The presence of embedded resistance efforts in a liturgical text like Psalm 82 speaks to the reality of a diverse people and a political resistance from within the historic Jewish community.

In today's world, Psalm 82 is still an active part of liturgy in many religious contexts. The Psalter is religious scripture to Christianity, Islam, and Judaism. Psalm 82 in particular retains its qualities as resistance literature which refuses to conform neatly to any singular ideology.

Conclusion

Reading an ancient biblical text as intentionally ambiguous is a recent trend in biblical studies. Though it has been somewhat broadly applied, understanding a poetic text, like Psalm 82, as ambiguous is complicated and must rely on an appeal to literary and linguistic comparisons. This has been taken up in previous chapters. Psalm 82 is also considered intentionally ambiguous based on William Empson's early twentieth-century model of ambiguity *types*. Ambiguity is a feature of implicitly ethical texts that is explored by Zimmermann. Considering the ambiguous nature of Psalm 82 provides one more aspect of support for reading the psalm as implicitly ethical, by the *Organon* model.

The significance of reading Psalm 82 as intentionally ambiguous is to assess its value beyond the scope of its mythological provenance. Psalm 82 was received in a Second Temple Period religious context. As an ambiguous text, its reach extends beyond the inner circles of religious community, so that it may be received also by readers and listeners in the periphery. These features also may recommend the psalm as evidence of resistance literature in Second Temple Judah.

Several twentieth- and twenty-first-century studies identified features of resistance literature which gained notoriety in the western world. These literary aspects have been found in ancient texts, such as those in the Hebrew Bible. The Psalter as a liturgical text has a history of usefulness to mainstream religious movements. However, Psalm 82 in particular includes certain features that align it with those found in resistance literature. When read alongside the criteria for resistance literature, the composition affirms a polysemic reading that opposes hegemonic religious influences at the time of its reception in post-exilic Israel.

The inclusion of Psalm 82 in the Psalter challenges a monolithic religious movement among Persian Era Jews and affirms the existence of nonconformist views which held to an early ancient Near Eastern tradition of advocacy for the poor. As resistance literature, Psalm 82 contains features that develop and present an implicit ethical message to a broad audience, that right justice is to actively care for the poor and marginalized, a message relevant to the community committed to the preservation of the Psalter in the Second Temple Period. This aspect of Psalm 82 considers the effects of embedded ethics on the community of its reception.

8

Conclusions

"Our lives begin to end the day we become silent about things that matter."
—Martin Luther King, Jr., Baptist minister and civil rights activist

AT FIRST GLANCE, PSALM 82 is a brief psalm and can appear fairly straight forward, especially for readers who are unencumbered with knowledge about the complexities of the Hebrew language, or the polyphony of ancient Near Eastern religious society. However, scholars have defended a variety of interpretations for the psalm. Furthermore, even though the dust had settled for centuries, Morgenstern stirred everything once again in the early twentieth century with his suggestion that mythology was central to the interpretation of Psalm 82. It is the rich linguistic and literary complexities in Psalm 82 that has prompted a long-standing interest in its exploration.

This study began by exploring linguistic and textual features of Psalm 82, particularly looking at main concerns held in translating the identity of the אֱלֹהִים. There are two: an unclear composition, which suggests ambiguity, and a concentration of language about the marginalized in one's community, which suggests an ethical reading. Both of these features in Psalm 82 recommend the text as implicitly ethical.

Scholarship of interpretation of Psalm 82 evidenced debate about particular meaning and significance for the Hebrew community. Pre-twentieth-century interpretations tended to focus on a justification of Israelite monotheism and geo-political positioning. Twentieth- and twenty-first-century scholarship dealt primarily with the questions raised by Morgenstern regarding the mythological provenance of Psalm 82 and also introduced a possible consideration for intentional ambiguity. The latter has been picked up in this study.

This thesis has prompted a reading of Psalm 82 with ethics in mind. Using Zimmermann's model for identifying implicit ethics in an ancient biblical text, certain aspects and features of the psalm have been explored in depth to demonstrate that there are multiple components of the psalm which contribute to an ethical understanding. As Zimmermann described his method in terms of Aristotle's *Organon*, which looks at aspects of a text like spokes of a wheel, so this study has identified various features of Psalm 82 which all point toward an ethical interpretation as primary. Psalm 82 is a composition which communicates justice and social ethics.

Past scholarship has flagged a number of issues in Psalm 82, some textual, and others literary, or compositional. These have been explored in Chapter One. The variety of "issues" in the text suggest there is room for a deeper exploration of the composition and language of the psalm. In this study, four aspects of Psalm 82 were explored in order to demonstrate the multiple ways that the psalm supports an ethical reading: textual features, mythological provenance in the early formation of the psalm, poverty and justice language in the psalm and its relationship with language in the Psalter, and ambiguity which suggests a potential for reading the psalm as resistance literature in its reception in Second Temple Judah.

A textual study of Psalm 82 revealed the psalm as a potential example of polysemy, in which certain terms have a semantic range in Hebrew. The composition lends itself to variant translations and multiple interpretations. The ambiguity of certain language in Psalm 82 does not impede a central concern for justice. These features of the text are consistent with findings that fit within Zimmermann's presentation of the *Organon* model for identifying implicit ethics in a biblical text.

The following chapter faced issues which surrounded a consideration of Psalm 82 as a mythological text. This study found that the psalm fits within models of Hebrew Bible mythology and also Ugaritic mythological literature, which has been previously suggested. The psalm's mythological themes also recommend an ethical reading, fitting with literature that emphasizes themes of justice and social ethics. There is a particular connection between Psalm 82 and literary and linguistic features in the Ugaritic *Epic of Aqhat*. These alignments confirm and clarify Psalm 82's mythological provenance as an early ancient Near Eastern composition.

The next component of this study took an in-depth look at the language of poverty and justice, as presented in Psalm 82. The issue central to the psalm is one of justice for the poor and marginalized in society. The language of poverty in Psalm 82 is richly condensed, drawing attention to this ethical concern. There are heavily contextualized statements of justice for the poor, which is aligned with themes of salvation and redemption in the Psalter, and in the Torah. The language of poverty, particularly in Ps 82:3–4 provides direct linguistic and literary evidence of an ethical concern for justice.

CONCLUSIONS

With the literary and linguistic features of Psalm 82 explored, the next section took a wider view of the field of psalmic hermeneutics. In this, a discussion of how psalms may be viewed as indeterminate in order to take a context-dependent approach to interpretation guided our reading of Psalm 82 as formed in one time, received in another, and functional as an ethical text in the modern world.

The final aspect of Psalm 82 explored in this study is intentional ambiguity, finding that the psalm fits reasonable descriptions of ambiguity. This suggests an internal quality of the psalm which was intentionally directed by its composer in an early ancient Near Eastern setting. It also suggests that in its later compilation as part of the Hebrew Bible Psalter in the Second Temple period, a decision was made to retain ambiguous features of Psalm 82. Furthermore, it is possible that the psalm is evidence of resistance literature in later periods of Israel's religion and reception of the Psalter. This is an important area of exploration for the future of biblical studies. The possibility of polyphonic voices in the Psalter contending to portray an ethical message, or even offer a warning about the dangers of injustice, should be considered an essential contribution of ancient religious texts. This especially because there are so many questions about right justice and social equity in today's world.

By communicating an ethic about the poor in the Psalter, the Hebrew Bible encourages a face-to-face encounter with the needy, the marginalized and the powerless in the context of worship. How is the community of worship shaped by consideration for the poor? In a legislative context, the poor are removed. Even in the teachings of the sages, wisdom literature feeds the elite by admonishing reckless behavior that may lead to poverty or other bad ends. It is easy to disregard the poor as a class of people that one does not wish to join. However, when a person encounters the plight of poverty face-to-face, that encounter inspires an ethical response. Psalm 82 provides an encounter between the reader and societal injustice against the poor.

By virtue of liturgical practice, the Psalter acts as a conduit to transfer an ethical paradigm from elite rulers to the broader community. The rhetoric of justice in Psalm 82 shifts ideologies of ethics from the upper echelon of social order into the hands of the commoner. Not only does the psalm advocate for the marginalized, but it stirs an obligation for advocacy in its audience. The ambiguity and ethical features of Psalm 82 decentralize its message, so that a complaint of unjust treatment toward the poor may be directed against the deity, but it may also apply to anyone, at any level of authority, and it must be addressed. Ambiguity in Psalm 82 is a means by which the composition encourages not only a diverse audience, but also reflect on a common central ethic of concern for the poor.

Demanding justice for the poor in the Psalter, Psalm 82 exposes the corruption of authority and provides a model by which someone in need could cry out for justice. This should impact the way we think about discussions of justice, righteousness, and concern for the poor in the Psalter. This study explored themes and aspects of Psalm 82 which evidence implicit ethics in the text. By these means, other psalms may be considered in a similar way. In *Psalms as Torah*, Gordon Wenham advocated for the necessity of considering an ethical teaching at the heart of practiced liturgy in the Psalter. Implicit ethics in the Psalter demonstrates how people should respond to problems in their community—a response that can be read about and repeated in a worship service, but then lived out in everyday life. The liturgy is just a starting point. Ethical messages in the Psalter should prompt the reader or worship participant to act on behalf of right justice.

Psalm 82 is a brief composition which is often sidelined as an obscure prophetic text, but it is meaningful. Psalm 82 provides insight into early ancient Israelite ideas about God and divine council. The psalm provides a powerfully relevant ethical message which warns against mistreatment of the poor and marginalized. Psalm 82 contains unique textual features that engage scholars interested in Ugaritic and Hebrew parallels in language and literature. Finally, the psalm suggests that the community of worship in late Israel was more diverse than is popularly conceived. Psalm 82 is potential evidence of resistance literature in Second Temple Period Judah. Its message may have been controversial, but it was relevant, and necessary in its inclusion.

Today's contemporary reception of Psalm 82 is not so different. The same properties that have made it difficult to place Psalm 82 in any particular genre, location, or temporal setting, easily extend the message of the psalm into the modern world. Its message of advocacy for the marginalized, and warnings about the dangers of injustice, could be applied for today's human society, unimaginable to an ancient composer. In fact, the message that Psalm 82 carries is relevant to all of humanity. As an ambiguous and resistant text, Psalm 82's message about justice may stretch beyond the boundaries of culture, language, and religion, into the hearts of those who seek truth and justice. It is a message of advocacy and hope for those who pursue justice. Psalm 82 is an appeal for redemption, forever sought by humanity, and appeal for someone great to rise up and save us all. An ethical reading extends this appeal to the heart of every human. Each person can respond to the cry of injustice. Each person can make a difference. The appeal of implicit ethics in Psalm 82 is a calling to persons at every level to respond and take a stand for right justice.

Bibliography

The Bay Psalm Book. Cambridge: Massachusettes Bay Colony, 1640.
Ackerman, James S. "An Exegetical Study of Psalm 82." PhD diss., Harvard Divinity School, 1966.
———. "The Rabbinic Interpretation of Psalm 82 and the Gospel of John: John 10:34." *HTR* 59 (1966) 186–91.
Adamo, David T. "The Poor in the Book of Psalms and in Yoruba Tradition." *OTE* 27 (2014) 797–815.
Albright, William. *Archaeology and the Religion of Israel.* New introduction by Theodore J. Lewis. Old Testament Library. Louisville: Westminster John Knox, 2006.
Alter, Robert. *The Book of Psalms: A Translation With Commentary.* New York: Norton, 2007.
Avigad, Nahman. "Excavations in the Jewish Quarter of the Old City of Jerusalem, 1971." *IEJ* 22 (1972) 193–200.
Baethgen, Friedrich. *Die Psalmen.* Handkommentar zum Alten Testament. Göttingen: Vandenhoeck & Ruprecht, 1892.
Barthes, Roland. *Writing Degree Zero, and Elements of Semiology.* Boston: Beacon, 1970.
Baudissin, Wolf Wilhelm. *Kyrios als Gottesname im Judentum und seine Stelle in der Religionsgeschichte.* Giessen: Töpelmann, 1929.
Beauvoir, Simone de. *The Ethics of Ambiguity.* New York: Kensington, 1976.
Berry, G. R. *The Book of Psalms.* Philadelphia: American Baptist Publication Society, 1934.
Binger, Tilde. *Asherah: Goddesses in Ugarit, Israel and the Old Testament.* JSOTSup 232. Sheffield, UK: Sheffield Academic, 1997.
Bovati, Pietro. *Re-establishing Justice: Legal Terms, Concepts, and Procedures in the Hebrew Bible.* Translated by Michael J. Smith. JSOTSup 105. Sheffield: JSOT Press, 1994.
Brathwaite, Kamau. *Roots.* Ann Arbor: University of Michigan Press, 1993.
Brooke, George J., ed. *Ugarit and the Bible: Proceedings of the International Symposium on Ugarit and the Bible, Manchester, 1992.* Münster: Ugarit-Verlag, 1992.
Brown, Francis, S. R. Driver, Charles A. Briggs, Edward Robinson, Wilhelm Gesenius, and Maurice A. Robinson. *The New Brown-Driver-Briggs-Gesenius Hebrew and English Lexicon: with an Appendix Containing the Biblical Aramaic.* Peabody, MA: Hendrickson, 1979.

Brueggemann, Walter, and W. H. Bellinger. *Psalms*. NCBC. Cambridge: Cambridge University Press, 2014.
Brueggemann, Walter. *The Psalms and the Life of Faith*. Edited by Patrick D. Miller. Minneapolis: Fortress, 1995.
Budde, Karl. "Ps 82:6f." *JBL* 40 (1921) 39–42.
Burnett, Joel S. *A Reassessment of Biblical Elohim*. SBLDS 183. Atlanta: Society of Biblical Literature, 2001.
Buttenwieser, Moses. *The Psalms, Chronologically Treated*. Chicago: University of Chicago Press, 1938.
Caláes, Jean. *Le Livre des Psaumes: Traduit et Commenté*. 2 vols. Paris: Beauchesne, 1936.
Callender, Dexter E. *Myth and Scripture: Contemporary Perspectives on Religion, Language, and Imagination*. SBLSBS 78. Atlanta: SBL Press, 2014.
Calvin, Jean. *Commentary on the Book of Psalms*. 5 vols. Translated by James Anderson. London: Tegg, 1840.
Chalmers, Scott. "Who Is the Real El? A Reconstruction of the Prophet's Polemic in Hos 12:5a." *CBQ* 68 (2006) 611–30.
Chesterton, G. K. *The Everlasting Man*. New York: Dover, 1925.
Cheyne, T. K. *The Book of Psalms*. 2 vols. London: Kegan Paul, 1904.
Childs, Brevard S. *Biblical Theology in Crisis*. Philadelphia: Westminster, 1970.
Claassen, W. C., ed. *Text and Context: Old Testament and Semitic Studies for F. C. Fensham*. JSOTSup 48. Sheffield: JSOT Press, 1988.
Clines, David J. A., ed. *The Dictionary of Classical Hebrew*. 9 vols. Sheffield: Sheffield Academic, 1993–2012.
———, ed. *The Dictionary of Classical Hebrew*. Vol. 1, *Aleph*. 9 vols. Sheffield: Sheffield Academic, 1995.
———, ed. *The Dictionary of Classical Hebrew*. Vol. 2, *Bet–Waw*. Sheffield: Sheffield Academic, 1995.
———, ed. *The Dictionary of Classical Hebrew*. Vol. 5, *Mem–Nun*. Sheffield: Sheffield Academic, 1995.
———, ed. *The Dictionary of Classical Hebrew*. Vol. 6, *Samech–Peh*. Sheffield: Sheffield Academic, 1995.
———, ed. *The Dictionary of Classical Hebrew*. Vol. 8, *Sin–Tav*. Sheffield: Sheffield Academic, 1995.
———, ed. *The Dictionary of Classical Hebrew*. Vol. 7, *Tsade–Resh*. Sheffield: Sheffield Academic, 1995.
———, ed. *The Dictionary of Classical Hebrew*. Vol. 4, *Yod–Lamed*. Sheffield: Sheffield Academic, 1995.
———. "Varieties of Indeterminacy." In *On the Way to the Postmodern: Old Testament Essays, 1967–1998*, 1:126–37. 2 vols. JSOTSup 292. Sheffield: Sheffield Academic, 1998.
Cohen, Aryeh. "Justice, Wealth, Taxes: A View from the Perspective of Rabbinic Judaism." *JRE* 43 (2015) 409–31.
Cooke, Gerald. "The Sons of (the) God(s)." *ZAW* 35 (1964) 29–34.
Craigie, Peter C. *Ugarit and the Old Testament*. Grand Rapids: Eerdmans, 1983.
Cross, Frank Moore. *Canaanite Myth and Hebrew Epic: Essays in the History of the Religion of Israel*. Cambridge: Harvard University Press, 1973.

Crüsemann, Frank. "Meine Kraft ist in den Schwachen mächtig: Eine theologische Reflexion." *Reformatio* 38.2 (1989) 117–21.
Dahood, Mitchell J. *Psalms*. Vol. 2, *Psalms 51–100*. 3 vols. AB 17. Garden City, NY: Doubleday, 1968.
Day, John. *The Old Testament's Utilisation of Language and Imagery Having Parallels in the Baal Mythology of the Ugaritic Texts*. Cambridge: Cambridge University Press, 1976.
Delitzsch, Franz. *Biblical Commentary on the Psalms*. Translated by David Eaton. 3 vols. Foreign Biblical Library. London: Hodder & Stoughton, 1887.
Dell, Katharine J. *Ethical and Unethical in the Old Testament: God and Humans in Dialogue*. LHBOTS 528. New York: T. & T. Clark, 2010.
Derrett, J. Duncan M. "An Ancient Buddhist Representation of Psalm 82." *Svensk Teologisk Kvartalskrift* 84.2 (2008) 65–67.
Dever, William G. "Iron Age Epigraphic Material from the Area of Khirbet el-Qom." *HUCA* 40–41 (1969) 139–204.
De Wette, W. M. L. *Commentar über die Psalmen*. Heidelberg: Mohr & Zimmer, 1811.
Dickson, C. R. "The Hebrew Terminology for the Poor in Psalm 82." *HTS* 51 (1995) 1029–45.
Dietrich, Manfried, et al. *The Cuneiform Alphabetic Texts: From Ugarit, Ras Ibn Hani and Other Places (KTU)*. ALASP 8. Münster: Ugarit, 1995.
Dijkstra, Meindert, and Johannes C. de Moor. "Problematic Passages in the Legend of Aqhâtu." *UF* 7 (1975) 171–215.
Dorfman, Ariel. *The Empire's Old Clothes: What the Lone Ranger, Babar, and Other Innocent Heroes do to Our Minds*. London: Pluto Press, 1983.
Duhm, Bernhard. *Die Psalmen*. KHC 14. Freiburg: Mohr Siebeck, 1899.
Ehrlich, Arnold B. *Randglossen zur Hebrèaischen Bibel: Textkritisches, Sprachliches, und Sachliches*. 7 vols. Leipzig: Hinrichs, 1908.
Eissfeldt, Otto. "El and Yahweh." *JSS* 1 (1956) 25–37.
Empson, William. *Seven Types of Ambiguity*. London: Chatto & Windus, 1947.
Epsztein, Léon. *Social Justice in the Ancient Near East and the People of the Bible*. London: SCM, 1986.
Ewald, Georg Heinrich August. *Commentary on the Psalms*. Translated by E. Johnson. Theological Translation Fund Library. London: Williams & Norgate, 1880.
Fensham, F. Charles. "Widow, Orphan, and the Poor in Ancient Near Eastern Legal and Wisdom Literature." *JNES* 21 (1962) 129–39.
Firth, David G. *1 & 2 Samuel*. ApOTC 8. Nottingham: InterVarsity, 2009.
———. *Surrendering Retribution in the Psalms: Responses to Violence in Individual Complaints*. PBM. Milton Keynes, UK: Paternoster, 2005.
Firth, David G., and Jamie A. Grant. *Words & the Word: Explorations in Biblical Interpretation & Literary Theory*. Downers Grove, IL: IVP Academic, 2008.
Frankfort, Henri. *Before Philosophy, the Intellectual Adventure of Ancient Man: An Essay on Speculative Thought in the Ancient Near East*. Harmondsworth, UK: Penguin, 1951.
Frazer, James George. *The Golden Bough: A Study in Magic and Religion*. New York: Macmillan, 1951.
Futato, Mark D. *Interpreting the Psalms: An Exegetical Handbook*. Grand Rapids: Kregel Academic, 2007.

Gafney, Wilda. *Daughters of Miriam: Women Prophets in Ancient Israel*. Minneapolis: Fortress, 2008.

Galil, Gershon. "The Hebrew Inscription from Khirbet Qeiyafa / Netaʿim: Script, Language, Literature and History." *UF* 41 (2009) 193.

Gamper, Arnold. *Gott als Richter in Mesopotamien und im Alten Testament*. Innsbruck: Wagner, 1966.

Gaster, Theodor Herzl. *Myth, Legend, and Custom in the Old Testament: a Comparative Study with Chapters from Sir James G. Frazer's Folklore in the Old Testament*. New York: Harper & Row, 1969.

Gates, Henry Louis. *The Signifying Monkey: A Theory of Afro-American Literary Criticism*. New York: Oxford University Press, 1988.

Gesenius, Wilhelm. *Gesenius' Hebrew Grammar*. Expanded by Kautzsch. Translated by A. E. Cowley. 2nd ed. Oxford: Clarendon, 1910.

Gillingham, Sue. "The Poor in the Psalms." *ExpTim* 100 (1988) 15–20.

———. "Praying to the Gods in the Psalms: Pursuing John Barton's 'Plain Meaning Approach'" in *Biblical Interpretation and Method: Essays in Honour of John Barton*, edited by Katharine Dell and Paul M. Joyce, 63–73. Oxford: Oxford University Press, 2013.

Goldingay, John. *The First Testament: A New Translation*. Downers Grove, IL: IVP Academic, 2018.

———. *Psalms*. 3 vols. BCOTWP. Grand Rapids: Baker Academic, 2006.

Gordon, Cyrus H. "History of Religion in Psalm 82." In *Biblical and Near Eastern Studies: Essays in Honor of William Sanford LaSor*, edited by Gary A. Tuttle, 129–31. Grand Rapids: Eerdmans, 1978.

Gordon, Robert P. "Standing in the Council: When Prophets Encounter God." In *The God of Israel*, edited by Robert P. Gordon, 190–204. UCOP 64. Cambridge: Cambridge University Press, 2007.

Goulder, Michael D., *The Psalms of Asaph and the Pentateuch: Studies in the Psalter, III*. JSOTSup 233. Sheffield, UK: Sheffield Academic, 1996.

Graetz, Hirsch. *Kritischer Commentar zu den Psalmen, nebst Text und Uebersetzung*. Breslau: Schottlaender, 1882.

Grant, Jamie A. "Determining the Indeterminate: Issues in Interpreting the Psalms." *Southeastern Theological Review* 1 (2010) 3–14.

———. "The Hermeneutics of Humanity: Reflections on the Human Origins of the Laments." *A God of Faithfulness: Essays in Honour of J. Gordon McConville on His 60th Birthday*, edited by J. A. Grant et al., 182–202. New York: Bloomsbury, 2014.

———. *The King as Exemplar: The Function of Deuteronomy's Kingship Law in the Shaping of the Book of Psalms*. SBL Academia Biblica 17. Leiden: Brill, 2004.

Groenewald, A. "Mythology, Poetry and Theology." *HTS* 62 (2006) 18.

———. "Psalms 69:33–34 in the Light of the Poor in the Psalter as a Whole." *Verbum et Ecclesia* 28.2 (2007) 425–41.

Gunkel, Hermann. *Introduction to Psalms: the Genres of the Religious Lyric of Israel*. Completed by Joachim Begrich. Translated by James D. Nogalski. Mercer Library of Biblical Studies. Macon, GA: Mercer University Press, 1998. Reprint, Eugene, OR: Wipf & Stock, 2020.

———. *The Psalms: A Form-Critical Introduction*. Translated by Thomas M. Horner. Facet Books. Philadelphia: Fortress, 1967.

Handy, Lowell K. "Sounds, Words and Meanings in Psalm 82." *JSOT* 15.47 (1990) 51–66.

Hanway, Jonas. *Songs, Hymns, and Psalms, Collected, Altered, or Composed, Adapted to Moral and Instructive Amusement and the Religious Part of the Education of the Scholars of the County Naval Free-Schools, Proposed for the Breeding Up of Poor Boys to Agriculture, and the Theoretical Practice of Common Seamanship.* London: n.p., 1783.

Harlow, Barbara. *Resistance Literature.* New York: Methuen, 1987.

Harris, R. Laird, et al. *Theological Wordbook of the Old Testament.* 2 vols. Chicago: Moody, 1980.

Hart, H. L. A. *The Concept of Law.* Clarendon Law Series. Oxford: Oxford University Press, 2012.

Hatton, Peter T. H. *Contradiction in the Book of Proverbs: The Deep Waters of Counsel.* Society for Old Testament Study Series. Burlington, VT: Ashgate, 2008.

Heard, Christopher. *Dynamics of Diselection: Ambiguity in Genesis 12–36 and Ethnic Boundaries in Post-Exilic Judah.* SemeiaSt 39. Atlanta: Society of Biblical Literature, 2001.

Heiser, Michael S. "The Divine Council in Late Canonical and Non-canonical Second Temple Jewish Literature." PhD diss., University of Wisconsin, 2004.

———. "The Mythological Provenance of Isa XIV 12–15: A Reconsideration of the Ugaritic Material." *VT* 51 (2001) 354–69.

Hengstenberg, Ernst Wilhelm. *Commentary on the Psalms.* 3 vols. The Biblical Cabinet. Edinburgh: T. & T. Clark, 1845.

Hitzig, Ferdinand. *Urgeschichte und Mythologie der Philistäer.* Leipzig: Weidmann, 1845.

Holladay, William L. *The Psalms through Three Thousand Years: Prayerbook of a Cloud of Witnesses.* Minneapolis: Fortress, 1993.

Hood, J. C. "I Appeared as El Shaddai: Intertextual Interplay in Exodus 6:3." *WTJ* 76 (2014) 167–88.

Hoppe, Leslie J. *There Shall Be No Poor among You: Poverty in the Bible.* Nashville: Abingdon, 2004.

Hossfeld, Frank-Lothar. "Ps 82 und das vierte Psalmenbuch (Ps 90–106)." In *'Mein Sohn bist du' (Ps 2,7): Studien zu den Königspsalmen*, edited by Eckart Otto and Erich Zenger, 173–83. Stuttgarter Bibelstudien 192. Stuttgart: Katholisches Bibelwerk, 2002.

Hossfeld, Frank-Lothar, and Erich Zenger. *Psalms 2: A Commentary on Psalms 51–100.* Translated by Linda M. Maloney. Hermeneia. Minneapolis: Fortress, 2005.

———. "The So-Called Elohistic Psalter: A New Solution for an Old Problem." In *A God So Near: Essays on Old Testament Theology in Honor of Patrick D. Miller*, edited by Brent A. Strawn and Nancy R. Bowen, 35–51. Winona Lake, IN: Eisenbrauns, 2003.

Houston, Walter. *Contending for Justice: Ideologies and Theologies of Social Justice in the Old Testament.* LHBOTS 428. London: T. & T. Clark, 2008.

Huehnergard, John. *An Introduction to Ugaritic.* Peabody, MA: Hendrickson, 2012.

Huffmon, Herbert B. "The Covenant Lawsuit in the Prophets." *JBL* 78. (1959) 285–95.

Hulst, A. R. *Old Testament Translation Problems.* Helps for Translators. Leiden: Brill, 1960.

Human, Dirk J. "Psalm 82: God Presides in a Deflated Pantheon to Remain the Sole Just Ruler." In *"From Ebla to Stellenbosch": Syro-Palestinian Religions and the Hebrew Bible*, edited by Izak Cornelius and Louis Jonker, 154–68. Abhandlungen des Deutschen Palästina-Vereins 37. Wiesbaden: Harrassowitz, 2008.

———. *Psalmody and Poetry in Old Testament Ethics*. LHBOTS 572. New York: T. & T. Clark, 2012.
———. *Psalms and Mythology*. LHBOTS 462. New York: T. & T. Clark, 2007.
Ingram, Doug. *Ambiguity in Ecclesiastes*. LHBOTS 431. New York: T. & T. Clark, 2006.
James, Joshua T. *The Storied Ethics of the Thanksgiving Psalms*. LHBOTS 658. New York: T. & T. Clark, 2017.
Johnson, Aubrey R. *The Cultic Prophet and Israel's Psalmody*. Cardiff: University of Wales Press, 1979.
Joüon, Paul. *A Grammar of Biblical Hebrew*. Translated and revised by T. Muraoka. 2 vols. SubBi 14. Rome: Editrice Pontificio Istituto Biblico, 1993.
Jüngling, HansWinfried. *Der Tod der Götter: Eine Untersuchung zum Psalm 82*. SBS 38. Stuttgart: Katholisches Bibelwerk, 1969.
Kanafānī, Ghassān. *Adab al-muqawamah fī Filasṭīn al-muḥtallah*. Beirut: Dār al-Adāb, 1966.
Kee, Min Suc. "The Heavenly Council and Its Type-Scene." *JSOT* 31 (2007) 259–73.
Keel, Othmar. *The Symbolism of the Biblical World: Ancient Near Eastern Iconography and the Book of Psalms*. Timothy J. Hallett. London: SPCK, 1978.
Kilmer, Anne Draffkorn. "Ilāni/Elohim." *JBL* 76 3 (1957) 216–25.
Kim, Hyun Chul Paul. *Ambiguity, Tension, and Multiplicity in Deutero-Isaiah*. SBLStBibLit 52. New York: Lang, 2003.
Kirkpatrick, A. F. *The Book of Psalms*. 3 vols. CBSC 16. Cambridge: Cambridge University Press, 1891.
Kittel, Rudolf. *The Religion of the People of Israel*. Translated by R. Caryl Micklem. London: Allen & Unwin, 1925. Reprint, Eugene, OR: Wipf & Stock, 2015.
Köhler, Ludwig. *Deuterojesaja (Jesaja 40–55) stilkritisch untersucht*. Giessen: Töpelmann, 1923.
Kraus, Hans-Joachim. *Psalms 1–59: A Commentary*. Translated by Hilton C. Oswald. Continental Commentary. Minneapolis: Augsburg, 1988.
———. *Theology of the Psalms*. Translated by Keith R Crim. Continental Commentary. Minneapolis: Augsburg, 1986.
Kuczynski, Michael P. *Prophetic Song: The Psalms as Moral Discourse in Late Medieval England*. Philadelphia: University of Pennsylvania Press, 1995.
Landgraf, Virginia W. "Competing Narratives of Property Rights and Justice for the Poor: Toward a Nonannihilationist Approach to Scarcity and Efficiency." *JSCE* 27 (2007) 57–75.
Lee, Seong Hye. "The Psalter as an Anthology Designed to be Memorized." PhD diss., University of Bristol, 2011.
Levin, C. "The Poor in the Old Testament: Some Observations." *R&T* 8 (2001) 253–73.
Lévy-Bruhl, Lucien. *How Natives Think*. Translated by Lilian A. Clare. London: Allen & Unwin, 1926.
Lewis, C. S. *An Experiment in Criticism*. Cambridge: Cambridge University Press, 1961.
Lipton, Diana. "Desire for Ethics or the Ethics of Desire?" In *Ethical and Unethical in the Old Testament: God and Humans in Dialogue*, edited by Katharine J. Dell, 34–55. LHBOTS 528. New York: T. & T. Clark, 2010.
Lohfink, Norbert. "Poverty in the Laws of the Ancient Near East and of the Bible." *TS* 52 (1991) 34–50.
Lord, Albert Bates. *The Singer of Tales*. HSCL 24. Cambridge: Harvard University Press, 1960.

Machinist, Peter "How Gods Die, Biblically and Otherwise: A Problem of Cosmic Restructuring." In *Reconsidering the Concept of Revolutionary Monotheism*, edited by Beate Pongratz-Leisten, 189–240. Winona Lake, IN: Eisenbrauns, 2011.
Mandela, Nelson. "Nelson Mandela in London's Trafalgar Square." BBC, 2005. http://news.bbc.co.uk/2/hi/uk_news/politics/4232603.stm.
Margalit, Baruch. *The Ugaritic Poem of AQHT: Text, Translation, Commentary*. BZAW 182. Berlin: de Gruyter, 1989.
Mason, Rex. *Propaganda and Subversion in the Old Testament*. London: SPCK, 1997.
May, Herbert G. "A Sociological Approach to Hebrew Religion." *JBR* 12 (1944) 98–106.
McCann, J. Clinton, Jr. "The Single Most Important Text in the Entire Bible: Toward a Theology of the Psalms." In *Soundings in the Theology of Psalms: Perspectives and Methods in Contemporary Scholarship*, edited by Rolf A. Jacobson, 63–76. Minneapolis: Fortress, 2011.
———. "Righteousness, Justice, and Peace: A Contemporary Theology of the Psalms." *HBT* 23 (2001) 111–31.
McClellan, Daniel. "The Gods-Complaint: Psalm 82 as a Psalm of Complaint." *JBL* 137 (2018) 833–51.
McKane, William. *A Critical and Exegetical Commentary on Jeremiah*. ICC. Edinburgh: T. & T. Clark, 1986.
McKenzie, John L. *Myths and Realities: Studies in Biblical Theology*. Milwaukee: Bruce, 1963.
Mein, Andrew. *Ezekiel and the Ethics of Exile*. Oxford Theological Monographs. Oxford: Oxford University Press, 2001.
Miller, Patrick D. "Cosmology and World Order in the Old Testament: The Divine Council as Cosmic-Political Symbol." *HBT* 9 (1987) 53–78.
———. "El, The Creator of Earth." *BASOR* 239 (1980) 43–46.
———. *Interpreting the Psalms*. Philadelphia: Fortress, 1986.
———. "When the Gods Meet: Psalm 82 and the Issue of Justice." *Journal for Preachers* 9.4 (1986) 2–5.
Miller, Suzanna. "Open Proverbs: Exploring Genre and Openness in Proverbs 10:1—22:16." PhD diss., University of Cambridge, 2018.
Miranda, José. *Marx and the Bible: A Critique of the Philosophy of Oppression*. Translated by John Eagleson. 1971. Reprint, Eugene, OR: Wipf & Stock, 2004.
Moberly, R. W. L. *The Old Testament of the Old Testament: Patriarchal Narratives and Mosiac Yahwism*. OBT. Minneapolis: Fortress, 1992.
Möller, Karl. "Reading, Singing and Praying the Law: An Exploration of the Performative, Self-involving, Commissive Language of Psalm 101." In *Reading the Law: Studies in Honour of Gordon J. Wenham*, edited by Karl Möller et al., 111–37. LHBOTS 461. New York: T. & T. Clark, 2007.
Morgenstern, Julian. "The Mythological Background of Psalm 82." PhD diss., Hebrew Union College, 1939.
Mowinckel, Sigmund. *Psalmenstudien*. 6 vols. 1921–1924. Reprint, Amsterdam: Schippers, 1961.
———. *The Psalms in Israel's Worship*. Translated by D. R. Ap-Thomas. 1961. Reprint, Grand Rapids: Eerdmans, 2004.
Nasuti, Harry Peter. *Tradition History and the Psalms of Asaph*. SBLDS 88. Atlanta: Scholars, 1988.

Niditch, Susan. *Oral World and Written Word: Ancient Israelite Literature.* LAI. Louisville: Westminster John Knox, 1996.

———. *Underdogs and Tricksters: A Prelude to Biblical Folklore.* New Voices in Biblical Studies. San Francisco: Harper & Row, 1987.

Niehr, Herbert. "Gotter oder Menschen—eine Falsche Alternative: Bemerkungen zu Ps 82." *ZAW* 99 (1987) 95–98.

Oesterley, W. O. E. *Ancient Hebrew Poems.* London: Macmillan, 1938.

Olshausen, Justus. *Die Psalmen.* HAT 8. Leipzig: Hirzel, 1853.

Otto, Eckart. "Myth and Hebrew Ethics in the Psalms." In *Psalms and Mythology*, edited by Dirk J. Human, 26–37. LHBOTS 462. New York: T. & T. Clark, 2007.

Otzen, Benedikt, et al. *Myths in the Old Testament.* Translated by Frederick Cryer. London: SCM, 1980.

Page, Hugh Rowland. *The Myth of Cosmic Rebellion: A Study of Its Reflexes in Ugaritic and Biblical Literature.* VTSup 65. Leiden: Brill, 1996.

Parker, Simon B. "The Beginning of the Reign of God: Psalm 82 as Myth and Liturgy." *RB* 102.4 (1995) 532–59.

———. *The Pre-Biblical Narrative Tradition: Essays on the Ugaritic Poems Keret and Aqhat.* RBS 24. Atlanta: Scholars, 1989.

Parker, Simon B., and Mark S. Smith. *Ugaritic Narrative Poetry.* WAW 9. Atlanta: Scholars, 1997.

Parris, LaRose. *Being Apart: Theoretical and Existential Resistance in Africana Literature.* Charlottesville: University of Virginia Press, 2015.

Pelikan, Jaroslav, et al., eds. *Luther's Works.* American ed. St. Louis: Concordia, 1955.

Perowne, J. J. Stewart. *The Book of Psalms: A New Translation, with Introductions and Notes Explanatory and Critical.* 7th ed. 2 vols. London: Bell, 1890.

Petersen, Claus. *Mythos im Alten Testament: Bestimmung des Mythosbegriffs und Untersuchung der mythischen Elemente in den Psalmen.* BZAW 157. Berlin: de Gruyter, 1982.

Peterson, Eugene H. *The Message: Psalms.* Colorado Springs: NavPress, 1994.

Prinsloo, Willem S. "Psalm 82: Once Again, Gods or Men?" *Bib* 76 (1995) 219–29.

Purtill, Richard L. *J. R. R. Tolkien: Myth, Morality, and Religion.* San Francisco: Ignatius, 2003.

Rendsburg, Gary. *Linguistic Evidence for the Northern Origin of Selected Psalms.* SBLMS 43. Atlanta: Scholars, 1990.

Ro, Johannes Un-Sok. *Poverty, Law, and Divine Justice in Persian and Hellenistic Judah.* AIL 32. Atlanta: SBL Press, 2018.

Rodd, Cyril S. *Glimpses of a Strange Land: Studies in Old Testament Ethics.* OTS. Edinburgh: T. & T. Clark, 2001.

———. *Psalms.* Epworth Preacher's Commentaries. London: Epworth, 1964.

Rogerson, J. W. *Myth in Old Testament Interpretation.* BZAW 134. Berlin: de Gruyter, 1974.

Rogerson, J. W., and J. W. McKay. *Psalms.* 3 vols. CBC. Cambridge: Cambridge University Press, 1977.

Rokay, Zoltan. "Vom Stadttor zu den Vorhöfen: Ps 82—Sach 1–8 (ein Vergleich)." *ZKT* 116 (1994) 457–63.

Roth, Martha T. *Law Collections from Mesopotamia and Asia Minor.* With a contribution by Harry A. Hoffner. WAW 6. Atlanta: Scholars, 1995.

Salters, R. B. "Psalm 82:1 and the Septuagint." *ZAW* 103 (1991) 225–39.

Sauvy, Alfred. "Trois Mondes, Une Planéte." *L'Observateur* 118, August 14 (1952) 14.
Scheffler, Eben H. "The Poor in the Psalms: A Variety of Views." *Verbum et Ecclesia* 36 (2015) 1–9.
Schiffman, Lawrence H., and James C. VanderKam. *Encyclopedia of the Dead Sea Scrolls*. 2 vols. New York: Oxford University Press, 2000.
Schlisske, Werner. *Gottessöhne und Gottessohn im alten Testament; Phasen der Entmythisierung im Alten Testament*, BWA(N)T 5. Stuttgart: Kohlhammer, 1973.
Schmid, H. H. "Creation, Righteousness, and Salvation: 'Creation Theology' as the Broad Horizon of Biblical Theology." In *Creation in the Old Testament*, edited by Bernhard W. Anderson, 102–17. IRT 6. Philadelphia: Fortress, 1984.
Schniedewind, William M. *Society and the Promise to David: The Reception History of 2 Samuel 7:1–17*. New York: Oxford University Press, 1999.
Schreiner, David B. "Double Entendre, Disguised Verbal Resistance, and the Composition of Psalm 132." *BBR* 28 (2018) 20–33.
Schroeder, Christoph O. *History, Justice, and the Agency of God: A Hermeneutical and Exegetical Investigation on Isaiah and Psalms*. BibIntSer 52. Leiden: Brill, 2001.
Schutte, Flip. "Myth as a Paradigm to Read a Text." In *Psalms and Mythology*, edited by Dirk J. Human, 1–8. LHBOTS 462. New York: T. & T. Clark, 2007.
Scott, James C. *Domination and the Arts of Resistance: Hidden Transcripts*. New Haven: Yale University Press, 1990.
Segal, Robert Alan. *Myth: A Very Short Introduction*. 2nd ed. Very Short Introductions 111. New York: Oxford University Press, 2015.
Seibert, Eric A. *Subversive Scribes and the Solomonic Narrative: A Rereading of 1 Kings 1–11*. LHBOTS 436. London: T. & T. Clark, 2006.
Silver, Morris. *Prophets and Markets: The Political Economy of Ancient Israel*. Social Dimensions of Economics. Boston: Kluwer-Nijhoff, 1983.
Sissons, Nick. "Psalm 82 Re-Written." *Epworth Review* 20 (1993) 91.
Slivniak, Dmitri. "Our God(s) is One: Biblical and the Indeterminacy of Meaning." *SJOT* 19.1 (2005) 3–23.
Smick, Elmer B. "Mythopoetic Language in the Psalms." *WTJ* 44 (1982) 88–99.
Smith, Mark S. *God in Translation: Deities in Cross-Cultural Discourse in the Biblical World*, 131–39. FAT 57. Tübingen: Mohr Siebeck, 2008.
———. *The Origins of Biblical Monotheism: Israel's Polytheistic Background and the Ugaritic Texts*. New York: Oxford University Press, 2001.
———. *The Ugaritic Baal Cycle*. VTSup 55. Leiden: Brill, 1994.
Smith-Christopher, Daniel L. *A Biblical Theology of Exile*. OBT. Minneapolis: Fortress, 2002.
Staerk, Willy. *Studien zur Religions- und Sprachgeschichte des Alten Testaments*. 2 vols. Berlin: Reimer, 1899.
Sternberg, Meir. *The Poetics of Biblical Narrative: Ideological Literature and the Drama of Reading*. Indiana Studies in Biblical Literature. Bloomington: Indiana University Press, 1985.
Strawn, Brent A. "The Poetics of Psalm 82: Three Critical Notes along with a Plea for the Poetic." *RB* 121 (2014) 21–46.
Sun, Chloe. *The Ethics of Violence in the Story of Aqhat*. Gorgias Dissertations 34. Piscataway, NJ: Gorgias, 2008.
Tate, Marvin E. *Psalms 51–100*. Word Biblical Commentary 20. Grand Rapids: Zondervan, 1991.

Thalhofer, Valentin. *Hauspralaten und Dompropstes in Eichstätt Erklärung der Psalmen und der im römischen Brevier Vorkommenden Biblischen Cantica: Mit Besonderer Rücksicht auf deren Liturgischen Gebrauch*. Manz: Regensburg, 1895.

Trotter, James M. "Death of the אלהים in Psalm 82." *JBL* 131 (2012) 221–39.

Tsevat, Matitiahu. "God and the Gods in Assembly: An Interpretation of Psalm 82." *HUCA* 40–41 (1969) 123–37.

Usue, Emmanuel O. "Theological-Mythological Viewpoints on Divine Sonship in Genesis 6 and Psalm 2." In *Psalms and Mythology*, edited by Dirk J. Human, 91–103. New York: T. & T. Clark, 2007.

Van Leeuwen, Raymond C. "Wealth and Poverty: System and Contradiction in Proverbs." *HS* 33 (1992) 25–36.

Wagner-Tsukamoto, Sigmund. "State Formation in the Hebrew Bible: An Institutional Economic Perspective." *JSOT* 37 (2013) 391–421.

Waltke, Bruce K., and Michael Patrick O'Connor. *An Introduction to Biblical Hebrew Syntax*. Winona Lake, IN: Eisenbrauns, 1990.

Weinfeld, Moshe. *Social Justice in Ancient Israel and in the Ancient Near East*. Minneapolis: Fortress, 1995.

Weiser, Artur. *The Psalms: A Commentary*. Translated by Herbert Hartwell. OTL. Philadelphia: Westminster, 1962.

Wellhausen, Julius. *Die Kleinen Propheten*. Skizzen und Vorarbeiten 5. Berlin: Reimer, 1898.

Wenham, Gordon J. *Psalms as Torah: Reading Biblical Song Ethically*. STI. Grand Rapids: Baker Academic, 2012.

———. "Prayer and Practice in the Psalms." In *Psalms and Prayers*, edited by Bob Becking and Eric Peels, 279–95. OtSt 55. Leiden: Brill, 2007.

Westermann, Claus. *Praise and Lament in the Psalms*. Translated by Keith R. Crim and Richard N. Soulen. Atlanta: John Knox, 1981.

———. *The Psalms: Structure, Content, and Message*. Translated by Ralph D. Gehrke. Minneapolis: Augsburg, 1980.

Wilcock, Michael. *The Message of Psalms 73–150: Songs for the People of God*. Downers Grove, IL: InterVarsity, 2001.

Wilfand Ben-Shalom, Yael. *Poverty, Charity and the Image of the Poor in Rabbinic Texts from the Land of Israel*. SWBA 9. Sheffield: Sheffield Phoenix, 2014.

Wilson, Gerald H. *The Editing of the Hebrew Psalter*. SBLDS 76. Atlanta: Scholars, 1985.

———. "The Shape of the Hebrew Psalter." *Int* 46 (1992) 129–42.

Wilson, Lindsay. "Educating Calvin about Elihu." Paper presented at the Tyndale Fellowship Conference. Tyndale House, Cambridge, UK, 2017.

Younger, K. Lawson. "'The Gods of Aram' (Judges 10:6) in Light of Recent Research." Paper presented at the Tyndale Fellowship Conference. Tyndale House, Cambridge, UK, 2017.

Zimmermann, Ruben. *The Logic of Love: Discovering Paul's "Implicit Ethics" through 1 Corinthians*. Translated by Dieter T. Roth. Lanham, MD: Lexington/Fortress Academic, 2018.

You may also be interested in:

Charting the Course of Psalms Research

Essays on the Psalms, Volume 1

Erhard S. Gerstenbgerger
Edited by K.C. Hanson

Erhard Gerstenberger (1932-2023) has been a highly influential exegete of the Psalms for several decades. He demonstrated how the Psalms were able to modulate the deepest feelings of individuals and communities, encompassing a wide variety of existential experiences relating to God and the world. Gerstenberger believed that psalmic poetry grew out of diverse and real-life situations.

The first two essays in *Charting the Course of Psalms Research* deftly review the secondary literature. The first covers the 'lyrical literature' of the Old Testament, and the second considers the history of interpretation of the Psalms. The remaining essays explore the social settings of the Psalms and their connection to theology and communication theory, and include two chapter translated into English for the first time and edited by K.C. Hanson. Student and researcher alike will be enriched by the insights Gerstenberger provides.

Erhard S. Gerstenberger (1932-2023) was Professor Emeritus at the University of Marburg, where he taught Old Testament from 1985-1997, and served as Dean of the Department of Protestant Theology from 1993-1994. His numerous works have been translated into many languages, and he remains an influential biblical scholar.

K.C. Hanson is Editor in Chief of Wipf and Stock publishers, and has numerous theological publications. Hanson worked closely with Gerstenberger on the translations for this book.

Published 2024

Paperback ISBN: 978 0 227 18001 3
PDF ISBN: 978 0 227 18002 0